MW01485569

DESIGNED FOR SUCCESS

DESIGNED FOR SUCCESS

BETTER LIVING AND SELF-IMPROVEMENT WITH MIDCENTURY INSTRUCTIONAL RECORDS

JANET BORGERSON
AND JONATHAN SCHROEDER

THE MIT PRESS
CAMBRIDGE, MASSACHUSETTS
LONDON, ENGLAND

© 2024 Massachusetts Institute of Technology

All rights reserved. No part of this book may be used to train artificial intelligence systems or reproduced in any form by any electronic or mechanical means (including photocopying, recording, or information storage and retrieval) without permission in writing from the publisher.

The MIT Press would like to thank the anonymous peer reviewers who provided comments on drafts of this book. The generous work of academic experts is essential for establishing the authority and quality of our publications. We acknowledge with gratitude the contributions of these otherwise uncredited readers.

This book was set in ITC Century Std and Helvetica Neue by New Best-set Typesetters Ltd. Printed and bound in the United States of America.

Library of Congress Cataloging-in-Publication Data

Names: Borgerson, Janet, author. | Schroeder, Jonathan E., 1962– author.
Title: Designed for success : better living and self-improvement with midcentury instructional records / Janet Borgerson and Jonathan Schroeder.
Description: Cambridge, Massachusetts : The MIT Press, [2024] | Includes bibliographical references and indexes.
Identifiers: LCCN 2023024653 (print) | LCCN 2023024654 (ebook) | ISBN 9780262048835 (hardcover) | ISBN 9780262377874 (epub) | ISBN 9780262377867 (pdf)
Subjects: LCSH: Self-culture—United States—Audio-visual aids. | Self-culture—United States—History—20th century. | Sound recordings in education—United States—History—20th century.
Classification: LCC LC31 .B67 2024 (print) | LCC LC31 (ebook) | DDC 371.39/430973—dc23/eng/20231117
LC record available at https://lccn.loc.gov/2023024653
LC ebook record available at https://lccn.loc.gov/2023024654

10   9   8   7   6   5   4   3   2   1

DEDICATED TO THE MEMORY OF PAUL E. SCHROEDER, MD

CONTENTS

INTRODUCTION
ACHIEVING THE GOOD LIFE WITH MIDCENTURY RECORDS

Midcentury vinyl records presented rock and roll, cool jazz, and stereophonic symphonies, but record albums also expressed broader US goals of global influence, self-improvement, and individual success. While celebrated discs delivered Chuck Berry's rockin' dance rhythms, Miles Davis's musical innovations, and Beethoven's concertos, rarely remembered records lectured listeners on child rearing, wine drinking, and music appreciation. For go-getters, the Success Motivation Institute's training records divulged *The Seven Secrets of Selling to Women* and provided a template to *Think and Grow Rich*. As cannons boomed on now-classic recordings of Tchaikovsky's *1812 Overture*, adventurous voyagers—or aspiring Cold War spies—repeated phrases from "Learn in Your Own Home" language instruction LPs.

Albums such as *Hear How to Play Winning Bridge*, *The Family All Together*, and *Sing Out for Free Enterprise* not only provided purposeful listening pleasure but also served pedagogical functions that connected to countrywide concerns. Many of these LPs take up business and career success, encouraging postwar listeners—including US workers and consumers—to embrace ideal environments and economic ideologies as part of everyday life. Concurrently, staying ahead of the Soviets was a task passed on to US citizens during the Cold War. In this sense, all efforts at self-improvement, especially in arenas that had a patriotic ring, such as physical fitness, economic competitiveness, improving US reputation abroad, counted as a unifying national project. Not surprisingly, then, midcentury instructional records tapped into wider anxieties, that is, around social status, gender roles, and world leadership, and played into fears of falling behind.

Midcentury instructional records reveal indicative goal-directed invitations to listen and learn, with pointed prompts to participation. Let's meditate! Practice a drum solo! Lose some weight! They champion a do-it-yourself aesthetic and form an unheralded chapter in the self-improvement movement. You, too, can pilot a plane.

However, instructional and self-improvement records have been largely overlooked. This is not surprising. As we have previously argued, the cultural significance of entire categories of midcentury vinyl has been underestimated when compared to research on film, television, and magazines. Instructional record albums came to include sales training, family life and sex education, beauty, fitness, and leisure lessons—basically, anything that could be taught might wind up on an instructional record. Yet no definitive history of instructional records has been written. Unlike rock, jazz, and blues records, few collectors obsess about them. The recording industry has compiled nothing similar to the *New York Times* bestseller list for Advice, How-To, and Miscellaneous books. No "Top 10" charts exist for instructional records.[1] Most have languished in record store bargain bins for years, relegated to obscurity—until now.

In *Designed for Success: Better Living and Self-Improvement with Midcentury Instructional Records,* we shed light on this genre of albums often deemed puzzling, quirky, or outright strange. We uncover intriguing treasures and sample surprisingly sage advice. Detailed liner notes, illustrated booklets, pedagogical design, and album cover art advance the self-improvement project and provide rich material for observation, insight, and hopefully, some entertaining humor. As Conversa-phone's *Children's Spanish Language Course* promises, instructional records are "Simple! Fast! Modern! Fun!"

Clearly, the recorded content of instructional records varies depending upon which lesson lands on the turntable: rigorous repetition for learning Russian, training drills for mastering a sales pitch, or folksy foundations for "varmint calling" and bow hunting. We expose the ways in which midcentury instructional records contributed to a powerful US vision of personal success that reaches beyond the record titles' emphasis on stenographic practice, salesmanship, and even sex education toward a compelling sense of the US citizen who could navigate the American workplace and productively inhabit postwar home and leisure environments.

PARTICIPATORY DEMOCRACY, SELF-TRANSFORMATION, AND THE COLD WAR PROJECT

Records that were "designed for success" afforded an aspirational US populace access to achievement—in an easily consumed, portable format. Camouflaged in the mix of midcentury hi-fi aesthetics, modernist design, and technological progress, instructional and self-improvement records provided packaged instruction for training body and brain. They offered opportunities to challenge hometown shortcomings and gain a meaningful stake in postwar participatory democracy, wherein a promoted set of daily life patterns and practices taken up by the people had the potential to build a desired future. Instructional recordings imparted lessons for living a good life.

Designed-for-success records resonate with a distinctly US belief in self-transformation, touted through transcendentalist notions of aspirational striving and human development. By placing instructional records into the midcentury media context alongside foundational American cultural and philosophical notions of ontological fluidity—that transforming the self is possible and achievable—we gain new understandings of how these vinyl albums both shaped and reflected the spirit of the era. Indeed, midcentury records reveal crucial aspects of a nation's ambitions, desires, and longings.

With a turntable and a stack of enlightening records at hand, US learners lounging in living rooms could expand their horizons and contemplate more cosmopolitan conversations and career crescendos. Instructional records provide a motivational map for people whom historian Daniel Boorstin calls "the go-getters."[2] Expert advice from *Hear How to Improve Your Vocabulary and Speech* promotes transformation—from immigrant to American, rural resident to urban dweller, city slicker to suburbanite, lower class to middle class, beginner to expert. Related evolutions—modification of body, behavior, and mind—are possible with the help of albums such as *Keep Fit / Be Happy, On Wine: How to Select and Serve*, and *Developing Your ESP Powers*. Shifting insights about sexuality and gender? We'll introduce records such as *What You Can Learn from the Kinsey Report* and *Hear How to Achieve Sexual Harmony in Marriage*.

As the inner sleeve from a 1960s album proudly proclaims: "*Everything's* on long-playing records these days . . . your favorite artists, shows, comedy, movie sound tracks, concerts, drama, documented history, educational material, you name it." Increase typing speed? Create authentic South American dinners? Train your hunting dog? Vinyl records to the rescue.

LISTENING YOUR WAY TO A BETTER SELF IN THE "VALLEY OF THE STRANGE"

Instructional records helped spread the word: fitness, career, marital relations all could be improved through listening, learning, and doing. "It may be difficult to believe that a man's voice on a phonograph record can help his listeners to create a marvelous improvement" in their skills, begin the liner notes on *Outboard Motor Boating*. Nevertheless, the entire industry of designed-for-success records banked on doing just that. For example, Carlton Records' Hear How albums were promoted as "private lessons from experts." As an ad for the series puts it: "These instruction albums are on subjects that are most sought after for reference and advice because of their importance in the daily living habits of millions of people."[3] *Speed Reading Made Easy for Everyone* offers this motivational affirmation: "In turning on this record player, you have just taken a giant stride toward becoming a speed reader. You have shown interest and interest is a motivating force toward mastering speed reading." Along with basic lessons, then, instructional records offered guidance and psychological insight aimed at enhancing listeners' quality of life—a bargain at $3.98 in 1963.

Yet one recent guide to record collecting, published by the large online retailer Carolina Soul, doesn't mention instructional records at all.[4] In his book *Vinyl Junkies*, music critic Brett Milano observes that, for most record collectors, instructional records belong in the "valley of the strange."[5] Detroit radio station WDET broadcast a show in 2022 on "a mysterious and eccentric world" of instructional records.[6] Freeform radio stations, such as WFMU in East Orange, New Jersey, and WCBN in Ann Arbor, Michigan, often sample instructional records for humorous effect—as zany, "incredibly strange" programming. As BBC radio broadcaster Alan Dein has remarked, the "bizarre world" of instructional LPs with "oddball titles" occupies "the twilight zone of the commercial record industry" that has "slipped through the grooves of our audio social history, and out of sight."[7]

However, relegating midcentury instructional records to the realm of comedic relief or the merely weird drastically underestimates their significance to cultural history. Instructional records mark a modern moment, offering listeners a chance to learn from experts, travel vicariously, and gain appreciation for "the finer things in life" in a way that highlights expanding industries around music, food, and wine as well as self-development. Such records crucially link listening pleasure with learning productivity often in a combination that suggests business opportunities that harness self-improvement.

Instructional albums disseminate content for work on the self, launching "identity projects" by providing modern consumers the prompts and props for creating desired, and improved, selves. It's worth noting that television watching has been similarly analyzed: not simply a "passive activity" engaged purely for entertainment, "television can be the site of important identity work and moral reflection."[8] As such, instructional albums offer sites of self-definition, contributing to identity formation and a sense of difference from others, reflected in a statement such as: "My friends and I care about business careers, kitchen décor, and sports clubs, but we would never go fly fishing, learn Japanese, or take dictation." As personal, mobile objects, instructional records act as talismans in the quest for self-improvement and belonging.

We consider instructional records anthropological artifacts that speak to fundamental—and emergent—US attitudes, beliefs, and values. Further, these albums embody important social, pedagogical, and industrial practices that, at the time of their release, resulted in various, often invisible, inclusions and exclusions. Many midcentury albums that were designed for success seem to address a homogenized version of the US population—most obviously the White middle and aspiring upper middle class in a way that resonates with notions of "class rise."[9] With a few exceptions, largely confined to sports, music, and languages, instructional records express a White, English-speaking imagination, reflecting a logic of erasure typical of the era's mainstream culture.[10] Our aim, however, is not to explore nuances of White experience. Instead, we tell a largely untold story of how midcentury instructional records reflected and shaped culture; how they fed into anxieties about succeeding, getting ahead, and falling behind; and how they offer distinctive insights into midcentury goals and longings.

Thousands of instructional titles were produced by major companies like Columbia, RCA, and Warner Bros., smaller specialist firms such as Conversa-phone, as well as released on numerous private labels, on records pressed for product promotion, and for organizational training programs. Generally, though, in contrast to the world of sales charts, "Hot 100" hits, and pop stars, instructional records often appear as homespun productions and personal missives of advice. Some instructional titles feature famous spokespeople or recognized experts, and the most well-known how-to releases generally have some connection to a celebrity. *Jack La Lanne's Glamour Stretcher Time* capitalized on his popular television show in the late 1950s, while *Learn Tennis with Arthur Ashe* featured the celebrated sports star. A few instructional LPs sold well, such as *Play Guitar with the Ventures* and Bonnie Prudden's *Keep Fit / Be Happy*. Music Minus One's catalog of music instruction records have sold in the hundreds of thousands. Aebersold's "Play-A-Long" discs reportedly sold millions of copies.

In the current era of Instagram influencers, LinkedIn leadership gurus, and YouTube yogis, the overcommitted, overmessaged US consumer may not perceive sutras for slimming podcasts or paths to productivity platforms as part of a long-standing industry selling self-improvement and success. Yet advice, motivational messaging, and self-help have long provided plentiful content for rapidly evolving technologies. The twentieth century saw the rise of a burgeoning cadre of experts, creating a crucial phase in the industrialization of self-improvement.[11] Midcentury instructional records fit into this picture, engaging ear and eye in mainstream, postwar homes where seductive hi-fi systems promised not only stereo separation and music on demand but also lessons from wise—and, occasionally, witty—experts. Just put on a record.

Speaking of which, YOU BE A DISC JOCKEY, from 1963, offers listeners a chance to take to the airwaves. A banner wrapped around the *You Be a Disc Jockey* package effuses: "The perfect gift for the teen-ager: Fun, entertainment, perhaps the start of a career!" Bright, party-themed primary colors, along with celebratory secondary shades, fail to distract from career goals: Collegiate, albeit handmade, felt pennants hung behind Junior suggest he's considering his future—he's playing this LP after all. Mr. Established in red vest and complementary tie expresses jovial satisfaction with life in the studio. "DJ's have fun, and their listeners have fun. For this reason many people have wished that they too were, 'ON THE AIR.'" The two nonsquare photos center the cover, each featuring a turntable, a microphone, and a tidy rack of vinyl records, including Cameo Records' *3 Young Men from Montana* (1963) with folk song favorite "Sixteen Tons."

Producer and DJ Don Bruce provides the spoken script and instruction for producing your own show on side 2. An eight-page booklet feeds you your lines. Cameo/Parkway artists Dee Dee Sharp and Bobby Rydell appear for interviews. Songs by Chubby Checker and The Tymes provide the hits for the prerecorded program that puts you in the DJ seat. (The inner sleeve promotes a selection of Cameo/Parkway records as "the perfect gift.") On its release, *Billboard* named the package a "Special Merit Pick" (new releases of outstanding merit that deserve exposure and could have commercial success). The brief review noted "Top Deejay Don Bruce Is in Top Form."[12] One of the memorable radio DJs from our Michigan childhoods was Fred "Boogie" Brian, who spun tunes for oldies station WHND. He was fond of reporting the weather: "It's 69 degrees out today—Boogie's favorite temperature!" We thought of him when discovering this delightful radio career primer.

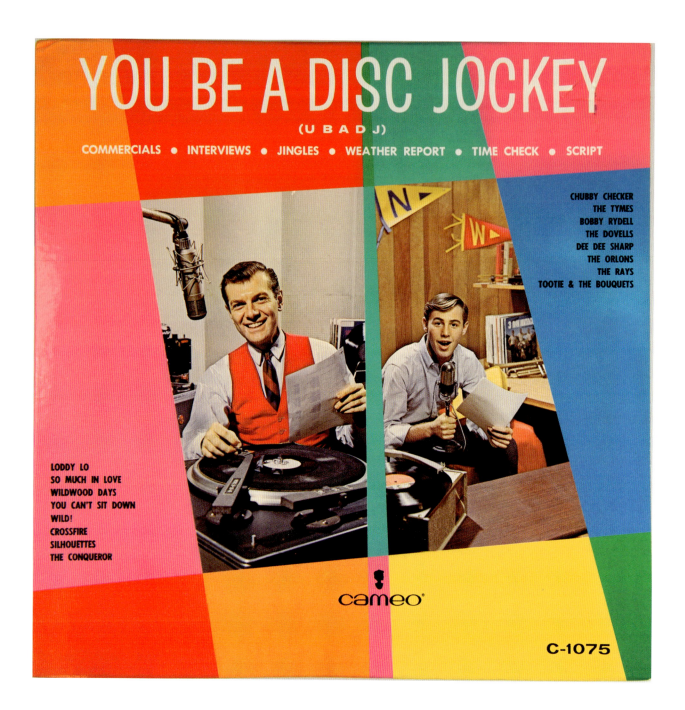

FIGURE 0.1

You Be a Disc Jockey,
Cameo C 1075, 1963.

TRANSCENDENTALISM, SELF-DEVELOPMENT, AND SUCCESS

Success! After effort, focus, and determination, success feels good. Notions of success lead to different ways of living and being—different lives, in fact. Midcentury self-improvement records call attention to the individual and their own resources, including a powerful and mutable mind that can alter the way a person sees and chooses to engage with the world, in a true phenomenological shift. These albums often tap into an American ideal in which "translating occupational achievement into status was the procedure for moving up within the middle class."[13] As such, instructional records formed an important front in the midcentury self-transformation project, offering listeners avenues to produce desired selves, or, as sociologist Erving Goffman puts it, to perform a presentation of (a successful) self in everyday life.[14]

The idea of success "stands as one of the most enduring expressions of American popular ideals."[15] Indeed, as a fundamental American belief, "the success myth has always joined the promise of material rewards to a supernaturalistic cosmology and remains rooted in the belief that in a universe of reason and of law, man is free to decide his own fate. These continuities may be likened to a single thread—winding, and of many colors—stretching across the whole of the American experience."[16] To expect success, to strive for success, and to speak about achievement appears to be particularly American. At its most base, the American ideal of success can be faulted for "encouraging a vulgar grasping for success and status as a testimony on one's worth."[17]

Foundational transcendentalist Ralph Waldo Emerson embraced perseverance, the work ethic, and rugged individualism. He wrote: "Self-trust is the first secret of success, the belief that if you are here the authorities of the universe put you here, and for cause, or with some task strictly appointed you in your constitution, and so long as you work at that you are well and successful."[18] Emerson's "first rule for success"? Attend to your aptitude, attend to yourself. Without "the brag and the advertisement . . . do your work."[19]

Inspirational author Horatio Alger mastered a mantra of the American dream: "Work hard and you will succeed." His rags to riches heroes begin with nothing, but end with something apparently worth having. That a patron—who knows potential when he sees it—must step in is often forgotten in the popular imagination. Of course, without personal experience of the related labors, a do-it-yourself attitude joined with a source of support may reduce to a myth of easy success. Yet attracting a patron—whether sugar daddy, sugar mama, angel investor—requires its own determination and consistent hard work, necessitating perhaps a questionable flexibility of character as well as a certain talent for seduction. Such talents are not completely without representation in designed-for-success LPs. Think vocal coaching, weight loss, and "closing the deal."

Emerson cast a cautionary eye on conceptions of success influenced by what he deemed "shallow Americanism": a term that designates a way of engaging the world that yearns for "skill without study, or mastery without apprenticeship, or the sale of goods through pretending that they sell, or power through making believe you are powerful."[20] Admittedly, this yearning resonates with a number of instructional albums, particularly those in the sales and persuasion categories. *Selling the Sizzle* summons a certain amount of hype, after all.

To take aim at scammers and those expecting more with the least effort is not difficult. Indeed, some LP "experts" who encourage others to "believe" and be their best selves are likely among these. Selling the public on the ease of their own success is a success and self-improvement industry in itself; we think of Amway motivational conference settings and related pyramid schemes. And how many "learn today, travel tomorrow" language records can one work through before realizing that the mission undertaken in this way—Listen. Repeat.—misrepresents cheerful delivery of "good morning" and "thank you" for fluency? Still, the desire to improve, to feel potential in oneself, and respond to expanded horizon hopes, pulses through instructional records.

A deepening commitment to self-development and success often requires adopting a new outlook. Ever relevant, Emerson defined the trait of true success as "The good mind chooses what is positive, what is advancing embraces the affirmative."[21] Many instructional records adopt the "power of positive thinking," and Norman Vincent Peale's premise regarding the positive's promise provides core content.

Put your mind to it, transform yourself, and everything is possible. Show initiative! Make the commitment! Buy this record! Listen, relax, think positive, and hear how to move up.

INSTRUCTIONAL AESTHETICS: THE STYLE OF SUCCESS

In general, designed-for-success records look different from most of the albums featured in our previous books, *Designed for Hi-Fi Living* and *Designed for Dancing*.[22] Instructional records center a style that creates a distinctive aesthetic feel, offering more sober, realist images, including everyday settings of office and family life and ordinary heroes just trying to get ahead. The less fantastical covers may seem to counter promotional wisdom: only colorful pictures attract the eye and communicate fulfillment of dreams! This visual bias belies, and helps to hide, the power of designed-for-success imagery. Just as black-and-white photography continues to communicate values and meaning in the wake of saturated, compelling color, instructional records, with their earnest aesthetics, contribute to the chronicle of postwar America. This story needs to be told, in conjunction with narratives fueled by chromophilic, eye-catching images.

CAPITALIST REALISM, MARKET VALUES, AND THE PRIVACY OF THE AMERICAN DREAM

Drawing upon conceptions of realism in the visual arts, historian Michael Schudson developed a notion of capitalist realism to express how advertising educates, informs, and persuades.[23] He compared US advertising to Soviet-era art that functioned as state propaganda supporting the communist system. Advertising imagery, Schudson argued, emphasizes the positive, assumes progress, and obscures class differences. In the US, "advertising messages that promise social mobility buttress the idea of the American Dream."[24]

Designed-for-success album covers often display an aesthetic of capitalist realism, altering the typical dynamics of album cover design in interesting ways. These practical records stress function over form and often eschew artistic touches. The utilitarian—dare we say, managerial—vision shifts many instructional album covers' graphic design to monochrome. Rather than embrace the full color covers of records geared toward entertainment, instructional records generally hew to the no-nonsense, scientific, black-and-white facts. Designed-for-success record albums visually embrace the grays of determination and grit required to succeed in the competitive environment of the American Dream.

During the twentieth century, advertising learned to draw on film's ability to capture mood and situation through strategic chromatic choices, promoting the play of shadows, or contrasting worlds of black and white versus color. Think of the legendary scene in *The Wizard of Oz* (1939) when Dorothy departs colorless Kansas and awakens in the technicolor dreamscape of the Yellow Brick Road. Watching *The Grapes of Wrath* (1940), one sees how director John Ford used the power of black and white to express the dire circumstances of migrant workers. The grays and dusty whites evoke a landscape without hope, specifically allowing lack of color to bleach the film of excitement and desire. In Wim Wenders's *The State of Things* (1982), Joe the Cameraman (played by Samuel Fuller) declares: "Life is in color, but black and white is more realistic." In other words, black and white has the potential to communicate an emotional tenor and a realism that captures aspects of the lived world in a way that color may not.

Instructional album covers borrow from the logic—as well as the graphic language—of advertising that animates capitalist realism. Like advertising, instructional records offer guidance in gaining knowledge, pleasure, and success. They incorporate other aspects of capitalist realism as well, including liner notes that promote upward mobility, equal opportunity, and the benefits of getting ahead. According to Schudson, such "values are put to work to sell goods, invoked in the service of the marketplace. And what is also distinctively capitalist is that the satisfactions portrayed are invariably private, even if they are familial or social; they do not invoke public or collective values. They offer a public portraiture of ideals and values consistent with the promotion of a social order in which people are encouraged to think of themselves and their private worlds."[25] The push to private spheres of subjectivity parallels the rise of radio, television, and record players, all consumed in the home, and motivates a profound shift for most households toward a more private lifeworld.[26]

In their emphasis on individual improvement, upward mobility, and success, instructional records exemplify how "the aesthetic of capitalist realism glorifies the pleasures and freedoms of consumer choice in defense of the virtues of private life and material ambitions."[27] A few of our selections represent an organizational effort, such as Xerox Corporation's *Effective Listening*, military training albums *Airman!!* and *The Making of a Marine!*, and records that were designed for school use, such as *Ethnic Dances of Black People around the World* and *Latin-American Game Songs*. However, most instructional records are aimed squarely at the individual do-it-yourself user.

Filled with lessons to facilitate social mobility and career advancement and drawing heavily upon advertising's aesthetics and pictorial innovations, they were meant for listening in the privacy of one's own home.[28]

CORPORATE USES OF PHOTOGRAPHY: EMPLOYEE MANAGEMENT, ADVERTISING TABLEAU, AND ALBUM COVER ART

Photography represents a key imaging technology, reflecting early twentieth-century beliefs that "science and system could solve the myriad problems of inefficiency, inequality, and poverty that plagued the United States' transition to urbanization."[29] As historian Elspeth Brown has shown, "by the early 1920s the corporate use of photographic representation had become an important element in managerial strategies to build employee loyalty, reduce labor turnover, manage public opinion, and sell more goods."[30] For example, photographs in company newsletters, such as *Western Electric News*, attempted to create an emotionally moving and persuasive visual marker of employee belonging and dignity. Such efforts emphasized individual skill and achievement and discouraged collective organizing and unions.

Advertising photography, once used more narrowly in corporate communication, transformed into a major cultural force, following advances in photographic technology, developments in stylistic expression, and shifting aesthetic tastes. During the twentieth century, advertising evolved from a source of information and persuasion to a fundamental facet of social communication. As a system, advertising not only promotes particular products, services, and brands but also works to support capitalism and encourage individual identity projects. Critical theorist Jean Baudrillard has observed that advertising acts "not so much to sell as to restore consensus, complicity, collusion."[31] Ads make upward mobility appear attainable and desirable.[32] As such, "advertising provides clues about how to live life and find well-being in contemporary market society."[33]

Advertising imagery emerged as an important visual idiom, building upon the innovations of photographers such as Lejaren à Hiller, whose early twentieth-century work "moved commercial photography from the tyranny of fact to the triumph of longing."[34] Subjective and emotional photographic inducements, strategically targeted toward a particular response, appeared in social, narrative tableaus, sparking identification with the pictured dream realities, which were presented as desirable and achievable for the American population. À Hiller's photograph of Greek physician *Aspasia* (1933), for example, presents a classical allegory reminiscent of private theatricals. Women, draped in togas—one breast exposed—converse near a Greek column, surrounded by scrolls, invoking notions of reflection, rationality, and balance championed by Aspasia's husband, Pericles. The album cover for *Calm Nerves for Self-Confidence* (discussed in chapter 7) wraps a revealing drapery around a female figure as she mimics an architectural column, embodying classical beliefs in greater human capacities.

Like film, fine art, and advertising, instructional album covers draw from a stock of cultural motifs to produce persuasive imagery designed to sell records. Similar to photographs more generally, midcentury album covers "have a multilayered patina of nostalgia, cultural history, and pictorial tradition, among other cultural and social codings, that cause us to read and react to them in a manner that supersedes their original context and intent."[35] Not surprisingly, then, record covers resemble other aspects of the era's visual culture, including iconic advertising images and other forms of corporate communication.

For example, a familiar genre of ads "show a single figure or small group wearing, holding, looking at, or otherwise involved with a product in a presentational sense."[36] Similarly, *How to Communicate Your Ideas* (from chapter 5) shows a group of men, dressed in suits, seated at a telltale boardroom table, demonstrating their membership in the managerial class. Many instructional album covers show records or a record player—either to communicate the connection between the enclosed product (the record) and instruction, or as an illustrative graphic detail.

RESONATING PHOTOGRAPHIC VISIONS AND THE STRATEGIC USES OF STYLE

As the industry expanded, advertising agencies hired photographers such as Lewis W. Hine, whose black-and-white portraits of people at work influenced visions of productivity and independent accomplishment: "Hine's heroicized workers were the most sophisticated photographic examples of a broader visual culture of capitalist realism in 1920s business journalism."[37] These photographs—such as the portrait of Frank Vrastil (1924), sleeves rolled up, hands on his tools; or high schooler Betsey Price focused on her sewing (1921)—have transitioned from the realm of corporate communication into distinguished examples of twentieth-century photography. In line with these portraits, advertising photographers could choose nonprofessional models "partly to appeal to a growing middle-class audience whose tastes and reading habits were reflected not in the haute couture fashion magazines . . . but in *Redbook*, *Ladies' Home Journal*, and *McCall's*."[38] Many of the instructional album covers discussed here, such as *Actual Business Letters* and *Play Electric Bass with the Ventures*, include ordinary people, quite distinct from the glamorous imagery of pop stars, jazz musicians, and celebrities prevalent on musical records.

During the 1940s and 1950s, advertising photography embraced fantasy and surrealism.[39] Several instructional records included in this book—particularly those in the "mind altering" genre, such as *Better Golf through Hypnosis*—demonstrate surrealistic elements of dreamlike spirals and bent lines. The cover for *Calm Nerves for Self-Confidence* captures the uncanny: a lunar landscape and a spaceship juxtaposed with an ancient Greek column.

Midcentury advertising photography was also driven by cinematic style and storytelling conventions—from thrillers, film noir, romantic comedies, Westerns. Photographers dreamed up mini-movies to promote products, creating attractive visions of adventure, love, and success. A few instructional album covers discussed in this book reflect cinematic touches, deploying cultural archetypes and expectations established through film.[40] *Music for Courage and Confidence* presents a rich vision of reflection in nature, with its lone figure perched on a promontory, staring at the stars. *Dinner in*

Rio captures a celebratory dinner, complete with half-empty champagne coupes, festive carnival streamers and balloons, and a couple's caress, full of passion and erotic possibility. A documentary film still provides the cover shot for *The Making of a Marine!*, which offers a close-up view of military induction: a sergeant screams at a sweaty recruit, setting the stage for another coming-of-age story, or perhaps a tale of conflict.

In a landmark 1988 exhibit of advertising photography, curator Robert Sobieszek proclaimed that, "more than any other kind of imagery, advertising photography has permeated our cultural consciousness."[41] Such photographs, he concluded, contribute "to a framework through which we view our past."[42] Among the midcentury photographers in the exhibit, Ralph Bartholomew Jr., Paul Outerbridge Jr., Victor Keppler, and Nickolas Muray provide useful context for thinking about instructional album cover art.

Ralph Bartholomew Jr., for example, was known for his carefully composed lifestyle imagery: he "created attainable fictions whose realities were based both in films and in a very narrow way of life found in the suburbs of the American northeast . . . these fictions . . . became the accepted formulaic aspirations of an entire generation of consumers."[43] His advertising photography showcased "wholesome, energetic middle-America liberated by consumerism."[44]

Bartholomew's 1950 ad for Columbia Records features two tidy teenagers, seated on the floor surrounded by records next to a hi-fi console. The built-in turntable is pulled out, likely playing a recently introduced vinyl format, the long-playing, 12-inch record—an LP. On the instructional album *How to Ski (A Living-Room Guide for Beginners)*, included in chapter 8, alpine racer Skeeter Werner strikes a similarly engaged pose, the hi-fi set as an integral après-ski companion.

Paul Outerbridge, whose work was castigated in 1973 by the influential Museum of Modern Art curator John Szarkowski as mere "commercial illustrations"[45] has recently "re-emerged as one of the 20th century's most intriguing photographers."[46] As an art critic has observed: "He was both an artist *and* a salesman."[47] For example, in a series of Eight O'Clock coffee ads for the A&P grocery store chain, "these colorful tableaux of smiling men and women clinking cups in ersatz dining rooms have an eerie verisimilitude that makes their imitation of social conventions seem like mockery. Whether Outerbridge intended this disjunctiveness is open to argument, but the pictures remain stylized, ironic and poignant."[48] The influence of his photographs, such as "Food Display," can be glimpsed on the covers of *Selling the Sizzle* and *Music to Barbecue By*. Both manage to elevate simple scenarios to inventively create and reflect consumer desire, and each may strike today's viewer as unintentionally humorous, yet pleasantly nostalgic.

Victor Keppler's and Nickolas Muray's photographs blurred the lines between advertising and editorial photography with their "highly realistic, vibrant and alluring color photographs."[49] Indeed, Keppler published an influential guide to color photography. Notably, his advertising work often "presented a serialized set of encounters featuring a real person in a real-life situation extolling the qualities [of a product]."[50] Such real-life encounters create many compelling—and quirky—scenarios on album covers.

FIGURE 0.2

Ralph Bartholomew Jr.,
Untitled, 1946, digital image.
© 2023 Museum Associates / LACMA.
Licensed by Art Resource, New York.

FIGURE 0.3

Paul Outerbridge, Jr.,
Food Display, 1937,
carbro print, 14¼ × 17⁷⁄₁₆ in.,
The J. Paul Getty Museum, Los Angeles.
© 2023 G. Ray Hawkins Gallery, Beverly Hills, CA.

FIGURE 0.4

Victor Keppler, Camel Cigarettes,
Woman in Red Convertible, 1951.
Courtesy of the George Eastman Museum.
Reproduced with permission from Thomas V. Keppler.

Let's Get Acquainted with Jazz (presented in chapter 11) features color imagery with just such an aesthetic: accented by bright red clothing and typography, a classroom setting with a student, a teacher, and a basic blackboard. In Keppler's 1951 ad for Camel cigarettes, a deep, saturated red animates the coat, scarf, gloves, and car of an exuberant redhead. The album *Seven Secrets of Selling to Women* (seen in chapter 2) highlights this passionate hue and expression.

Similarly, Muray's celebrated 1952 Hunt's Tomato Catsup ad, with its vibrant saturation and singular focus on sandwich, knife, and condiment bottle, might be compared to the vivid cover colors of *The Art of Mixing Drinks & Music*, which includes a close-up of a bottle opener, a knife, and a corkscrew against a bright red background. Further, David Hecht's multiple shots on *Coffee Break* and Wendy Hilty's cover for *Classical Music for People Who Don't Know Anything About Classical Music* can be productively compared to Keppler's and Muray's better-known photography. The unnamed photographer for *Let's All Sing by the Fireside* also seems to have been influenced by the realist-yet-staged aesthetics of much midcentury advertising imagery.

RECORDING TECHNOLOGIES OF THE SELF: INSTRUCTIONAL RECORDS AND SELF-TRANSFORMATION

Instructional records offered more than career related skills; they delivered knowledge and training to create sociologist William Whyte's "well-rounded" organization man and, indeed, new forms of humanity. More pedestrian accomplishments, such as teaching your children manners or learning how to play guitar, make earnest appearances as well. In affluent families, instruction might have been delivered by nannies, governesses, trainers, coaches, and tutors—not by instructional records or self-help books. The instructional recording industry made such training available to a mass audience eager to learn, improve, and succeed. Turning to LPs for training not only reveals something about one's origins but also one's curiosity and ambitions.

Dale Carnegie's phenomenally successful book *How to Win Friends and Influence People* (1936) inscribed the ethos of midcentury self-improvement. Many instructional albums take up Carnegie's ideas, including profound self-transformation through, for example, alterations in locution, speech, and vocabulary, as memorably dramatized in *My Fair Lady* (1956). Music scholar Tim Anderson observes, "Just as Professor Higgins lifts Eliza into ladyhood with the instrumental assistance of his phonograph, these records and their intents pose significant questions about the dynamics of listening and how the listener may learn how to perform around the demands of race, class, gender and genre."[51] Self-improvement records deliver educational content; they also promise fundamental shifts in the way the listener sees and chooses to engage with the world, and, further, they set expectations for how the world will respond. In other words, instructional records played an unheralded role in creating reciprocal visions and transformations for postwar US identities.

FIGURE 0.5

Nickolas Muray, color photograph, c. 1952.
© Nickolas Muray Photo Archives.
Division of Work and Industry, National Museum of American History,
Smithsonian Institution, gift of Nickolas Muray.

Communicating a steadfast belief in self-transformation, instructional records draw on what philosopher Michel Foucault calls the technologies of the self—"the procedures, which have doubtless existed in all civilizations, that are proposed or prescribed to individuals in order to fix, maintain or transform their identities with particular ends in view."[52] Technologies of the self "permit individuals to effect, by one's own efforts or with the help of others, a series of operations on his body or his soul, his thinking, his behavior and his mode of existence, with the aim to change oneself so that he has attained a certain state of happiness, purity, wisdom, perfection, or immortality."[53] Such "technologies," according to Foucault, can be codified in an instruction manual—or, as we would argue, on an instructional record.[54]

Instructional records provide a unique window into the ways in which midcentury Americans were encouraged to imagine themselves and develop fulfilling lives. The advertising industry made claims that passive consumption of the right automobile, hand cream, or beverage was the ticket to upward mobility—or, at least, the appearance of upward mobility. In contrast, most instructional records required an active participant, listening, practicing, *doing*, taking matters into one's own hands in an Emersonian mode of self-reliance to achieve enlightened results.

Albums that teach music are a successful and enduring category of the instructional genre. Music instruction records, such as releases by Music Minus One, encouraged listeners to learn by playing along, filling in the instrument that was "missing" from the recording. Thus, the use of a phonograph "underscores the modern element of the minus one concept and its promise to develop both a performer and listener through a record's ability to repeatedly display arrangements that address an imaginary 'you.'"[55] In other words, an activated self forms an integral aspect of learning to play music by listening to records and playing along.

Music Minus One's founder, Irv Kratka, a jazz enthusiast who produced his first record as a teenager, also ran the labels Inner City, Classic Jazz, and Proscenium Records. Dubbed "the godfather of karaoke," Kratka released over one thousand Music Minus One discs. His ambitious first effort was five recordings of Schubert's *Trout Quintet*, with each disc leaving out one instrument. Music Minus One recruited top names to play on their records, including first chairs at leading American orchestras and top names in jazz, including Max Roach, Stan Getz, and Hank Jones. Their motto: "For the first time, even hobbyist players could solo with a professional orchestra."[56]

Music Minus One records included a catalog that listed dozens of titles. Grouped into categories such as "The Wonderful World of Guitar," "Concert Band," and "Self-Instruction Kits," each Music Minus One volume "contains a 12" long play record of background accompaniment to each selection played by an All-Star rhythm section. The music ranges from easy through medium to difficult."[57] Music Minus One offerings included the Rutgers University Music Dictation Series, a ten-record course in "basic musicianship, ear-training and sight-reading." As Harold Schonberg, the venerable *New York Times* classical music critic noted: "There's a certain psychological benefit in MMO. You put the record on, alone in your own house. Nobody is going to raise depreciating eyebrows when you fluff a passage or come in on the wrong half of the measure. You can bluff to your heart's content."[58]

Music Minus One's BLUE DRUMS features pianist Mal Waldron and bassist Wendell Marshall, leaving space for "you" on drums. Waldron appears on a couple of other Music Minus One discs, including *The Blues Minus You—Ten Shades of Blue* and *For Singers 'N Swingers—Sing or Play with the Mal Waldron Trio.*

Waldron was a successful jazz musician and composer, playing with legends like John Coltrane, Eric Dolphy, and Charles Mingus, and a regular accompanist for Billie Holiday. He can be heard on many classic Prestige Records recordings. After a heroin overdose, he struggled to remember how to play the piano and "had to teach himself how to play again, partly by listening to his own records."[59] So, perhaps the Music Minus One records he contributed to reflect Waldron's own experience of learning by listening.

The album includes brief biographies of the musicians, notes on the "chorus form" and "song form," and sheet music for the ten original blues songs by Waldron. He provides a rationale for the LP: "Most jazz albums contain one or two blues and unless you can play them you never really make it with the cats." It's obvious that Waldron was a talented and inspired piano player, and one hardly misses the drums on the recording.

The cover photograph for *Blue Drums* is by David Gahr, whose photographs grace hundreds of album covers. His classic images of jazz and rock musicians include shots of Miles Davis and Janis Joplin that also appeared on US Post Office stamps.[60] He started at Folkways Records, where he shot covers for *Brownie McGhee and Sonny Terry Sing* (1958) and *It's My Way* by Buffy Sainte-Marie (1964), and he went on to create iconic covers for Van Morrison's *Moondance* (1970) and Bruce Springsteen's *The Wild, the Innocent & the E Street Hustle* (1973). Cover typography is by Sy Rudman, an artist and art director for *Argosy* magazine who designed many jazz album covers.

INSTRUCTIONAL RECORDS: JUST LISTEN AND LEARN

Most instructional records focus on a striving listener interested in education and self-improvement, not just entertainment or pleasure. As one commentor has observed: "Although it may seem unlikely now, the quest for the fledgling gramophone industry in the early years of the [twentieth] century was not simply to sell recordings of the great singers or music hall artists of the day, but to harness the power of the recorded spoken word in business. It was HG Wells who prophesied that 'the gramophone will one day be used for language teaching.'"[61]

From its beginning, the recording industry promoted phonographs as learning aids. For example, a 1901 ad for the Victor Talking Machine emphasized its usefulness for "listening and learning" and proposed that a phonograph was "the ideal gift for children."[62] Access to voices and sounds, to be repeated at will, created opportunities for relistening, memorization, mimicking, and in turn, learning. Moreover, the phonograph introduced sonic landscapes and listening experiences into new arenas and ears—outside the ken and typical taste tolerances of various audiences. Records included

FIGURE 0.6

Blue Drums,
The Mal Waldron Trio,
Music Minus One MMO 4005;
design by Sy Rudman,
photo by David Gahr, 1961.

incursions into auditory worlds beyond local language and music cultures, such as Conversa-phone records for learning Swedish or Arabic, or Capital of the World albums featuring music of Finland and Peru.

A singular focus on rock and jazz "made cultural historians deaf to postwar genres of recorded sound other than music."[63] Records fed the booming market for entertainment, and musical records commanded the most attention. But instructional records complicate understandings of the role of records in everyday life: the culture of recorded sounds encompasses a wide range of educational, instructional, and how-to recordings.

The admonition to listen and learn opens possibilities for an expansive self-conception, coupled with a willingness to change. Self-transformation requires a certain mutability, and self-reliance may involve taking to the woods. The cover of **SECRETS OF SUCCESSFUL VARMINT CALLING** shows a coyote creeping toward a camouflaged man, hands cupped over his mouth, apparently calling the "varmint." No-nonsense black-and-white typography is centered above the color photograph, and a signature-like script "by Johnny Stewart" names the record's narrator and producer. The LP includes a *How to Call Wild Game* manual and a detailed booklet that reproduces game caller Johnny Stewart's spoken-word script. He begins: "One of the most exciting moments in my life was the first time I saw a coyote running toward me in response to my call."

The booklet promotes the "Johnny Stewart Deluxe Electri-Call Wildlife Caller and Portable Public Address": a portable record player with an attached megaphone, "so lightweight a child can lift it with one finger," and "great fun on camping trips." Also available is a haunting hit parade of "Distress Cries" on 45 rpm singles, such as "Rodents Squealing," "Crows Fighting an Owl," and "Bleating of a Wounded Buck." Stewart urges: "Try always to put realism into your calling. Inject anguish, fear, and panic into the sounds you make." Side 1 features his folksy, knowledgeable guidance for the business of calling, and side 2 offers several distress calls, such as the eerie, terrified squeals of jackrabbits, "how a bobwhite quail sounds when caught by a predator," and a "woodpecker in distress, a terrific calling sound, especially for cats and coyotes."

Who was *Secrets of Successful Varmint Calling* for? Advertised in hunting magazines, we believe that it served a niche for urban men released into the suburban wilderness and eager to mingle with the wildlife, but protect their families from varmints. Lacking homegrown calling knowledge passed down from father to son? A turn to technology and a role for vinyl records. The album offers a unique artifact that demonstrates how recording technology enabled new forms of learning aligned with unfamiliar activities. Although the topic may seem primitive, the liner notes embrace modern pedagogical theories: "To gain maximum benefits, read the printed script while you listen to the recording. This 'Double Sensory' method of absorbing the information will greatly increase your powers of concentration and retention."

As Stewart recounts, "Wild game calling is an outdoor recreation that has in only a few years captured the interest of thousands. Hunters, hobbyists, photographers all

FIGURE 0.7

Secrets of Successful Varmint Calling,
Johnny Stewart,
Outdoor Products Records, 1967.

are intrigued by it. To blow a call, or play a recording and see a fox, coyote, or bobcat suddenly running toward you is a thrill you'll never forget." Johnny Stewart Game Calls is still in business, building upon his sterling reputation: "Stewart pioneered the most powerful weapon in the war on predators more than 50 years ago. As the first person to successfully record the sounds of wild rabbits, Stewart understood the importance of achieving just the right pitch and volume for attracting coyotes to gun before anyone else had even conceived of using audio recordings." Listening to the distress calls reproduced on *Secrets of Successful Varmint Calling* was indeed distressing—as difficult to listen to as any record we have heard. The squeals of "baby cottontail in distress" still echo in our ears.

THE LIMITS OF MIDCENTURY SELF-TRANSFORMATION: CORPORATE CULTURE, MIND POWER, AND SEX ROLES

With fundamental postwar shifts and changes, and as organizational life with its rules and regulations came to dominate the workplace, how could the US population uphold belief in economic independence through individual achievement? Receding echoes of the capitalist entrepreneur boldly striding toward the frontiers of fortune must now usher in the new sounds of corporate culture and hierarchies of expertise.[64] Such "adjustments" were often perceived as requiring capacity and temperament to conform to organizational manners and mores, relinquishing visions of individualist success.

In his landmark *The Organization Man* (1957), William Whyte bore witness to an increasingly organized and hierarchical culture.[65] In financier Henry Clews's infamous 1908 Darwinist discourse, Whyte found an efficient, if self-serving, articulation of the Protestant ethic and a stark contrast to Whyte's own characterization of the conforming corporate man at midcentury. Whyte stresses Clew's go-getter attitude: "Success comes to the man who tries to compel success to yield to him," and "Birth is nothing. The fittest survive. Merit is the supreme and only qualification essential to success."[66] As presented here, moral and ethical roots bind wealth acquisition and display to a divine plan embodied and carried forward by individuals' "natural qualities" in a national economic context of unhindered choice and participatory enterprise. Choose your own trade, work as hard as you want, set the price for your own labor or products.

But, warns Whyte, as large organizations provided career paths for greater numbers, the experience of being passed over in favor of someone with questionable "merit" became a common event not to be overcome by admonition to greater effort. Personal disappointment yielded sober understandings of the potential to "rise." As sociologist Micki McGee writes about midcentury US work-life reality: "Decreased opportunities for entrepreneurial advancement, coupled with vast new corporate structures, demanded additional adjustments to the ideal of success for American men."[67] These adjustments might involve shifting one's attention from workplace success to recreational pursuits. Enter leisure records like chapter 8's *Hear How to Improve Your Fishing* and *7 Days to Better Bowling*.

In his influential book *The American Myth of Success: From Horatio Alger to Norman Vincent Peale* (1969), historian Richard Weiss examines the evolution of the success myth in the wake of industrialization, with certain arenas of opportunity closing. He argues that "the belief in the autonomous individual remained but within a new framework of supporting ideas."[68] The core of this "new framework" to mitigate lessening opportunities? Mind power. Mind power mobilized inner strength and hidden talents, often drawing on psychological techniques for increasing motivation and clarity of purpose—a kind of "self-manipulation." As Weiss writes, "The use of mind to support an idealistic conception of man and the universe forms one of the central elements in the ideological climate of twentieth century America."[69] Work on the self could increase inner strength, mobilize undeveloped mental maps, and expand the promise of human potential.

Whyte's attention to men's dominant work-life milieu obscures the integral presence of female support and labor. One might ask what instructional records suggest about the cultural arrangements necessary to carry forward the postwar US project. With the likes of Mrs. Dale Carnegie urging US women to help their husbands "get ahead," the sexually stratified nuclear family undergirded midcentury American free enterprise and appeared fundamental to the "American Way." McGee writes, "Traditionally, the mythology of the self-made man had relied on the exploitation of women's labor in their roles of wives, mothers, sisters, as well as on a pejorative understanding of the 'feminine'"—in the sense that the "feminine" is defined in contrast to the characteristics touted as required for career and business success.[70] Ideally, children fell in line along these sex and gender expectations. The "family altogether" implied home-life roles that met the working man's needs and—with some luck and the skilled and thoughtful activities of designated wives and mothers—prepared the next generation to carry the nation forward in like form.[71]

Paul Goodman's best-selling book *Growing Up Absurd* (1960) addresses the lack—in the US "system" and associated organized society and culture—of meaningful engagement and self-justifying work for US youth, specifically boys. An organized US society proves incapable of meeting the meaning-creating needs of young men, leading to "delinquency," cynicism, and "wasted" human resources. For a moment, however, Goodman steps away from this discussion; he notes that he does not address the situation of "girls." It's unimportant, he writes, what "job" she works "till she is married." Girls are not expected to "make something" of themselves or have a "self-justifying" career path. Instead, "she will have children, which is absolutely self-justifying, like any other natural or creative act."[72] The "youth troubles" about which Goodman writes are apparently grander and more complex than would be the case if he were focused on "girls." Girls' "troubles" emerge as divergent steps, or missteps, on the natural and self-justifying path to childbirth. "Female delinquency," he writes, is straightforwardly sexual, presenting as "incorrigibility" and resulting in "unwanted pregnancy."[73]

That a social theorist so concerned with homogenizing social roles in an organized society fails to acknowledge the ways in which he positions females firmly within just such roles—as girlfriend, wife, and, of course, mother—is a stark statement of female subordination in the era's thought. Goodman's blind spot also witnesses to the disregard shown to female identity development, let alone female talent and ambition. Tellingly, for a female, any act that is socially legible—that is, recognizable in such a cosmology—must be conceptualized with childbirth as the ultimate end. Apparently, any alternative path for a female would be understood or visualized through sexuality or sexualization, as delinquency or perversion. On designed-for-success instructional records, we encounter these stringent sex role limitations. We also recognize the representational absences, what we don't see, that imply "delinquent" acts of self-creation—female and male.

Helen Gurley Brown's exploration in her "sensational best seller" *Sex and the Single Girl* (1962) might have emerged precisely from Goodman's offhand paragraph in *Growing Up Absurd*. It's as if she took Goodman at his word and expanded his observation into an etiquette and rule book for the "single" years of a female's life. "Single girls" will eventually marry and have children—that is their true path, Brown concurs. But, until they are married—and as part of their efforts to gain access to "better" men—exerting a bit of independence and flirting with sexual experience and carefully managed affairs was not a path from which to shy away. Marriage trumps career: "Sometimes a girl meets the wrong kind of man *for her* in her job. That calls for a job shift."[74]

The Hear How series from Carlton Records largely focused on skills—for example, *Hear How to Become a Better Bowler*, or *Hear How to Plan the Perfect Dinner Party* (a treasure from our book *Designed for Hi-Fi Living*). However, a few of their releases ventured into more intimate domains. HEAR HOW TO ACHIEVE SEXUAL HARMONY IN MARRIAGE depicts a boy and a girl, seemingly siblings, on swings being pushed by a couple, presumably their parents. The swinging motion—back and forth, up and down—performs a fitting segue into the first points of Dr. Rebecca Liswood's short lectures: "The Interpersonal Relationships in Marriage" and "What Is 'Love'?" Her advice for a successful sexual relationship in marriage? Allow for "preliminary lovemaking, the actual intercourse, and staying in each other's arms for a while." A husband and wife should be friends, she urges, relax in each other's company, and trust each other.

The more rudimentary material, much like that on Carlton's companion album *Hear How to Tell Your Children the Facts of Life* (interested readers may want to peek at chapter 6) concerns female and male "sex anatomy" and "conception and contraception." Dr. Liswood doesn't think much of the "rhythm method." Her discussion of female orgasm, sexual stimulation, and the concluding "sexual harmony in marriage" conjures "wonderful" and "satisfying" moments when spouses try not to blame or judge—and the wife (with diaphragm inserted before bedtime) is "always ready." Dr. Liswood's response to the complaint that after ejaculating a husband jumps up immediately to wash? "The boys have been indoctrinated that way in the army. Tell him he's not in the army now. He can stay put." Note: the military training records in this book—*Airman!!* and *The Making of a Marine!*—do not include that maneuver.

Hear How to Achieve Sexual Harmony in Marriage text on image:

HEAR HOW TO ACHIEVE SEXUAL HARMONY IN MARRIAGE

CARLTON HEAR HOW SERIES
CHH/28

DR. REBECCA LISWOOD, Exec. Director of the Marriage Counseling Service of Greater New York discusses the intimate relationships that can create a happy marriage.

FIGURE 0.8

Hear How to Achieve Sexual Harmony in Marriage,
Dr. Rebecca Liswood,
Carlton CHH 28, 1956.

LISTENING, MEMORY, AND LEARNING

Midcentury instructional records often delivered spoken information—lectures, focused lessons, scripted scenarios, foreign language phrases—with the important option of multiple repetitions, of listening again and again. Xerox Corporation's *Effective Listening* LP (explored further in chapter 1) presents listening as "the fundamental art on which all communication depends—the understanding and retention of spoken information." The elephant-evoking album *Modern Memory Methods* (chapter 1) designates memory training and recall as "the most important prerequisite" to schooling and learning. Thus, these records support a view of communication and learning that emphasize listening and retaining information. Listening is a skill, and a means of memorizing and potentially retaining information. Clearly, in combination, listening and memory capacities are essential to many forms of learning.

Without a doubt, a listener emerged as a key element to recorded sound: the listener "is figured as a subject whose auditory stance is determined by broader historical shifts in social identities and musical aesthetics."[75] As seen in the music appreciation movement, what is to be listened to is caught up in issues of identity—sex, class, and race. While the figure of the listener is generally "defined in predominately 'neutral,' nongendered, and nonracial terms, the Western aural self is deeply caught up with the history and politics of difference."[76] In other words, listening, as a personal and cultural practice, adheres to other socially prescribed paths, including what Jennifer Stoever calls "the sonic color line." Our identity, our background, and our geographical origins each help determine who and what we listen to, what we like, and how we experience sounds—particularly music.[77]

But what do the implicit assumptions of designed-for-success albums tell us about midcentury instructional philosophies? What about communication and learning that happen without spoken communication? Many experiences of "learning through doing" take place without speaking, and, therefore, with a different kind of listening. Critical theorist Sayan Dey, who writes on the mobilization of silence in what may be seen as non-Western and Native cultures, has argued that crucial forms of learning may indeed take place in silence.[78] What of those people, or cultures, who emphasize these other forms of learning?[79] What happens when they are up against educational systems that prioritize verbal communication and "the understanding and retention of spoken information" taken for granted on instructional records?

Sociologist Pierre Bourdieu recognized that educational institutions tend to perceive and promote as successful those children who begin school with certain learning dispositions already developed in the family and home environment—what he called the "primary pedagogic work."[80] This preparatory work facilitates children's verbal and language capacities, rather than their facility to make or do. Apparently diverse potentials, fostered in the home, bring benefits or deficits once children enter schools and encounter the ruling educational pedagogies that favor and promote students with mastery of abstract, symbolic realms, including language. Bourdieu associated these distinct modes with social class.[81] In other words, midcentury instructional records display familiar tendencies in their approach to teaching and learning, in part driven by the material characteristics and potential of the vinyl record itself.[82]

Tim Anderson, who focuses on the act of listening, writes, "We should recognize these instructional records for the clues about listening, both actual and idealized, that they are. They teach us how listening can instruct our attention and how we might listen to records to develop ourselves."[83] In his call for a sound studies to complement and contextualize the growth of visual culture studies, media theorist Jonathan Sterne argues that "sound, hearing, and listening are central to the cultural life of modernity, and sound, hearing, and listening are foundational to modern modes of knowledge, culture, and social organization."[84] He traces how listening was shaped by sound reproduction technologies, including the phonograph, and became more directive, private, and eventually, commodified.[85] Within what cultural theorist Kate Lacey calls the phonographic imagination, recordings "transformed the ways in which individuals and communities came to believe they could control who and what they listened to, and how they listened to it."[86]

Many instructional records rely on "the instructional style," in which speakers sound like teachers or mimic a lecturing professor, patiently intoning facts in a manly, authoritative mode.[87] In other words, a voice of credibility. The voice has been traditionally thought of as a vehicle of meaning and as a source of aesthetic admiration. Philosopher Mladen Dolar proposed that the voice can be considered a lever of thought that induces and influences thinking.[88] Instructional records, in their reliance on the narrator's voice, exemplify this notion. In particular, records aimed at influencing the mind, such as *The Burgess Method: Developing Your ESP Powers* and *Better Golf through Hypnosis*, deploy the voice in complex ways to induce relaxed concentration, utterly dependent on the narrator's voice.

Instructional records played on home hi-fi systems in concert with other LPs that supported cultural confidence and greater ease with cosmopolitan identities. These midcentury marvels offered guidance for boosting your bowling score, promoting your domestic dreams, and teaching your parakeet to talk.

PLAN FOR THE BOOK

Designed for Success is organized into four parts: "At Work," "At Home," "At Leisure," and "On Vinyl and Cultural History." The first three sections elaborate key assumptions and contours of the self-improvement and success movements, with chapters such as "Paths to Persuasion: Selling and Salesmanship," "Family Fidelity: The Harmonious Marriage and Well-Adjusted Children," and "Learning to Listen: Music Appreciation." Each chapter focuses on a designed-for-success theme that emerged from reflecting on the albums—their cover art, content, and the contexts in which they were released. Featured records in each chapter engage activities and lessons such as "selling the sizzle," "expanding your mind," or "learning to play the bongos." The final section offers wider reflections on the cultural history of vinyl records in midcentury media.

We have assembled illustrative and entertaining instructional records, turning again to a large vinyl archive—ours. In our selections, we were especially drawn to LPs that offer windows into practices and pleasures of bygone eras, including self-help titles *Music to Help You Stop Smoking* and *Training Your Dog to Hunt, Point, Retrieve*, and the entrepreneurial ruminations of *Think and Grow Rich* and *What It Takes to Be a Great Salesman*.

We include over 125 examples, released between 1950 and 1978. This era marks the golden age of instructional records, as the genre grew along with the recording industry: "After World War II, a resurgence of record sales and the development of long-playing formats set the stage for the reappearance of some of the diversity of the earliest days of recorded sound, making the postwar era a particularly dynamic period in which to study the phonograph industry."[89] We think the album covers are pretty great, too.

We describe these instructional albums, attending to salient elements that mark their role in the modernist project. We discuss how they encouraged US consumers to buy a record, bring it home, and turn the kitchen, den, or rec room into a classroom, a place for "doing," as well as a setting for incubating ambition. We consider social and cultural issues that animate these records via their photography, liner notes, graphic design, and sound. (Throughout the book, excerpts of liner notes and passages from spoken scripts on the records appear in quotes, without footnotes.) We reveal how instructional records provide listeners with guidelines for success, as well as lessons in listening your way to a better life: new career opportunities, sophisticated taste, and a path to the American dream. We revisit celebrated experts Jack LaLanne and Dr. Joyce Brothers, sports heroes Arthur Ashe and Arnold Palmer, as well as personalities relegated to obscurity, like choreographer, dancer, and educator Marie Brooks and hypnotist Russ Burgess. These successful figures offer an insightful glimpse of what counted for expertise in the era.

Along with the records, our sources include a range of archival material, including industry publications like *Billboard* and *Talking Machine World*; period advertisements from general magazines and music publications; record company brochures and catalogs; contemporaneous books, films, magazines and newspapers; and online resources. We concentrate on records selected from our own "analog archive" of records that we have collected, curated, and contemplated for over thirty years. Rather than provide a rote reading of each album, we vary the discussion—focusing on aspects that we think are illuminating, interesting, or inexplicable, and drawing connections to larger themes.

We find traces of midcentury modernism in unexpected places, and show how the imperatives of the era—economic growth, self-improvement, and personal success— are both reflected and encouraged by instructional records. We were inspired by legendary media theorist Marshall McLuhan's illuminating, influential, and idiosyncratic analysis of midcentury media, which he called "the folklore of industrial man."[90] We pay

close attention to visual aspects of album cover art, including graphic design and photography, as well as typography—"a tool for doing things *with*: shaping content, giving
language a physical body, enabling the social flow of messages."[91] Like McLuhan's, our
approach focuses on a specific set of examples that form an extended visual argument:
cumulative in its effect, but arbitrary in its preferred order of reading. In other words,
unlike when listening to records, skipping around is encouraged.

A close look at the instructional record provides unique insights into compelling
midcentury expectations, representations, and communication technologies that remain with us today. Instructional records represent an important precursor to contemporary social media obsessions with self-improvement and self-transformation. We
maintain our goal of changing—or enhancing—the way people look at and think about
midcentury record albums.

AT WORK

Jonathan's high school swim coach was fond of proclaiming "what the mind can conceive, the body can achieve" when encouraging the team to post faster times and attempt more difficult dives. He must have been thinking of legendary success writer Napoleon Hill's slogan "What the mind of man can conceive, it can achieve," from his famous self-help book *Think and Grow Rich*. Published in 1937 and still in print, *Think and Grow Rich* was purportedly based on interviews with famous and successful Americans like Luther Burbank, Thomas Edison, and George Eastman—although there is some controversy over whether Hill ever met any of his informants.[1] Nevertheless, his best-selling insights inspired millions and produced several spin-offs including *Think and Grow Rich: A Black Choice* (1991), *Think and Grow Rich for Women* (2014), and, of course, a *Think and Grow Rich* record, released in 1960.

With their straightforward titles and capitalist realist design, midcentury career training records often elicit laughter and surprise today—at least when we have introduced them to those (sadly) uninitiated into the earnest yet intriguing world of instructional albums. But they're not much different from LinkedIn Learning courses, personal branding videos, and mandatory online training classes that so many of us must endure. All draw upon that great reservoir of aspirational self-improvement that wells up when encountering records like *How to Succeed* and *What It Takes to Be a Great Salesman*—leading listeners to wonder, "Why not me?"

Self-improvement that sharpens work-related skills and expands opportunities springs from well-defined directives. Salespeople need more persuasive selling tactics, practice makes perfect for new stenographers, and leaders require enhanced listening techniques to support team communication. The midcentury workplace, whether office, factory, construction site, or recording studio, was a zone for productivity, evaluation, and the performance of new skills and burgeoning potentials. Instructional records delivered lessons and lectures, offering chances to get a leg up on the competition. Entrepreneurial ideas from industry leaders leapt from vinyl grooves—wisdom for the midcentury masses.

"At work" instructional records cater to a wide variety of careers that require a multitude of abilities. Ranging across office jobs, sales positions, military training—even breaking into the entertainment industry—work-focused albums embrace scientific management and the modern, efficient organization. For example, *How to Get Appointments by Telephone* offers basic advice about a fundamental business skill. *Actual Business Letters* focuses on secretarial work, a profession transformed by the introduction of electric typewriters in the 1940s and, later, of course, word processors. Many instructional albums were designed to improve cognitive skills like communicating, listening, and memorizing—useful outside of the office, as well. All encourage listeners to play them repeatedly.

Some, like Amway's *Sing Out for Free Enterprise* and *Selling America*, from Amway founder Richard DeVos, boosted enthusiasm in the interest of better sales and recruitment. Amway's albums combine work and pleasure, mixing speech and singing in often less-than-successful selections. Amway developed a potent combination of franchising and what would eventually be called the "gig economy." Much like Uber and Lyft today, Amway distributors were not considered employees; they often had other jobs and worked from home. At their peak, over one million distributers sold Amway products.[2] In the company's terms, "unique to the direct selling industry, the Amway Distributors Association has fulfilled its challenge through the years to uphold and support the effort that you and your fellow distributors put forth in building your own independent Amway businesses."[3] A critical aspect of their growth involved encouraging current "distributors" to recruit new ones.[4] In other words, selling the idea of selling Amway.

At midcentury, sales training records abounded. The Businessman's Record Club, modeled on the Book of the Month Club, delivered a stream of success records to subscriber's mailboxes. The Success Motivation Institute's "motivation, leadership development, and sales training recorded courses" included a printed copy of the entire recording script. One of their offerings, *Tough-Minded Management*, from 1966, boasted: "You now possess one of the world's finest combinations of personal communication and specialized knowledge. Simultaneously, through your own channels of sound and sight, you will acquire, retain, and be able to use the invaluable information, authored by one of the International Masters of Success." Sign us up!

Instructional records reflect changing aspects of the workplace, including the growing field of design thinking and the march of technological advancement. Industrial designers like Donald Deskey, Henry Dreyfuss, and George Nelson sought to streamline workspaces with specialized furniture and discrete zones for concentrated work and coffee breaks. Meanwhile, a rising tide of occupational experts were eager to offer advice for every aspect of working life. Training records such as *Effective Listening*, *Speed Reading Made Easy for Everyone*, and *Tough-Minded Management* reflect the influence of scientific management in their quest for efficiency.

In the age of laptops, spell-check, and voice recognition software, it may be hard to understand the importance of skills like shorthand, stenography, and typing for corporate life. Business letters were but one context for stenography; reporting and re-cording in courtrooms or for other matters of public concern made accurate shorthand critical for getting the story right and creating the historical record.

Steno Booster opens a window into the gendered nature of office roles. This "dic-tation speed and accuracy training course" record aimed at aspiring secretaries. As design curator Ellen Lupton observes: "Whereas the traditional clerk often had been responsible for mentally *composing* as well as physically *writing* a text, workers in the mechanized office were assigned limited functions as stenographers (who captured ex-ecutive's words in shorthand) and typists (who mechanically transcribed such words.)"[5] Of course, "executive" meant "male," and "stenographers and typists" implied "female" at midcentury. In that way, innovations in office technology fostered ever more spe-cialized jobs, with arguably less leeway for individual creativity or for breaking down gendered (and raced) occupational roles.

Notably, self-improvement inhabits a porous boundary between work, home, and leisure arenas. Well-pronounced phrases gleaned from *Hear How to Improve Your Vocabulary and Speech*, or the behavior of a well-behaved dog, trained with the help of *Training Your Dog to Hunt, Point, Retrieve*, might impress the boss. Basic social graces, an appealing appearance, and some simple dance steps might smooth the path to career success. Although some instructional records are artifacts of corporate training programs, most represent the do-it-yourself ethos of self-improvement. For example, LPs for mastering motivational sales techniques depict sober—if heroic—achievement, yet evoke an optimism of individual progress and new opportunities. As a category, at-work instructional records reveal unexpected insights into the yearnings of an era.

Let's get to work.

1 BECOMING A BETTER WORKER
EFFICIENCY, PRODUCTIVITY, AND CAREER TRAINING

Veterans occasionally refer to the recruiting slogan that was popular when they signed up, as in "We're 'Be All You Can Be' soldiers" or "He's 'Army Strong.'" We can remember seeing, throughout high school, a US Armed Forces recruitment television ad that stated: "Army. Navy. Air Force. Marines. We Don't Ask for Experience. We Give It. You Won't Read It in a Book. You'll Live It."

In the late 1960s, the Army's recruiting efforts focused on success. The album HOW TO SUCCEED includes "messages"—meant for radio play—that provide glimpses into the military's efforts to continue to recruit amid growing unrest about the Vietnam War. One of a series of *How to Succeed* recordings "Presented as a Public Service by the United States Army," the record includes twenty-four tracks, ranging from twenty to sixty seconds. The label's fine print states: "This record is the property of the Government of the United States and must be used as public service material only." And, in bold capital letters: "Do not use after 1969." The Saturday-morning-cartoonish cover shows an adventurous group of recruits, including paratrooper, helicopter pilot, and scuba diver, as well as more familiar figures of nurse, radio operator, surveyor, and air traffic signaler.

With no immediate plans to embark on a late military career, we decided nevertheless to subject ourselves to the Army's recruiting messages. First up, a sixty-second spot, "High School." This musical number includes rock instruments with singers that sound a bit like the Beach Boys meet the Mamas and the Papas. The song urges impressionable listeners: "With Army a future you can choose. With Army the future's up to you." Spoken parts inform you that you can learn to "tell a computer what to say" and "move a mountain that's in the way." A more mature-sounding narrator closes with a stern command: "Your future. Your decision. Choose Army." A few spots feature short dramatic scenarios, enhanced with military sound effects, like pulsing helicopters and firing rifles. Other spots include "Professional Nurse," "Sounds of Leadership," and "While You're Young." On one called "Communication," we're introduced to Jane Andrews, a captain in the Women's Army Corps. She's stationed in Munich, and on weekends she "sees the sites"—"the timeless heart of Old Bavaria, Paris, Amsterdam, Venice." Jane "didn't want an everyday-type job. She wanted responsibilities. She

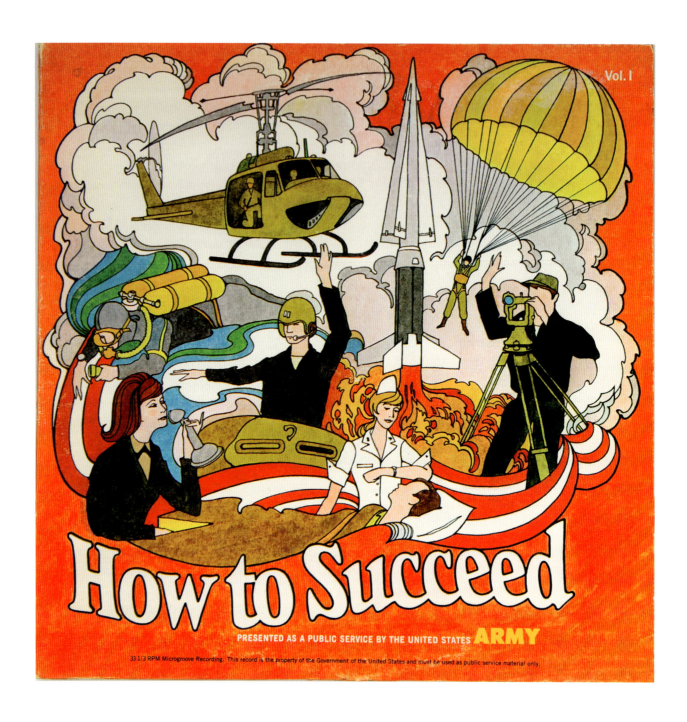

FIGURE 1.1

*How to Succeed: Presented as a Public Service
by the United States Army,*
Government of the United States, ca. 1968.

wanted challenges." The spot ends: "A chance to put your talents to work, while you see the world." No mention of Southeast Asia.

On the cover of an unusual rectangular album package (10¼ inch by 11¾ inch) of muted turquoise, apricot orange, and olive green, a cartoon-like Boy Scout dressed in familiar khaki uniform, with neckerchief and cap, reaches out with distended arm, tapping a telegraph sounder in an effort to LEARN THE INTERNATIONAL MORSE CODE. In a nice visual touch, Morse code dots and dashes emanate from the sounder. The cover's diverse size type, set at various angles, strikes us as similar to album cover design originator Alex Steinweiss's legendary layouts for midcentury Columbia Records.[1] Such creative typography may signal the record's young audience, as if a Scout had designed it to earn a graphic arts merit badge.

Promising "faster, easier" learning with the Raybrun Code-Voice Method, the recording was produced for the Boy Scouts of America, which was responsible for training thousands in Morse code during World War II. The album includes two ten-inch 78 rpm discs, since "the best way to learn code is by listening to it—by hearing." *Learn the International Morse Code* was advertised in popular magazines such as *Boy's Life* and *Popular Mechanics*, as well as *QST*, the official publication of the American Radio Relay League. An amateur radio association commended the album in a post from 2017: "Together, the BSA's classic album and booklet are an efficient, effective method of teaching the Morse code to interested young Americans and is highly recommended."[2] (A recording of the album is available on YouTube.)

The liner notes begin:

> Drums throbbing in the jungle . . . the flash and boom of a cannon at sea . . . puffs of smoke rising from a mountain top . . . bonfires blazing in the night . . . Paul Revere's signal lantern in the Old North Church Tower . . . those are just a few of the means that men throughout history have used to "get the message through" in peace and war.

The recording communicates the enthusiasm and competence of a scout troop leader: "Today we're going to have fun and learn something at the same time. Morse code is used to send messages between ships at sea and airplanes in the sky, and trains and railroad stations, too." The notes chime in, "if you know the Morse Code, you can tap out secret messages with your finger to a friend in the same room, qualify as a First Class Scout, and earn the Signaling Merit Badge." *Learn the International Morse Code* embraces self-improvement, pledging that learning Morse code opens a path to future success, both in the Scouts and beyond. Teaching a language that is "likely to be more useful to you than mastery of Latin, Greek, French, or Spanish," the album offers a quick, comprehensive course in the code, allowing the listener to hear the signal tones and memorize the correct letter relation.

FIGURE 1.2

Learn the International Morse Code,
Raybrun E1 KB 1894,
pressed by RCA Victor, 1951.

Manual typewriter, rotary telephone, and portable turntable form a gray midcentury tableau for the secretary whose similarly hued gray dress, nylon-band diamond wristwatch, prim curls, and puritan collar with secured pearly buttons subdue sex appeal. Perhaps she imagines a rosier, dreamier future in the grooves of Steno-disc Records' ACTUAL BUSINESS LETTERS.

The LP's goal? To develop shorthand for "added speed and confidence." Shorthand, or stenography, has roots in antiquity as a simplified, efficient writing method that helps stenographers write faster and in less space. Media historian Lisa Gitelman places shorthand and stenography within a history of writing and recording systems, all driven by claims of quickness, efficiency, and "naturalness."[3] For those charged with putting the marks and symbols on paper, success in mastering the system required diligence and skill: "So knowing and complying with a specific shorthand system, amid its rigorous structure of approved rules and its vociferous promotion of 'best' systems, must have lent its users a sense of rightness, of authority, of being in step, which comprises so much of the ideology of literacy."[4]

Actual Business Letters includes band after band of recorded dictation, 80 to 90 words per minute on side 1, and up to 100 wpm on side 2. Not merely a family member or friend reading out simplistic sentences or hypothetical business concerns—this LP presents the real thing. "Dear Sir," begins side 1, leading the way into varied, well-articulated, and quick-paced dictations. Letters present informative marketing and sales pitches, brief resumés, and layoff notifications with strong concluding lines: "Very Cordially Yours." Additional options in this record series include "all standard word phrases" and "business letters for students" in speeds up to a breathtaking 240 words per minute. In an era of "never-ending need for qualified stenographers and secretaries," the notes inform, company lending libraries made certain all the gals could check out a practice record and "use them at their leisure at home." So much for home as a place of leisure.

"Practice at home today . . . a better paying job tomorrow" promises the cover of STENO BOOSTER, a record that offers a "new easy way to boost your shorthand speed!" *Steno Booster* was part of a well-developed "listening at home" curriculum of recordings, including those for boosting steno speed, shorthand, typing, and "sound spelling" to "help poor spellers become good spellers." Although the terms on the record—dictation, shorthand, stenography—may seem outdated, many autofill functions on our laptops and smartphone apps offer equivalents for common phrases and terms; shorthand lives on in our electronic devices. The record presents several business letters dictated at speeds varying from 90 to 130 words per minute. Lucky for the learner, each letter is reproduced in the enclosed booklet. In a nice cross-promotional ploy, the letters include one from the Conversa-phone company that describes the benefits of their line of instructional records, including this one. We like the cover photograph of a budding stenographer, smartly dressed and snuggled up on her midcentury couch, dutifully listening to an instructional record player, writing pad in hand. "Remember, better work means more pay for you!"

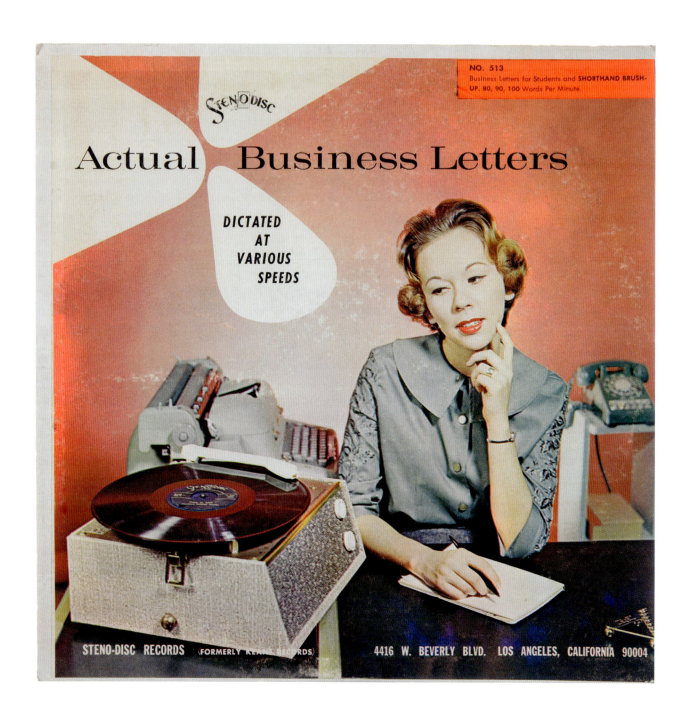

FIGURE 1.3

Actual Business Letters,
Stenodisc No. 513, ca. 1950.

FIGURE 1.4

Steno Booster,
Conversa-phone S 202, 1961.

A spider's web spiral, echoing the era's *Twilight Zone* and ESP graphics, centers a Janus-faced chiaroscuro woodcut in black, muted orange, and yellow, embedded in chocolate brown—a familiar palette from late 1960s interior and textile design. Modernist typography, evocative of early computing, announces the future of EFFECTIVE LISTENING on this box set released by Xerox Learning Systems. Drawing on design technologies of the day, the elaborate package holds a brown die-cut cardboard insert with perforated inverted folds and cutaways that house two identical rectangular eighty-plus-page "listener response booklets" that repeat the album cover image. The enclosed materials include a 1957 *Harvard Business Review* article, "Listening to People"; an "Effective Listening Pre-test"; space for writing in recording-prompted responses; and a "post-test." The back cover page could be filled in, detached, and sent in for a "Certificate of Accomplishment that is suitable for framing." Thus, unlike most corporate training films, this material was meant to be used at home as well as the office. Three LPs in complementary beige, yellow, and orange inner sleeves deliver opportunities to practice "the fundamental art on which all communication depends—the understanding and retention of spoken information."

The listening begins with a number of conversational monologues, including a drunken man buying more booze and secretarial patter in a high-pitched nasal female voice. An authoritative male narrator introduces the notion of important versus unimportant information, as he recites statistics about how much detail most of us miss in daily interactions (75 percent), and explains Xerox Learning System's commitment to education and improvement. Being "an active participant with ample opportunity to respond the same as you would in real life" translates into five sides of exercises geared toward advancing abilities to "outline with the use of key words," "discriminate between relevancies and irrelevancies," and "cut through distractions such as unusual accents and dialects," as well as "speaker bias, disorganization, and emotion." Not meant as a solitary activity, one may "enjoy taking the program most with another person" or order extra response booklets and make a "social gathering" out of it.

MODERN MEMORY METHODS offers a course in memory training—"by far the most important prerequisite to all schooling, training or learning." The record starts by inferring that "you are probably taking the course because you feel a need for more earning power, more job security, greater knowledge, more free time, increased social popularity or a boost in self-confidence." Wow. Sign us up!

A graphically compelling cover image of an elephant, taking the shape of a capital "M," presents the enduring symbol of powerful memory. Textured dark gray cardboard mimics an elephant's hide, and a string around the elephant's trunk signals a reminder. Donald A. Robinson, the man behind the record, taught courses for such corporations as General Dynamics. The narrator, Blaine P. Worrell, DDS, is described as "one of California's leading radio and TV announcers." He provides personal inspiration for switching careers: "After completing this memory course, he decided to become a dentist." The Modern Memory Methods liner notes suggest answering a few questions if you're

FIGURE 1.5

Xerox: Effective Listening,
Columbia CSM 1205 7, 1970.
Courtesy of Xerox Corporation.

FIGURE 1.6

Xerox: Effective Listening,
interior, Columbia CSM 1205 7, 1970.
Courtesy of Xerox Corporation.

considering the course—for example, "How often are you embarrassed by forgetting a name?" or "Are you uneasy around your boss because you have to keep 'looking it up'?" Furthermore, "Did you lose a sale, client or customer due to forgetting?" Affirmative answers? "Then this course will be of tremendous value to you."

Invoking "positive thinking," Robinson recruits a stellar cast of quotes from Norman Vincent Peale, William James, and the Bible to convince would-be listeners that "if you put your whole heart and effort into any project, never doubting your success, you will achieve it." The key revelation? "Memory is based on a formula we call the 4 Rs: Record, Retain, Recall, and Remember." The material is straightforward and fairly easy to take in. Side 1 offers several rules for remembering names: ask the person to repeat his name. Repeat the name immediately (everyone likes to hear the sound of his own name). Associate the name with something or somebody you know. Side 2 provides a somewhat more intricate system of matching words to remember numbers. It's a classic associative way of memorizing things—perhaps the effort needed to remember the system develops memory on its own.

Those who watched US television in the 1970s surely recall ads for Evelyn Wood speed-reading courses that promised free introductory lessons in "reading dynamics." Wood epitomized the speed-reading fad that peaked long before today's apps and YouTube videos reanimated claims to improve reading speed and comprehension. SPEED READING MADE EASY FOR EVERYONE, endorsed by the American Reading Society, promises: "You can read faster . . . understand more . . . enjoy your reading more! This album tells you how!" Bold claims for reading success pronounce: "Actual tests prove that you can at least double your reading speed by using this record for thirty days." The album cover features a checkerboard pattern of blue, black, and yellow squares, with graphic illustrations of the wide range of realms in which your new speed reading skills will come in handy: food preparation, bricklaying, rocketry, agriculture, technical drawing, and manufacturing.

The speed reading method's basic requirement involves training your eyes in visual techniques, including something called "rapid serial visual processing." As the liner notes remind the eager student, "The key to speed reading is smooth, effortless eye movement." *Speed Reading Made Easy* was produced by Stacy Keach Productions, specialists in theatrical, commercial, and industrial films and radio programs, run by the father of the actor Stacy Keach.

After close listening, we opened books and gave the techniques a try. While fresh in our minds, our reading focus seemed improved. But, after a couple of days, old habits returned. Clearly we would have to follow the note's reminder: "For the quickest results, practice every day!"

For decades, McGuffey Readers taught students to read and "democratized the arts of the spoken word."[5] Elocution, grammar, oratory, and rhetoric were regularly taught in schools, and rhetoric formed a cornerstone of liberal arts programs at universities.

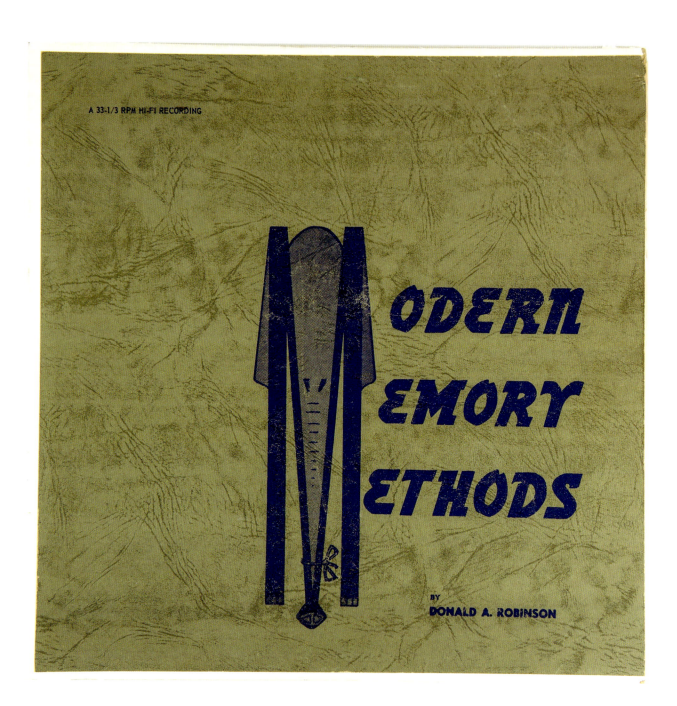

FIGURE 1.7

Modern Memory Methods,
no label, 1966.

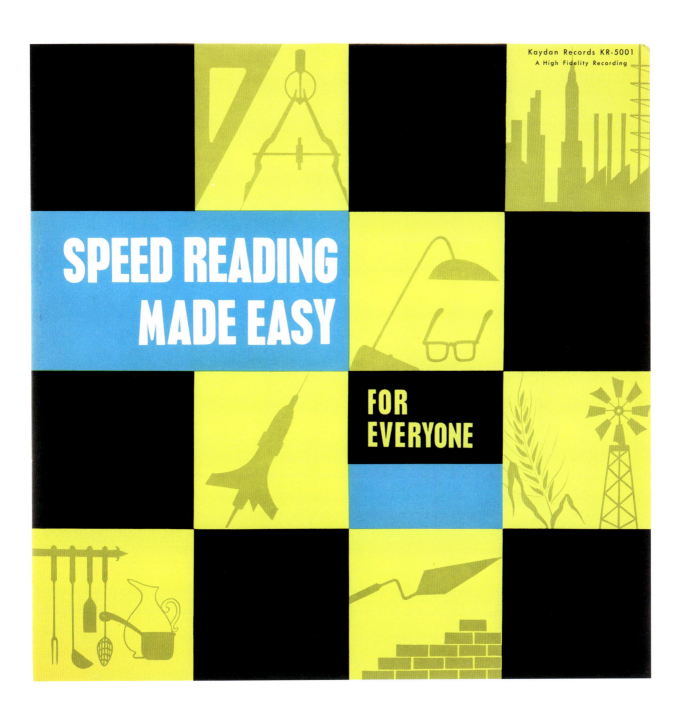

Within the image: Kaydan Records KR-5001 / A High Fidelity Recording / SPEED READING MADE EASY / FOR EVERYONE

FIGURE 1.8

Speed Reading Made Easy for Everyone,
Kaydan Records KR 5001, 1963.

Professor Richard Norman begins HEAR HOW TO IMPROVE YOUR VOCABU-
LARY AND SPEECH with English-language students' common complaint: "One can't
always tell from the way it's spelled how a word is pronounced." He runs through a list
of 150 words "you may be mispronouncing and/or misusing," such as "admirable," "eschew," "obsequious," and "victuals." A few examples strike the contemporary listener
as archaic holdovers from a mid-Atlantic accent. Should one pronounce "almond" with
the "l"? Norman says "the box of *amonds* is on the table." The album cover, with char-
acteristically understated *Hear How* graphics, presents photographs of three situations
in which improved speech and vocabulary may seal a deal. We see the boss at a board
meeting, standing and leaning into his pronouncement; a tea or coffee party with three
well-dressed women; and a telephone conversation.

    Hear How to Improve Your Vocabulary and Speech is straightforward—Norman
marches through the word list alphabetically in a conversational style. Not much ex-
planation appears as to why these particular words were selected, but, as Norman is
reportedly "one of the most distinguished speech teachers in the country," we'll assume
they were worthy of the recording. A favorite: "'chimera'—a fancy sort of word referring
to a horrible creature of the imagination."

"How well we express ourselves often determines our success in human relations,"
intone the liner notes for SPEAK WELL, "a self-teaching guide for better speech" from
Columbia Records. "We question the educational and social background of a person
who says 'The goil lives in New Joisey,'" writes producer Paul Mills, a specialist "in
developing the selling personality through better oral communication." As a scholarly
review of *Speak Well* primly noted, "Some listeners may find Mr. Mills' New York speech
and his occasional dentalization of initial (t) and (d) sounds distracting. The exercises
on the record are clearly aimed at correction of common New York speech faults."[6]
(Native New Yorkers may bristle at the suggestion that their way of talking is filled
with "faults.")

    This remarkably technical album offers "a modern method to overcome lisping,
nasality, fundamental pronunciation errors and many other incorrect speech habits"
for "voice personality development." When pronouncing "s" sounds? "Keep your tongue
up," and "do not touch your teeth." The notes "recommend learning correct speech
through a correct mechanical approach." A detailed booklet included with the disc
presents an anatomical drawing of the "speech organs" and a "vowel chart" for the
super studious.

    Billboard gave *Speak Well* a three-star review (good sales potential) upon its re-
lease in 1959: "Aimed primarily at business people and others who are in constant con-
tact with the public."[7] A sample of speaking situations illustrate the cover in a folksy
cartoony style—a public lecture, an Elizabethan-costumed theatrical production, a
teacher at a blackboard (remember those?), a clerk at a grocery store. There's also
a small drawing of the Statue of Liberty, hinting at a significant goal of the speech
exercises: to minimize "thick foreign accents" of immigrants. Listening to this record

FIGURE 1.9

Hear How to Improve Your Vocabulary and Speech,
Carlton CHH 23, 1961.

FIGURE 1.10

Speak Well: Off the Record,
Columbia CL 1361, 1959.

brought up a bunch of questions. What's "proper" English today? Who gets to decide how to pronounce certain words? How has the global diversity of English speakers influenced the language?

"Here within your grasp is your most valuable selling aid," the notes for HOW TO GET APPOINTMENTS BY TELEPHONE assure the listener. Released by the Success Motivation Institute, whose motto was "Breaking the success barrier," the record offers more than mere hints about how to get appointments. It's more of an all-inclusive sales course, with selections such as "How to Listen Effectively," "How to Overcome Objections," and "How to Be a Successful Salesman." The cover pairs a red graphic rocket with a bright red phone, suggesting technology's role in a modern and success-filled future.

How to Get Appointments by Telephone was created by Mona Ling (born Mona Rosenbalm), whose "training courses have been presented to thousands of salesmen across the continent." Somewhat disappointing, though, is the fact that Ling is not heard on the recording, but replaced with a standard, chipper male radio announcer. Sounding eerily contemporary, the record begins, "Today each of you has in your possession an Aladdin's Lamp. It's your telephone."

A small phone-book size "Reference Guide for Narration" includes the recorded script, "the commandments in telephone selling ('You shall think about the prospect's viewpoint at all times.' 'You shall not show off your technical vocabulary.' 'You shall not leave any objections unanswered')." How to Get Appointments by Telephone urges listeners to set high goals, as "low goals do not inspire a salesman to perfect his techniques." Echoing the principles of scientific management, listeners are encouraged to think about their "prospect time bank" and to establish a "prospecting control system." The notes quote UK prime minister William Gladstone: "Ninety men in every hundred in the crowded professions will never rise above mediocrity because the training of the voice is entirely neglected." Also included are handy checklists "for the real estate salesman," a "rating quiz" for personality traits, breathing exercises, and, of course, "correct voice work." The record heroically rallies excitement around telephone sales with noteworthy—if bombastic—declarations, such as "Telephoning is a creative adventure," and "Writing a telephone presentation is like writing a hit play."

"Here is a documentary record of where our nation's might begins" announces AIRMAN!! UNITED STATES AIR FORCE BASIC TRAINING IN SOUND! Recorded at Lackland Air Force Base in Texas, "with the cooperation of the United States Air Force," the album is one in a series of basic military training documentary records. Airman!! was an early project of documentary filmmaker George Casey, who went on to garner several Oscar nominations for short documentaries, including the 1980 IMAX film The Eruption of Mount St. Helens!

The lively recording intersperses field recordings of basic training exercises and interactions from "bus arrival at Lackland" to "processing out through assignments"

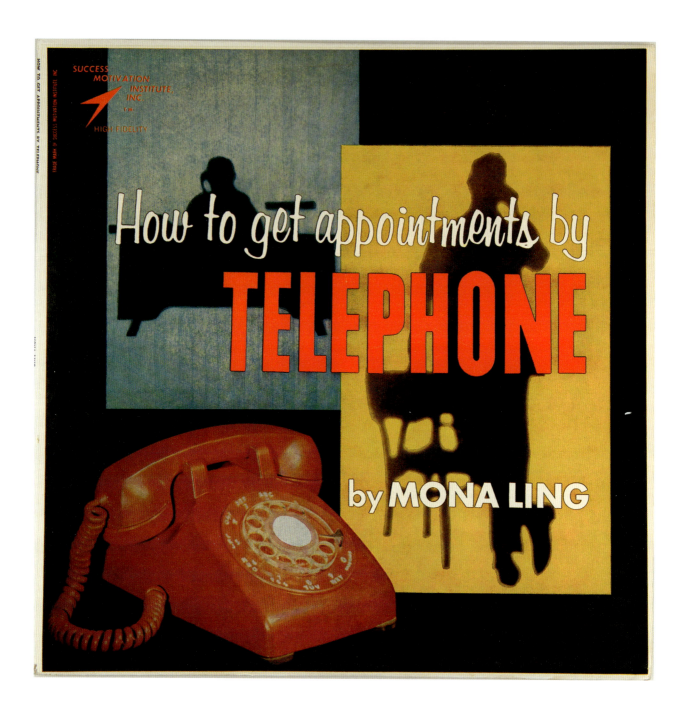

FIGURE 1.11

How to Get Appointments by Telephone,
Success Motivation Institute SMI 1318, 1965.

with narration and commentary from officers and recruits. The cover shows an extreme close-up of a training instructor—"TI" in military jargon—barking a command at a sweaty, bug-eyed recruit. The album title, spelled out in a stencil-like font called, ironically, Army, punctuated with two exclamation points, captures the exclamatory, enthusiastic, and exhausting environment of basic training.

Airman!! offers a poignant observation about basic training, "perhaps the most memorable period in the lives of hundreds of thousands of young American men." Fun facts are interspersed: "Total time for an Air Force haircut: twenty-nine seconds"; basic training "usually takes eleven weeks. The eleven busiest, most confused, colorful, KP-filled weeks of his life." Much like a movie trailer, the notes boast: "Here are the voices of basic training: the fearsome shouts of the TIs, the groan-filled cadence of PT [physical training], the barracks bull session, the stammered security instructions of the big inspection, and the recruit's piercing scream before he lands in the icy waters of the obstacle course." A training instructor's declaration—"It's not intended that you should like it"—captures the spirit of this "documentary in sound."

Documentary Recordings also released *A GI's Germany in Sound & Music!* volumes 1 and 2. *Airman!!* claims to be pressed on "polymax vinyl"—perhaps this was an innovative military development. In any event, the LP merits a listen as a proto–reality show document of an important experience in many lives and a fundamental aspect of military training designed to produce "self-reliance, responsibility, military polish and Air Force know-how."

On **THE MAKING OF A MARINE!** a giant exclamation point anchors blazing yellow capitals against striking scarlet and mimics sensationalist movie headline marketing. The cover incorporates several aspects of the Corps' official iconography, including the color scarlet and the anchor, eagle, and globe emblems. Filling much of the gatefold sleeve, a black-and-white documentary style shot of camouflaged members of the 1st Marine Division Reconnaissance Battalion reaffirms heroic realism. Shown storming from a Sikorsky H-34 "Choctaw" helicopter, carrying M1 rifles, the liner notes report: "This unit is currently in action in South Vietnam."

Descriptive notes and photos add detail to Marine "training in sound," commencing with "reception processing" and "rifle inspection in ranks," traveling through "rocket launcher training," and concluding with a segment captured during Operation Big Top off the California coast—an "amphibious and vertical envelopment" operation. "These are the real sounds, unstaged, and recorded on-the-spot." Microphones, recorders, and "twenty miles of recorded tape" as well as "the cooperation and the candor" of the US Marine Corps set the stage for fifty minutes that "should be played loudly."[8]

"Listen here to a record packed with all the necessary information needed to start an acting career," beckon the notes for **DO YOU WANT TO BECOME A MOVIE STAR?** The album offers an aspiring movie star real-life lessons: "Presents acting as a business, a business that that can be mastered by many to fill the growing talent needs of

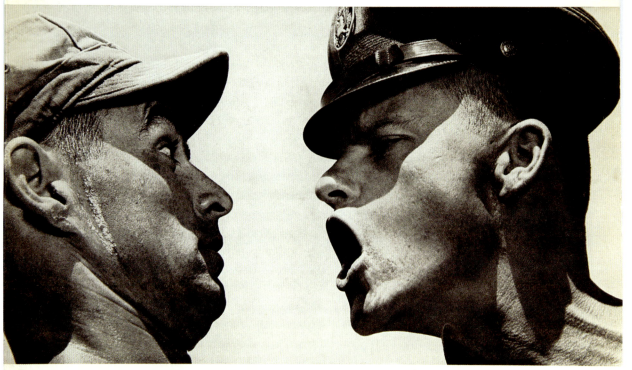

FIGURE 1.12

Airman!!,
Documentary Recordings LP 803, 1959.

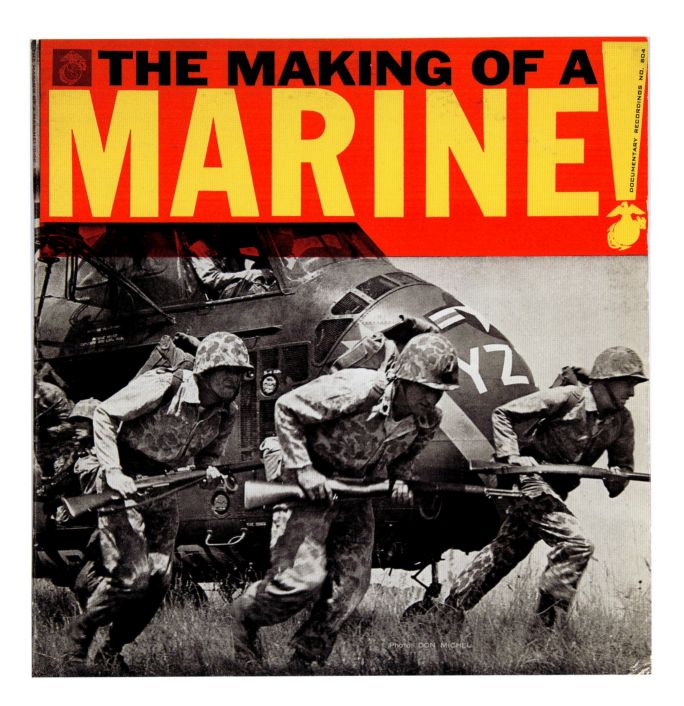

FIGURE 1.13

The Making of a Marine!,
Documentary Recordings LP 804;
photo by Don Michel, ca. 1959.

FIGURE 1.14

Do You Want to Become a Movie Star?,
Imperial LP 9130, 1960.

television, movies and the stage." On the cover, a Jayne Mansfield lookalike wearing a light pink, low-cut dress and formal white gloves beams at a man standing near her, while another man sits at a table stacked with actor headshots. A door in the background announces "Casting Office." (Given the notorious reputation of the "casting couch" it's disconcerting to follow the seated man's lascivious gaze—it seems clear what role he has in mind for her.)

Do You Want to Become a Movie Star? is presented by Jerry Bloom, a casting director for hit television shows *77 Sunset Strip, Alfred Hitchcock Presents*, and *The Outlaws*. According to the "About the Teacher" blurb on the back cover, Bloom "gave up a flourishing legal career for show business," A few name actors, such as Richard Evans, Robert Fuller, and Kathy Nolan, lend their talents to the disc, each divulging how they got their big break. All had worked with Jerry—after listening we felt like we were on a first-name basis—as a casting director. The LP opens with keen questions: "Do you want to be a star?" "Do you want to see your name in lights?" Quickly, though, Jerry offers a reality check: "Not everyone can be a star. Some of you must content yourself with a lessor place in the theatrical world." Given the rough shape of our copy, we hope that after many listenings the original owner found success.

PATHS TO PERSUASION
SELLING AND SALESMANSHIP

BIRTH OF A SALESMAN, we are informed, "is not a mere training program or a lecture. With all the tools of dramatization, full music, cast and effects, this record takes us back in time to catch a glimpse of the selling age of yesterday." Producer Bert Tenzer, whose records such as *The Secret for Perpetual Life* (1963) and *The Sky's the Limit* (1963) "carry an impact seldom achieved in the world of business," went on to produce television programs and films, and was known for his protoinfomercials in the guise of TV shows. A man of "unlimited resources of imagination and creativeness," Tenzer obviously had a passion for promotion. His liner notes report "years of preparation and research . . . months of script writing . . . weeks of recording studio production with a full cast and music." He brags that *Birth of a Salesman* "belongs in the record library of the all-time greats," and that "listening to it is, in itself, a thrilling experience."

The recording begins with a solemn narrator—a bit like a sales-oriented Rod Serling (of *Twilight Zone* fame)—intoning "the ticking of a clock sets a pace and no one dare fall behind." Spooky sound effects accompany a "flashback to another era" of patent-medicine men and snake-oil salesmen, who would have "no chance against the consumer of today." Salesmen need to "keep pace with the times," listeners are told, as several scripted scenarios play out. Tactics like "strategic questioning" are explained to help salesmen "hit the target" with "precision selling."

The drumbeat of self-improvement—as well as a fear of failure—pulses through the recording, urging listeners to be better than past salesmen, improve their sales tactics, and never fall behind. *Birth of a Salesman*, while not quite reaching the dramatic heights of Arthur Miller's Pulitzer Prize–winning play *Death of a Salesman* (1949), the tragic tale of Willy Loman, was entertaining to hear. Listening wasn't quite the thrill the notes promised, but the creatively produced record surpasses most Businessmen's Record Club selections for contemporary interest and introspective presentation.

Birth of a Salesman's cover design is credited to Don May, who worked for Chicago design firm Hoskinson, Rohloff, and Associates.[1] Against a big city nightscape, a lone salesman, with briefcase in one hand and overcoat in the other, walks an animated path, dotted lines marking his sales territory while indicating his movement within it.[2] His graphic, clip art–like form allows him to stand in for every (sales)man, his uniform of suit, hat, and tie visible as details, as he strides on to the next customer. Unadorned sans serif font spells out the album title, with "Sales" emphasized in white and slightly misaligned with "Man." Aptly, the cover art resembles a poster for a play or Broadway show.

With a literary imagination, one can see inspiration from Miller's *Death of a Salesman* prologue: "Before us is the Salesman's house. We are aware of the towering, angular shapes behind it, surrounding it on all sides. Only the blue light of the sky falls upon the house and forestage. . . . [A]n air of the dream clings to the place, a dream rising out of reality."[3] The humble *Birth of a Salesman* cover also hearkens back to Alex Steinweiss, the legendary inventor of modern cover design, and one of his early efforts, *Columbia Records Presents Gershwin's Rhapsody in Blue* from 1942, with its strikingly similar building forms and dotted lines. Connections can also be made to Reid Miles's illustrious designs for Blue Note records. For example, his classic cover for Sonny Clark's *Cool Struttin'* (1958) features similar typography.[4] The *Birth of a Salesman* cover might be considered a bargain basement Blue Note, its aspirational themes drawing inspiration from the prestigious jazz label's standard setting designs.

"80% of the Nation's Buying Power Is Controlled by Women" hypes a heading on the back cover of DOTTIE WALTERS REVEALS THE SEVEN SECRETS OF SELLING TO WOMEN. Listeners are offered not just "seven selling secrets," but "seven keys to reaching this unlimited buying power." The author of numerous books, including *Speak and Grow Rich* and *Never Underestimate the Selling Power of a Woman*, Walters was a founding member of the National Speakers Association.[5] The liner notes report: "Her counsel on the distaff side of sales psychology is based on the sound experience of directing and operating her own advertising firm." The album is endorsed by none other than *Think and Grow Rich*'s author Napoleon Hill: "How does it feel to be a girl who has just blown the world a blast of inspirational star dust?" (Hmm. That sounds like a backhanded compliment to us.)

The cover highlights the color red: vibrant red roses, red typography, and Walters's red lips pop out from the black background and play off of her red hair. This cover recalls Victor Keppler's 1950 photograph for Camel cigarettes, with a vivacious redhead behind the wheel of a Cadillac (see fig. 0.4). The notes wax lyrically: "This album marks the first time her unique and practical counsel has been recorded."

Dottie Walters Reveals was released by Success Motivation Institute, which produced dozens of similar records and continues today as a global Christian organization that "helps people permanently motivate themselves to realize the success they desire." In the enclosed "Reference Guide to Narration," Success Motivation Institute's founder Paul J. Meyer offers advice for "how to get the most from this album," claiming, "You now possess one of the world's finest combinations of personal communication and specialized knowledge. Simultaneously, through your own channels of sound and sight, you will acquire, retain, and be able to use the invaluable information, authored by one

FIGURE 2.1

Birth of a Salesman,
Businessman's Record Club BRC 129;
cover design by Don May, 1962.

of the International Masters of Success." Emphasizing the record's convenience, he recommends repeated listenings: "The album will be a slightly different album every day!"

Side 1 begins with Walters's sweeping statement: "For centuries, woman has been like the Sphinx of Egypt, an eternal mystery to men. Men have cursed her, loved her, enslaved her and worshiped her, but they've always been mystified by her. Now, in our modern, commercial world, man must try to sell to her." Her final secret: "Infuriate them. . . . Make a woman mad," she urges and quotes Ralph Waldo Emerson: "Infuriating a woman is to press a powerful thing." She recounts numerous episodes in which furious women rose up, from mythical Greek Furies to Harriet Beecher Stowe, and suggests: "You, too, can unleash them in order to sell to women."

The liner notes for THE MAN IN SALESMAN tout that "this long-awaited volume was literally produced by popular demand and is no doubt the finest thing of its kind." And, if that wasn't enough, the record is endorsed "by such eminent authorities as Mrs. Dale Carnegie and Norman Vincent Peale." The record's speaker, Kenneth McFarland, who is enthusiastically described as "America's Number One Spokesman," parlayed a background in educational administration into a successful public speaking career. The speech was recorded at something called "the Distinguished Salesman Award Banquet" and was "not made under artificial conditions." The record's inner label includes the motto "Man Building . . . Business Building, Educational and Inspirational."

Apparently not addressing the Parke-Davis pharmaceutical convention audience captured on the album cover—a sea of suit-and-tie organization men—McFarland proclaims pleasure at seeing "the ladies" in the audience. Great! A midcentury believer in equal opportunity, who, then, promptly sinks into a schtick of sexist jokes, seemingly to defuse any simmering male anxiety about underperforming and losing out to savvy saleswomen. The low point? When McFarland lays out for laughs the story of a stuttering colleague. Alcohol abuse, dishonesty, and disloyalty earn his hearty derision with plentiful petty asides infused with anti-unionism, xenophobia, lightly veiled racism, and more sexist stereotypes.

The Man in Salesman was released by Edward M. Miller and Associates, which specialized in conservative self-help and sales training records such as *Are We Raising the Red Flag over Ourselves?*, *Selling America to Americans*, and *America, You're the Greatest*, all from the 1960s. These records trumpeted ambitious goals: "The McFarland records glorify the American system and the magnificent opportunities that exist within its framework for all those who understand it, appreciate it, and are willing to 'play by the rules.'" In his midwestern twang, with brisk delivery, McFarland declares that "gas and oil is the basis of the free enterprise system." The liner notes chime in: "Our people do not inherit in their blood streams the vital understandings that are necessary to preserve the American system of free competitive enterprise, and to succeed under this system." *The Man in Salesman* makes clear that capitalist logic needs to be taught.

A charcoal drawing against an ochre background depicts the signature moment: a signed contract demonstrates WHAT IT TAKES TO BE A GREAT SALESMAN.

FIGURE 2.2

Dottie Walters Reveals the Seven Secrets of Selling to Women,
Success Motivation Institute SMI 1345, 1963–1964.

Released by the Businessman's Record Club, which followed the Book-of-the-Month Club and the Columbia Record Club models, the record features a straightforward, no-nonsense, let's-get-down-to-business graphic style. Lecturing over two sides with casual, smarmy declarations, Phillip J. Kelly, "former Advertising Manager, B. F. Goodrich," tells semi-inspiring tales of salesmen being the best and meeting their mark. Proving manhood by "knowing product" and "making the sale" sets a competitive tone and a slap on the back camaraderie. Success in salesmanship stands in for success in life: "If you can't get happiness out of your work, you're never going to be happy. . . . The real producers, the real pros" overcome doubt and sustain faith with a "think big and act big" strategy, where knowing you're going to succeed is the same as succeeding.

A Businessmen's Record Club "Record of the Month," **SELL YOURSELF RICH** features G. Worthington Hipple—"Worth" to his customers—"one of America's most dynamic salesmen and sales managers." (Instructional record trivia—Hipple's twin brother was actor Hugh Marlowe, who appeared in such films as *All About Eve* [1950] and *The Day the Earth Stood Still* [1951] as well as the long-running soap opera *Another World*.) It's another recorded talk, lightly sprinkled with comedic efforts, along with "simple truths," such as "Sell the benefit," "All sales are made through enthusiasm," and "Everyone must train himself for what he wants to do in life. And the salesman is no exception." The record promises answers to important questions like "Who makes the big money?" and "Why does one product sell more than its competitors?" Our copy was sealed, so, apparently, no one tapped its riches.

PROFIT IN PERSUASION begins with a riotous rocket blast and a game observation: "Isn't it great living and selling in the space age!" The record was aimed at retailers for the Toro Manufacturing Corporation, producers of motorized lawn equipment for homes, businesses, sports fields, and golf courses. (Jonathan recalls firing up a trusty Toro to mow his family's grass in the 1970s.) "Intelligent, well directed, enthusiastic persuasion is the basis of effective retail Salesmanship" begin the notes. A letter appears on the back cover, signed by John C. Norton, general manager, sales and advertising, who went on to become executive vice president and founder of Toro International. Addressing "The Toro Program Dealer," the liner notes explain the "P.I.P" (Profit in Persuasion) program—"the kind of persuasion that closes sales and creates profits."

On the Sales-Sonics Recording inner label, the record is called "The Profit's in Persuasion" and consists of a presentation "especially prepared" by Larry Wilson, "an early pioneer in reimagining the role of the salesperson [who] revolutionized the way people sell." Introduced in the notes as having "the ability to take a lot of the mystery out of selling," Wilson's approach to sales training was "to help people and organizations be all that they can be—to achieve performance with fulfillment."[6] Coauthor of the perennial best-seller *The One-Minute Sales Person*, he founded Wilson Learning, which is still in operation today, assisting "executive sales and leadership teams with employee engagement, salesforce development, leadership development, business transformation, and workforce upskilling."[7] On *Profit in Persuasion*, Wilson urges his audience

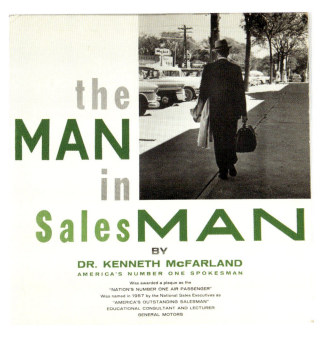

FIGURE 2.3

The Man in Salesman,
Edward M. Miller and Associates, EM 1170;
cover by L. Berthaum, 1961.

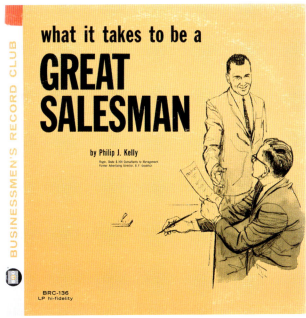

FIGURE 2.4

What It Takes to Be a Great Salesman,
Businessman's Record Club,
BRC 136, 1963.

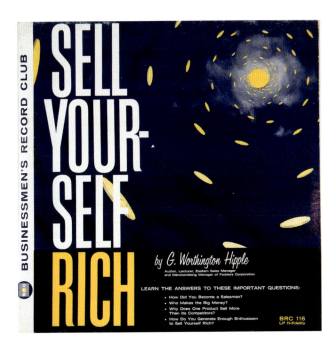

FIGURE 2.5

Sell Yourself Rich,
Businessman's Record Club,
BRC 116, 1962.

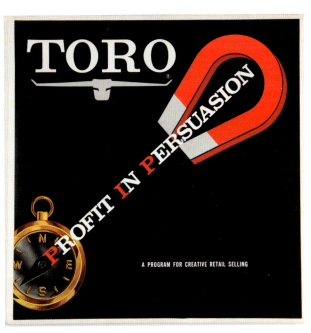

FIGURE 2.6

Profit in Persuasion,
Toro, Kaybank KB 3443, 1963.

FIGURE 2.7

Selling the Sizzle,
Success Motivation Institute SMI 1315, 1960.

of salesmen to ask themselves, "How are we advancing and changing to keep pace in this age of space?"

A white-coated waiter with a skinny black bow tie holds out a silver platter decorated with dark green parsley and slices of raw tomato and onion surrounding a hefty, well-marbled T-bone steak. White steam, obviously added to the photograph, wafts up, dramatizing the sizzle, the sight, the smell of the big sale. A mesmerized, well-coiffed couple enjoying cocktails in etched glasses and candlelight contemplate the upsell benefits. A flourish of handcrafted yellow script suggests the standout success of **SELLING THE SIZZLE**. Not just for businessmen, this LP's recorded lecture captures "the world's greatest salesman," Elmer Wheeler. He generously offers help to all by revealing his "Wheelerpoints," which include "Everybody is a salesman. Doctors, lawyers, merchants, housewives, students . . . all are trying to sell something during their lives. Some sell products, some sell services, and every one of us spends our lives trying to sell the people around us on ourselves." Sounds familiar, no doubt, to today's social media influencers.

Wheeler—with his odd and, at times, grating mix of a Jimmy Durante delivery and Jack Kerouac's droning, exclaiming phrases and rhymes—modulates between sincere intensity, with an occasional forced chuckle, and a snide meanness, especially when describing female prospects. In his hackneyed stories from the field, Wheeler recalls his own early sales experience on the farm: sitting roadside, with a crudely painted "Eggs for Sale" sign, he lured "city" women into thinking he was too ignorant to know market prices. Still, he got the customers to pay more with his "Just out of the chicken fresh" slogan. The marketing sizzle? "Farm freshness," not eggs.

Traveling around the world, Wheeler reports, he gleaned tricks from retailers in Tokyo, Turkey, Rome, London, Paris, Cairo, "and even Tangiers." Among his insights: "Don't sell the steak, sell the sizzle," emphasizing emotions and multiple senses, including hearing and scent. Being sizzle-conscious highlights "the tang in the cheese, the crunch in the cracker, the whiff in the coffee, the pucker in the pickle." Move hearts, he says: "The heart is closer to the pocket book than the brain." Wheeler recommends saying it "with flowers," "showmanship stunts," and learning to incorporate winning expressions and gestures. Never "ask if"; instead, "ask which." Watch how you say what you say. Smile with your eyes and heart. And work on "clockwork timing," which boils down to keen manipulation to get what you want: a better position and higher sales, as well as "more social success." Although he tends toward hucksterism, his focus on the customer's emotional connection to products would fit in perfectly with a contemporary marketing campaign.

3

MAKING MONEY, MANAGEMENT, AND MOTIVATION

After a long day of mind-numbing meetings, evening ushers in uplifting hours and a BUSINESSMAN'S BOUNCE for the still-suited executive murmuring sweet selling secrets in the ear of a fashionable blonde. The liner notes helpfully explain: "This is music for the tired businessman who isn't so tired once he gets a young and pretty out-of-town buyer in his arms." On the table to seal that deal? A martini and a bucket of champagne. The notes effuse: "This is expense-account music, night-on-the-town music, makes-you-want-to-dance music." Muted salmon tulip dress with matching hair accessory, creamy pumps, and elbow-length gloves garlanded by glittery bracelets embrace a golden glow among cane café chairs, a classical Greek baseboard motif, and an elaborate crystal chandelier torchiere. The notes go on: this is "tea dance music that features much dancing and absolutely no tea at all." The blonde's body twist suggests more tango than tea dance, possibly owing to the bounty of beverage.

"It's Only a Paper Moon" begins with tinkling piano, high-spirited muted horns, and, yes, a bit of bounce. Sentimental schmaltz on "I'll String Along with You" and a ragtime-inflected up tempo on "The Very Thought of You" affirm that this is "dance music for people who are old enough to have stopped learning new steps." Eddie LeMar at the piano brings cascading notes and an "updated" band sound: "It's a rhythmic organization, one that always has a beat!" The night's final sale's pitch? The winning flattery of "You Oughta Be in Pictures," hinting that the long-standing sexism of casting directors, movie directors, and producers plays out in the business world as well. *Businessman's Bounce* exposes the gender roles of the era, in which selling was masculine and consuming feminine, and females entertained and provided "bounce."

FINDING ATTRACTING SELECTING TRAINING MANPOWER, from Elba Corporation, offers "Tomorrow's Sales Methods Today!" Elba, an insurance company, developed an audiovisual method that pre-dates the PowerPoint deck by decades.[1] Along with producing records such as *Tax Free Dollars for Retirement* and *While You Can*, they used portable Bell & Howell projectors to show filmstrips accompanied by records and, later, cassette tapes to wow would-be prospects. (For interested collectors, Elba Model 1151 projection kits can occasionally be found on eBay.)

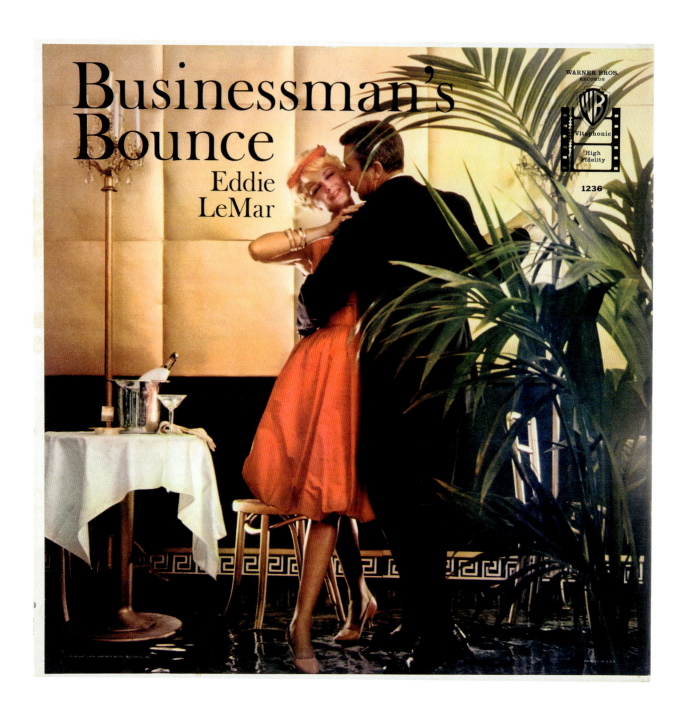

FIGURE 3.1

Businessman's Bounce,
Eddie LeMar, Warner Bros. W1236;
Photo by Hal Adams, 1958.

Vitaphonic

High
Fidelity

Music for the expense account set

Businessman's Bounce

Eddie LeMar, *his piano and orchestra*

SIDE ONE:
1. It's Only A Paper Moon
2. I'll String Along With You
3. The Very Thought Of You
4. With Plenty of Money and You
5. Ev'ry Day
6. Remember Me?

SIDE TWO:
1. Sweet Madness
2. Why Shouldn't I
3. You're An Old Smoothie
4. Love Is The Sweetest Thing
5. I Only Have Eyes For You
6. You Oughta Be In Pictures

This is music for the tired businessman who isn't so tired once he gets a young and pretty out-of-town buyer in his arms.

This is music that you might hear at the El Morocco, the Pump Room, or the St. Francis—tea dance music that features much dancing and absolutely no tea at all.

This is expense-account music, night-on-the-town music, makes-you-want-to-dance music. It's not the sort that will bring you spellbound to the bandstand to listen raptly to some instrumental virtuoso. It's not music that's hot, cool or rockin' and rollin'. It's dance music for people who are old enough to have stopped learning new steps. It's dance music based on familiar and great popular songs, played with the melody way out in front all the way, and with a bright and comfortable beat that is made for grown-up dancing.

Eddie LeMar is a veteran of this kind of music. For many years his transcribed dancing parties have been featured on hundreds of radio stations throughout the country. In the past, and in keeping with the usual tonal qualities of a "society band," Eddie has always featured violins and accordion. Now, updating his group to a more modern sound, he has four brass, four saxes, a rhythm section and himself featured at the piano. As a matter of fact, this new sound, with Eddie playing a dominant lead at the piano and backed up with the rich and brilliant brass-reed combination, offers a striking and delightful dance band personality. Above all, it's a rhythmic organization, one that always has a beat!

It's the Tom Collins of dance music—refreshing, spirited and easy to take. It's got a little kick and a lot of tingle. It's for dancers who are no longer gymnasts; it's for the young at heart who are no longer kids; it's for sentimentalists who aren't afraid to remember; it's for everyone who could have danced all night, if they'd had the music of Eddie LeMar to dance to. ∗ ∗ ∗

For Your Listening Pleasure May We Suggest:

COCKTAILS, DINNER, AND DANCING, SHEP FIELDS	Jubilee 1056
AT THE TIFFANY BALL, LESTER LANIN	Epic LN-3410
AM I IN LOVE?, MARVIN WRIGHT	Warner Bros. W 1232
DANCE, ERNIE HECKSCHER	Verve 4007
AN EVENING AT THE PUMP ROOM	Mercury 20280

Master Control at Warner's

Warner Bros. Records, Inc.
THE FIRST NAME IN SOUND

VITAPHONIC HIGH FIDELITY, THE FIRST NAME IN SOUND, is the optimum in modern sound recording technique, conforming to the fine tradition of sound reproduction that has been the standard of Warner Bros. for more than thirty years. Only the finest materials and equipment are used in these recordings, from actual studio recording session to final pressing.

TECHNICAL DATA: Recorded range, 20-25,000 cycles. Three channel Ampex 300 tape recorders, latest condenser microphones in conjunction with Vitaphonic FNV optimum frequency range control. Mastering on specially designed, electronically controlled variable pitch Scully lathes, and Westrex feedback cutters. RIAA playback curve. Rolloff, 13.75 DB at 10 KC.

CAUTION: Be sure your playback stylus is in good condition. A worn needle will not reproduce the full fidelity of this recording, and will shorten its life.

COPYRIGHT 1958, WARNER BROS. RECORDS, INC.

Cover photo: Hal Adams

PRINTED IN U.S.A.

FIGURE 3.2

Businessman's Bounce,
rear cover, Eddie LeMar, Warner Bros. W1236;
photo by Hal Adams, 1958.

While the title on the label is "To Be Somebody," the cover spells out the words "Finding," "Attracting," "Selecting," and "Training," with the first letter of each boldly highlighted in yellow, calling attention to "fast." The stock photograph of a man breaking a pencil in half contrasts with the otherwise bright graphic lettering and creates a no-nonsense layout—nothing on the back cover, however. Interestingly, the record opens with a brief musical interlude and a series of sketches about frustrated workers. We hear a woman talking about how her boss, Mr. Wells, "has worked harder than anyone," but can't get a promotion "unless someone dies or retires"; one man grumbling that he's "fed up" with his work; and another man telling his wife that "no matter how hard I work. . . . it's a dead end." He muses, "I just want to get out and be somebody." A calm narrator consoles us that "any kind of work has its frustrations and irritations."

The recording is punctuated by beeps that signal a move to the next image on the accompanying film strip. Listening brought back fond memories of midcentury classroom technologies: Didn't the sound and images invariably get out of sync? The rest of *Finding Attracting Selecting Training Manpower* consists of a film-like story of how "Dave" rose to success in insurance sales—with scripted scenarios of sales advice from experienced salesmen —how hard the work is, and how many sacrifices must be made. A key takeaway: how much money you make "depends entirely on you."

Quality oak paneling, broad polished wood desk, and dark suit/white shirt/tie set the scene for **TOUGH-MINDED MANAGEMENT**, with documents delivered from a bevy of ring binders. Narrator Joe D. Batten—a consultant riding the conceptual coattails of legendary business gurus W. Edward Deming and W. A. Shewhart and their quality control and continuous improvement concepts—discerned, at the US Constitution's core, Bible scriptures and "the master plan for free and individual enterprise in our country." Without doubt, Batten reckons a God-granted, and Founding Fathers' foretold, free enterprise capitalism that required the postwar–Cold War US work force to embrace hierarchical organizations and accept management expertise.

Tough-minded management requires "guts" as well as "applying the full power of your *mind* to the development of all the other minds with which you interact daily." "Domains for action" include "Men, Money, Materials, Time, and Space." One walks willingly, purposefully, into this management mind shift. There are "principles" to engage (purpose, motivation, performance), phases (present climate, objectives, planning, control), and notions of executive accountability. Ideas, the booklet intones, are more likely to be taken up after six exposures to them: from rejection to cautious adoption to "I used that idea today—it's terrific."

Not unlike hypnosis albums, among other recordings that relied on repetition to take listeners through relaxation exercises or "suggestion" ("Butter and fat will be disgusting to you"), the Success Motivation Institute understood that desire for success could open minds to the self-improvement and nation-building rhetoric of the day: relax! Be completely relaxed. Not everyone could be the manager, but all intelligent

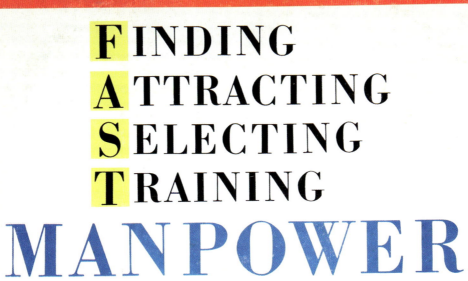

FIGURE 3.3

Manpower: Finding, Attracting, Selecting, Training,
Elba Systems V 26662, 1970.

FIGURE 3.4

Tough-Minded Management,
Success Motivation Institute SMI 1349, 1966.

motivated men could hold in mind hope of promotion and adjust behaviors, visions, and ideas of reasonable sacrifice to conform with company performance standards.

HOW TO COMMUNICATE YOUR IDEAS promotes the basic promise of management instruction records: "These ideas are not inborn, but can be learned by the ambitious manager." Described as a "*Nation's Business* Execudisc," the recording dramatizes articles that appeared in the US Chamber of Commerce's monthly magazine, *Nation's Business*.[2] In the late 1960s and early 1970s, *Nation's Business* also produced several Executive Seminars in Sound, including the promising titles *Mastering the Art of Delegating* and *How to Live with Your Own Success*.

The cover shows two older—and possibly more experienced—businessmen in a paneled room listening intently to a younger man, pen in hand, attempting to communicate his ideas. A pen shows up on the back cover as well, next to *Nation's Business* editor Jack Woolridge's signature. He lets the listener know that "nothing happens until someone has an idea. But ideas must be communicated to others before action can begin." *How to Communicate Your Ideas* provides "dramatized solutions, designed by experts, to everyday human relations problems in business." Clearly, diverse understandings of human relationships map onto possible avenues for communication, creating in the business context not only openings for strategic management insights but also opportunities for workers to adapt to management expectations and adopt organizational mores in hopes of promotion. Straightforward selections include "You Can Make the Boss Listen," "How to Say No When You Have To," and "Avoid the Jargon."

The narrator has a dry sense of humor that makes the record refreshingly entertaining: "Use the excess capacity of your mind to analyze constantly what is being said, even if the speaker is boring. Don't use it to plan that weekend fishing trip."

After all that managing, it's time for a coffee break! A thermos and red steel girder; a paper cup, typewriter, and file cabinet; a stovetop percolator, white china, and kitchen utensils; a Georg Jensen porcelain pot, demitasse cups, and framed *Porgy and Bess* LP cover (RCA, of course): these constitute multiple settings for the common COFFEE BREAK. "The coffee break," the liner notes laud, "is as much a part of life today as peanut brittle, carbon paper, filter-tipped cigarettes and liquid detergents." The people who populate coffee-consuming spaces? Construction workers, office flirters, midmorning chatters, and evening-out romancers all share in this workday ritual.

Photographer David Hecht divided the cover scenarios into five sections, one set aside for the LP title—in mocha brown sans serif bold capital font. "In Rome, at the height of Empire, the cry was 'Nullus Sucrum'—which means the Romans liked theirs black and hearty," hail the lighthearted notes by Ferris A. Benda, a mainstay on mid-century RCA albums. "There are songs here for every coffee break mood," he assures listeners: "Ask Anyone Who Knows," "Please Don't Talk about Me," "A Little Kiss Each Morning," and "Suddenly" provide a soundtrack of strings suggesting a bit more romance than caffeinated rally.

FIGURE 3.5

How to Communicate Your Ideas,
Nation's Business NB 101, 1967.

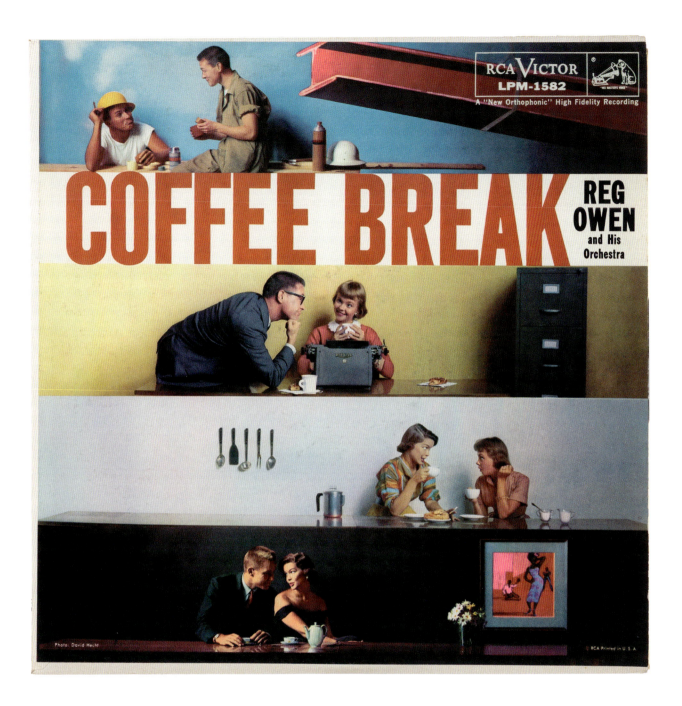

FIGURE 3.6

Coffee Break,
Reg Owen and His Orchestra,
RCA Victor LPM 1582;
photo by David Hecht,
china courtesy of Georg Jensen, 1958.

THINK AND GROW RICH invokes a pithy and inspirational quote from Ralph Waldo Emerson to illuminate the first principle of desire, "the starting point for all achievement": "There's nothing capricious in nature, and the implanting of a desire indicates that its gratification is in the constitution of the creature that feels it." Based on Napoleon Hill's enduring bestseller, *Think and Grow Rich* (1937), the recording offers timeless tips on, well, thinking and growing rich.

Think and Grow Rich—the record—promises "the essence of the immortal book by Napoleon Hill" and is narrated by Earl Nightingale, "a personal friend of the author." He's also a believer: "I searched for twenty years to find a formula that would enable a person to utilize every possible element in his favor. It wasn't until I discovered the works of Napoleon Hill that I found all the answers." Nightingale also produced his own self-help record, *The Strangest Secret*, inspired by *Think and Grow Rich*. Nightingale's rapid-fire recording reviews Hill's "Thirteen success principles that will provide you with money . . . happiness . . . success when they are applied to your life!" We hear Hill's famous maxim from "one of the most amazing books ever written": "By controlling your mind, you can control your destiny here on earth." The cover of *Think and Grow Rich* is credited to the Three Lions studio, which produced dozens of album cover photographs, ranging from Charles Mingus's *The Clown* (1957) to the Ronettes' debut, *The Ronettes Featuring Veronica* (1964).

The red capital-letter font on SELLING AMERICA underscores a black-and-white shot of Amway cofounder Richard DeVos, haloed with auditorium light strips as he hovers above a large and attentive audience. A small Amway logo, set with a map of the United States and Canada, announces: "Home-care know-how at your doorstep." Amway—a "direct selling" company that for product distribution relies upon human individuals who, in the best cases, come with their own loyal client rolodex—wove together notions of "free enterprise," "democracy," and "belief in the dignity of man." *Selling America* won the Alexander Hamilton Award for Economic Education from the right-wing Freedoms Foundation.

More than just a run-of-the-mill multilevel marketing business, "Amway is a monument to the free enterprise system in this country."[3] Selling Amway products—and recruiting others to do the same—represents a chance for energetic people to make money in their spare time. Involvement in the company is also portrayed as strengthening a sense of family and patriotism."[4] Amway founders Jay Van Andel and Rich DeVos's "lifestories have attained the status of modern-day legend: how two high-school buddies, both college drop-outs, went into business together after World War II and, after dabbling in several smaller operations, founded Amway Corp. in Van Andel's basement in 1959."[5]

Selling America is not merely one more instructional record; it's quite a document of American free-enterprise mythology. Paired with the enthusiastic enticement "Let me tell you how great it is in America!," a highlighted box on the back cover presents "DeVos' Comparison of Economic Systems." The comparisons champion familiar Cold-War, anti-Soviet, anti-communist understandings of "free enterprise system" superiority. The

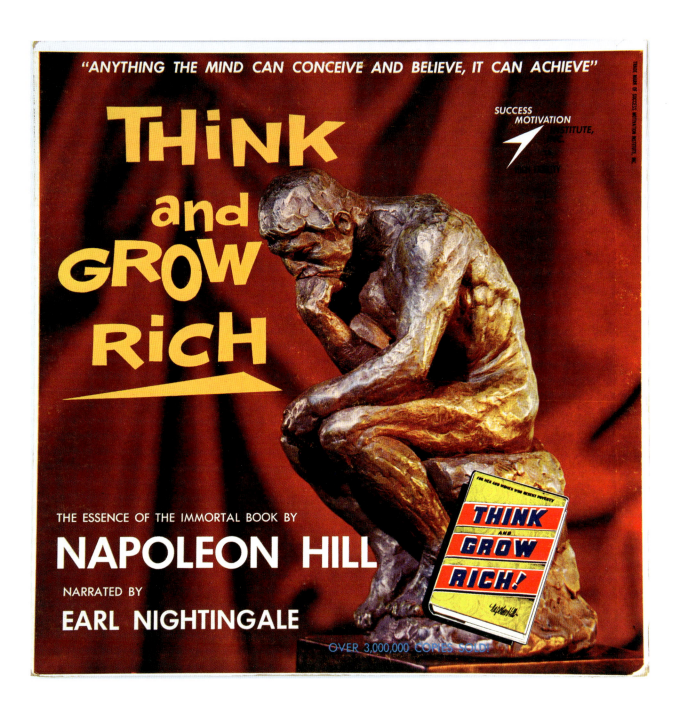

FIGURE 3.7

Think and Grow Rich,
Success Motivation Institute SMI 1313;
photo by Three Lions, 1960.

FIGURE 3.8

Selling America,
Richard De Vos, VA 650, 1967.

FIGURE 3.9

Sing Out for Free Enterprise,
Sanborn Singers, VA 993, 1969.

heading sarcastically states, "To 'enjoy' the same 'privileges' as the Russians, Americans would have to: abandon three-fifths of our steel production capacity; rip up 14 of every 15 miles of our paved highways; cut our standard of living by three-fourths; scrap 19 of every 20 automobiles; smash 40 million TV sets; remove 9 of every 10 telephones; put 60 million people back on the farm." Pictured awards apparently presented to Amway cite "preservation of our cherished American institutions," "bringing about a better understanding of the American Way of Life," and "effort on behalf of free speech . . . 'the basis of government', the foundation of our precious liberty." DeVos and Van Andel suggest that their company assists others in grasping "the opportunity that is their birthright as free men in a free land."

"Before you go out to rebuild the world, have you learned how to clean up your bedroom?" DeVos begins this talk, recorded at the National Association of Junior Achievers Conference in Bloomington, Indiana. More jokes and one-liners follow and generate huge applause: "Do you know that most people who favor birth control have already been born?" DeVos wants his followers, his future leaders, to go out into the world and say to all, "You can do it!"

As a true believer in "the individual" and dismissive of system-based explanations, DeVos asserts: "Anyone who wants to can solve their own poverty problem. I think that being poor is something people do." How to solve a "poverty problem"? Though it's never directly stated, the solution is clear: boost income with Amway sales. This can-do attitude isn't without responsibility. In his crusade for recognizing fellow Americans' respectability, and his efforts to bring them into the Amway salesforce, DeVos chides his potentially contemptuous junior achievers toward a more benevolent entitlement, suggesting that you, the more privileged and capable, can change others' lives. Do not insult. Do not say, "He's just a bus driver." In the guise of a joke, DeVos baits his young audience with lightly veiled in-group condescension, getting them to laugh, then shaming them for putting down a "fellow American." It's a manipulative strategy for breaking down defenses familiar to anyone who has been unknowingly lured to a cult recruitment meeting.

In honor of Amway's tenth anniversary, the Sanborn Singers muster their collective entrepreneurial talents and SING OUT FOR FREE ENTERPRISE. The "Singers," with welcoming arms open wide, pose near a white Amway van. Each beaming team member proffers a household product from behind a low wall of Amway "laundry compound" that evokes the readymade art of Andy Warhol's Brillo Boxes. White dresses and sport coats, blue pants and dresses, topped off with red, white, and blue scarves and ascots: Need we remind readers that Amway is "a contraction of 'American Way'"? Songs such as "Recruit—Train—Motivate," "What is Amway," and a "Patriotic Medley" (with dire versions of "Comin' Round the Mountain," "Workin' on the Railroad," "Whistle While You Work," and "Climb Every Mountain") that move into gospel-inspired hand clapping and "uplifting," unifying chorus. The eighteen-member "all-Amway-Distributor Sanborn Singers," led by Jan and Fred Sanborn (Amway Diamond Direct Distributors), performed for years at Amway conventions.

II

AT HOME

Escaping outmoded traditions drawn from English-manor visions of formal dress, Victorian manners, and silver candlesticks struck midcentury industrial designers Mary and Russel Wright as key to moving into the modern era's democratic subjectivity. In their best-selling *Guide to Easier Living*, from 1950, housing needed to serve postwar, Cold War US citizens in novel ways—"a new way of living, informal, relaxed, and actually more gracious than any strained imitation of another day could be."[1] The modern suburban home casts off the burdens of imitative traditionalisms, including fussy furniture, staid unused rooms, and housework worthy of a servant fleet.

So, after a streamlined one-pot, no-salad-plate dinner, why not convene mom, dad, and kids in the multipurpose living room—a flexible space of track lighting, area rugs, and stackable chairs? An area free from "even leisure-hour work" with areas for conversation, reading, and certainly a music corner, "radio-phonograph-television with record storage handy." Yes, the music corner stocked with vinyl records wins our approval. Though, given what we know about instructional records, a bit of leisure-hour work may intrude.

The innovative and influential Wrights proclaimed the postwar dwelling a percolating core of US productivity—and, most importantly, a comfortable, harmonizing space for gathering the family altogether. Indeed, this lionized family unit materialized strategic values and roles, forming a nucleus conceived to drive forward national goals. Yet, "as the assembly line encroaches more and more on our working life, crowding out individual creative expression, the need for a home in which we can realize ourselves as individuals becomes increasingly urgent."[2] Thus, the home must also provide respite from increasing industrialization and the imposed conformity and homogeneity of work as an organization man.

Home and family concerns anchor major categories of midcentury instructional and self-improvement albums. These records addressed vital domestic tectonics with musical accompaniments, soothing suggestions, and an urgency to learn the lessons of modern living. For women, in particular, instructional records rose up and commanded attention as part of a daily domestic soundscape.[3] Whether attempting to morph the mood after a long day at work, to socialize the children, or to understand the connection between television snacks and weight gain, midcentury records joined in a growing chorus of advice, guidance, and training. In an era when the metronome set the beat behind organ- and piano-driven melodies, the midcentury female with "toes pointing and back straight" attempted to winnow her waist and lift her bust to keep her husband happy and love alive. An aging body was thought to be deficient, sexually unattractive, calling out for cosmetic solutions to wrinkles, gray hair, and extra poundage.[4]

Betty Friedan's best-selling book *The Feminine Mystique* (1963) contested "the 1950s consensus that women's place was in the home."[5] She critically assessed the state of midcentury American women: "Experts told them how to catch a man and keep him . . . how to buy a dishwasher, bake bread, cook gourmet snails . . . how to dress, look, and act more feminine and make marriage more exciting; how to keep their husbands from dying young and their sons from growing into delinquents."[6] Friedan showed how a cabal of educators, health professionals, and Freudian psychologists fostered a feminine ideal that limited the imagination of women by focusing so much attention on family, child-rearing, and personal appearance.[7]

For example, the advertising industry promoted "the belief among women that by controlling their bodies through diet and exercise, women can achieve success in all aspects of their lives, from relationships to careers."[8] Thanks in large part to fitness celebrities Jack LaLanne, Bonnie Prudden, and Debbie Drake, "the cultural perception of exercise as a leisure pastime began to change in the early 1960s. While it remained unclear if exercise was effective in controlling one's weight, the active lifestyle and physical activity as a leisure pursuit grew in appeal, thanks to a new president and Hollywood's influence."[9] Via television shows, books, and fitness records, exercise was promoted for its positive effects in maintaining youthful appearance, providing psychological uplift, and even making "a woman more interesting."[10] Yoga also grew in popularity in the United States, where an emphasis on physical and health benefits helped to demystify the ancient practice.[11] Discourses about weight loss evolved from self-*control* to self-*improvement*.

LaLanne, first to host a televised fitness program, emerged as a midcentury fitness guru. He embodied a distinctive type of masculinity: "In an era when few stars displayed such developed musculature, LaLanne's formfitting jumpsuit left little to the imagination. His clothing was so tight that at times (in this pre-Lycra/spandex era) LaLanne had to unbuckle the waist clasp on the suit to perform certain exercises."[12]

In her books and on her records, Bonnie Prudden offered exercise routines and choreographed workouts, along with "a call to brutal self-evaluation."[13] Women who remained unfit, she warned, would experience "chronic fatigue, an unsatisfying sex life, a loss of courage, or the feeling you are growing old."[14] Less manual labor and walking as part of daily life meant less exercise and fitness. Midcentury moderns needed to compensate.[15] Prudden, and her husband at the time, Hans Kraus, argued: "The affluent lifestyle of 20th century America was making life so easy that American adults and children were rapidly losing muscle tone." Prudden reported that "56 percent of American children tested had failed at least one of a battery of fitness measures, including leg lifts and toe touches. By contrast, only 8 percent of European children had failed even one test component."[16] Her report spurred the creation of the President's Council on Youth Fitness (now the President's Council on Fitness, Sports, and Nutrition) to correct what has been called a "muscle gap" in Cold War discourse.[17]

For fitness enthusiasts like Prudden and Debbie Drake, maintaining an attractive figure was important for marital satisfaction.[18] On her illuminating *How to Keep Your Husband Happy* workout record, Drake gets straight to the point: "Do you know that overweight is a threat to the happiest of marriages? . . . Fighting against weight is one of the surest ways of fighting for her husband's continued love, and getting it." Her advice, "while strict and sexist, wasn't expensive," emphasized three essentials for happiness—"a good diet, good exercise, and a good marriage."[19] Luckily, Drake's workout records were cheaper than a gym.[20]

For husbands, in contrast, "discussions of exercise usually occurred in the context of burgeoning efforts to promote healthy lifestyles."[21] Wives, aware of the growing heart attack rate for men and the emerging concerns for healthier habits, were responsible for both their own and their husbands' exercise regimes, as well as the food placed on the family dining table—creating some conflict with the postwar penchant for eating and drinking.

Food and drink albums, such as *Music to Barbecue By* (produced by Adolph's meat tenderizer), *The Music & Food of Italy* (cookbook included), and *Dinner and Music in the Pacific* (with color centerfold of a food-laden luau table) supported visions of well-stocked supermarkets, backyard cookouts, and, importantly, disposable income. *On Wine: How to Select & Serve* details European wine regions (Let's take a trip!) and cooking with wine (Let's make beef bourguignon!), as well as guidance that has aged well for stocking a wine cellar.

Beyond useful tips and tempting recipes, these records reflect larger themes of postwar affluence: jet travel, growing appetites for foreign food, and sophisticated cooking at home, as promoted by best-selling cookbooks like *Mastering the Art of French Cooking* (originally published in 1961). In *The Midcentury Kitchen* (2019), Sarah Archer writes: "Television worked in tandem with the travel industry to make 'foreign' or 'exotic' food from abroad both desirable and something that could be imitated at home. Servicemen and women who had spent time overseas in World War II or the Korean War brought back new tastes, too."[22] Midcentury instructional records resonated.

Instructional records also reflected Cold War concerns. The infamous "kitchen debate" heated up the question of national superiority at the 1959 American National Exhibition in Moscow, where an array of American appliances such as washing machines, refrigerators, and gas stoves enameled in striking colors suggested certain advantages of capitalism over communism, at least in the consumer arena.[23] US vice president Richard Nixon and Soviet premier Nikita Khrushchev debated quality of life as a smiling American "housewife" imported from the United States showed off the demonstration kitchen, displaying perfectly baked cakes. The LP *Music for Cooking with Gas* included a soundtrack as well as instructions for using your new Caloric gas oven. Backyard barbecues, country-club dances, and weddings: at the Moscow Exhibition, young Americans serving as cultural ambassadors performed these rituals of midcentury American life, allowing Soviet citizens to see US bounty for themselves.

Urgings toward self-improvement begin early, even as self-consciousness is still developing. From its earliest days, the record industry targeted children, as well as their doting parents.[24] By the 1940s, children accounted for as much as 25 percent of yearly record sales.[25] Educational records enjoyed a postwar boom: "Parents increasingly saw children's leisure time as a crucial aspect of preparation for the job market."[26] As a 1955 *New York Times* article exhorted: "Parents interested in the total development of their children would do well to follow the lead of the experts, who recognize that some records are educational as well as entertaining."[27] School grading systems tracked the average, the above average and, of course, what needed improvement. Following the lead of schools, which often encouraged listening to records as music appreciation, families embraced educational records.[28]

Attracting children's attention was crucial, so record companies splashed out on recording personnel, promotion, and packaging. Walt Disney released "educational and entertaining" instructional records, such as Disneyland Records' *Learning to Tell Time Is Fun* (1964) and *Multiplication and Division* (1969) with Jiminy Cricket and Rica Moore. The Family Achievement Institute produced a series of instructional and motivational albums under the banner "The secret of success in anything is to first find success at home." Narrated by celebrities Pat Boone, Art Linkletter, and Norman Vincent Peale, the records were "filled with wholesome content about how to maintain family unity or teach your children character."[29] Sold in five-record sets by door to door salesman, Family Achievement Institute titles included *Adventures in Family Living* and *The Time of Your Life*, both from 1967.

At midcentury, New York City's famous FAO Schwartz toy store carried records and featured a selection of instructional titles in their catalogs, which were sent out to eight hundred thousand customers.[30] As their record buyer reported: "Parents are more concerned about their children's studying a foreign language than ever before. Many of the instructional recordings are geared to school courses the child will encounter in coming years. '*The New Math*' is now one of the most popular items."[31] Who shopped at FAO Schwartz? Through the wide glass door guarded by a giant toy soldier came "the Kennedy children, Washington people, royalty, movie stars, tourists and the average parents looking for toys and records for his child."[32] FAO Schwartz also sold Music Minus One titles along with music instruction records, spoken-word recordings from Caedmon, and Peter and the Wolf albums, all in a separate record department. Albums such as *How to Think* introduced the younger set to the functions of the brain and the basics of critical thinking.

Instructional records promoted the transformation of the body and, perhaps more importantly, the mind. Muscle relaxation techniques, emotionally affecting music, and precursors to neurolinguistic programming open the midcentury subject to suggestion, expanded perception, and a path to confidence, mental control, and even joy. In addition, one's own mind power can influence other people's minds. Crystallized in Carnegie's *How to Win Friends and Influence People,* "the personality ethic of manipulating other people has been the dominant means to success in self-help literature since the 1930s. It is not a philosophy to live by but a technique to earn a living with."[33] Carnegie's maxims pop up on sales and motivation records as well as *Psycho-Cybernetics.*

Home provides a space beyond prying eyes, a place to try out new recipes, relax with high-fidelity sound, and, according to multitudes of instructional records, explore new routes to self-improvement and success. Kitchen, living room, recreation room, bedroom: all provide props and resources for listeners learning new skills, developing hidden talents, improving their minds, and expanding their horizons. Home harbors private discussions and secluded physical realms. Family relationships grow and possibly self-destruct here as years go by and priorities and desires shift. Together, the records in the At Home section offer prescriptions for how to live a successful life.

4 FITNESS AND BEAUTY

Black-and-white typography and a model in modest bra and underwear add comic-book print advertisement styling and a chance to REDUCE THROUGH LISTENING. The cover image visually demonstrates the record's results; the model's slimmer figure appears within a gray shadowy outline—a less svelte version of herself. Multiple font sizes promise an "easy new method" that "helps you develop a dislike for fattening foods." Part of a self-improvement series that "operates on proved psychological principles of subconscious re-education," and delivering messages to the "subconscious mind," the LP transmits the voice of behavioral modification proponent Edwin L. Baron to relaxed listeners who are "open to suggestion," one listening session a day. Habits of overeating, along with the desire for sugar and cream "vanish," although "some people may find it necessary to play the records several times daily."

The producers of *Reduce through Listening* seem to have worked with a reduced budget, as sides one and two are identical. On each, a slow, measured voice, intoning with religious authority, hypnotically drones for several minutes through a repetitive basic relaxation exercise ("You will be completely relaxed, completely calm"). Once deep in proper relaxation, the "suggestion" begins associating "sugar, starches, fats, oils" and alcohol with visions and recollections of the worst things "you have ever tasted" and smelled. Over and over, listeners are told to eat only three meals a day and to eat half their usual amount. No snacks. Subconsciously, "pleasantly" determined and "completely relaxed" in the face of temptation, the record provides the bridge to achieving and maintaining ideal weight.

JACK LA LANNE'S GLAMOUR STRETCHER TIME was released on beautiful blue translucent vinyl. On the cover, fitness guru LaLanne, shot on a diagonal, bisects the deep blue background as he demonstrates a "glamour stretcher" with his impressive biceps and muscular physique. The cover describes the recording as "the wonderful new way to acquire a lovelier, more exciting figure." LaLanne found success and fame with *The Jack LaLanne Show*, which began broadcasting in San Francisco in 1951, went nationwide in 1959, and continued into the 1980s. Many viewers will remember

FIGURE 4.1

Reduce through Listening,
Improvement Services MR 1006, 1964.

HOW THIS RECORD CAN HELP YOU LOSE WEIGHT
or Stay as Slim as You Are
QUICKLY...SENSIBLY...WITHOUT CONSCIOUS EFFORT!

This special double-life record,* REDUCE THROUGH LISTENING, can help you completely avoid high calorie foods and liquids . . . and can condition you to prefer low calorie foods and liquids — until you reach the weight you desire. It can help you lose weight (or maintain your present weight, if you happen to be slim) without the use of will power, pills, or gimmicks . . . without the need to exercise . . . with no impairment of your health . . . and without the substitution of other unpleasant habits, (1) If you sincerely want to reduce, or maintain your present weight; (2) If you can respond to suggestion; (3) If you listen to it just a few minutes daily.

HOW THIS RECORD WORKS

If you listen to this record daily, you will no longer be preoccupied with the thought of food. Your excess pounds will disappear because your desire for high calorie and excess food will vanish. You will "think thin" without being aware of it. After listening to this record, as directed, you will find yourself unwilling to eat any foods containing sugar, starches, fats, or oils. You will develop a preference for such low calorie foods as lean meats, eggs, fresh fruits, and leafy vegetables. You will eat no more than three meals a day — and smaller quantities than you are accustomed to eat at each meal — until you reach the weight you desire. You will have no urge to nibble snacks between meals, while watching TV, or before retiring at night.

It is a psychological principle that a habit is formed when a certain degree of pleasure is derived from repeating an act — such as eating pleasant tasting, fattening foods. Conversely, the same habit can be broken when a similar degree of displeasure is associated with the same act. REDUCE THROUGH LISTENING attempts to associate displeasure with the eating of high calorie foods — and with overeating — until the latter activities are both distasteful and undesirable.

REDUCE THROUGH LISTENING is not a "fad" method of reaching, or maintaining, the weight you desire. It is a tried, tested, and proved way of losing, or maintaining, weight sensibly and effortlessly. The record operates on proved psychological principles of subconscious re-education . . . helps you listen your harmful eating habits away through completely harmless and beneficial reinforced suggestion. RE-DUCE THROUGH LISTENING can bring about a state of complete physical and mental relaxation during which a continual flow of suggestions is fed to your subconscious mind. As you are responsive, these suggestions can completely erase your desire for fattening foods. You will diet without giving it a second thought. You will no longer be afraid to stand on your bathroom scale. "Raiding the refrigerator" will be a thing of the past.

Since the effects of suggestion last for varying lengths of time with different individuals, suggestions should be reinforced accordingly. Although a single playing daily will normally suffice, some people may find it necessary to play the record several times daily — others only occasionally. As a person becomes increasingly conditioned to the suggestions in the record, REDUCE THROUGH LIST-ENING can be played at less frequent intervals until the desire to eat fattening foods, and the habit, no longer exist. A small percentage of people find it necessary to listen to this record for 15 to 30 days before their subconscious minds are conditioned and results observed. If you should find yourself in this category, please be patient . . . and be persistent.

IF YOU ARE ALREADY SLIM...

If you have already reached the weight you desire — or are just beginning to fight the Battle of the Bulge — listening to this record can help you maintain your weight while foregoing the painful mental and physical effort normally associated with resisting the temptation to eat fattening foods.

GETTING THE MOST OUT OF "REDUCE THROUGH LISTENING"

To properly use this record, you should lie down, or sit back in a comfortable chair. Relax your hands and legs, making them as comfortable as possible. Close your eyes and keep them closed during the entire record. Then . . . just listen your weight away.

EDWIN L. BARON HAS HELPED THOUSANDS OF OVERWEIGHT PEOPLE REACH THE WEIGHT THEY DESIRE

Edwin L. Baron — who created REDUCE THROUGH LISTENING and whose voice you hear on this record — is one of the world's most famous behavior therapists. He has lectured before groups of physicians, surgeons, and dentists; has given talks and demonstrations at universities all over the world; has made innumerable appearances on radio, television, the speaker's platform, and in motion pictures; and has been the subject of many articles in national magazines, as well as the press.

Mr. Baron graduated from Northern Illinois University, and later majored in Psychology at Loyola University in Chicago, where he received his Ph.B degree. Post-graduate study was taken at the University of Virginia and the University of Chicago.

He is one of the world's foremost researchers and practitioners in the areas of behavior modification, auto-suggestion, and relaxation. During World War II, as an officer in the U. S. Army Medical Department, Mr. Baron participated in the treatment of cases involving shell shock neuroses and anesthesia. Among many other achievements, he has helped women bear children painlessly, and has helped amnesia victims out of their dilemmas. He originated the idea of helping groups of people lose weight through subconscious re-education, as reported in TIME, NEWSWEEK, SCIENCE DIGEST, and most leading newspapers. His accomplishments have also been featured in LIFE and LOOK.

At the present time, in addition to a crowded lecture schedule, Mr. Baron conducts regular classes in mental relaxation and subconscious re-education. He has helped thousands give up the smoking habit, and has helped additional thousands overcome faulty study habits, cope with tensions, and overcome a multitude of other problems, including shyness, inferiority feelings, lack of self-confidence, and sleeplessness.

EDWIN L. BARON

*(Note: REDUCE THROUGH LIST-ENING is a unique "double-life" record. Improvement Services, Inc. is the only organization, to our knowledge, offering such a record. Since this particular record is meant to be played daily over a long period of time, and may eventually lose some of its quality, we are providing an identical message on both sides.)

THE SELF-IMPROVEMENT SERIES

REDUCE THROUGH LISTENING is one of several behavior modification recordings created and produced by Edwin L. Baron in conjunction with a group of men who comprise the Improvement Services, Inc. organization. Other records in the series are:

SMOKE NO MORE

An easy way to quit smoking, completely erasing the desire for tobacco. If you have tried to give up smoking, without success, just play this extraordinary record a few minutes daily . . . and throw your cigarettes away!

RELAXATION AND SELF-IMPROVEMENT

An easy way to achieve relaxation of mind and body . . . relieve tensions and worry . . . overcome sleeplessness . . . attain keener mental ability . . . develop initiative and drive . . . eliminate self-consciousness and shyness . . . and acquire faster and deeper conditioning for auto-suggestion. Used by physicians, dentists, and hospitals to relieve anxieties prior to surgery.

SELF-IMPROVEMENT SERIES

a division of

IMPROVEMENT SERVICES, INC.

Chicago, Illinois

©1964 Improvement Services, Inc.

A SELF-IMPROVEMENT SERIES RECORD Long Playing Micro Groove 33⅓ RPM High Fidelity Recording

---

FIGURE 4.2

Reduce through Listening,
back cover,
Improvement Services MR 1006, 1964.

his striking white German Shepherds, who often made an appearance. Janet's mother, a singer, dutifully kept up core strength by exercising along with LaLanne, and both authors have fond memories of watching the show as children and occasionally joining in. Reruns gained new life on the ESPN Classic channel and YouTube.

Glamour Stretcher Time's liner notes begin: "Jack LaLanne has dedicated his life to helping others acquire the physical well-being he found for himself. His driving ambition has been to help the millions who watch him on TV to look better and feel better through scientific exercises and sensible diet." LaLanne pioneered televised fitness regimens, laying the groundwork for today's telegenic fitness gurus. His "obsession with grueling workouts and good nutrition, complemented by a salesman's gift, brought him recognition as the founder of the modern physical fitness movement."[1] LaLanne had to battle oddball, outdated notions about fitness, claiming that "the doctors were against me—they said that working out with weights would give people heart attacks and they would lose their sex drive."[2]

On his death at age ninety-six in 2011, his *New York Times* obituary summed up LaLanne's achievements: "Expanding on his television popularity, he opened dozens of fitness studios under his name, later licensing them to Bally. He invented the forerunners of modern exercise machines like leg-extension, squat, and pulley devices. He marketed a Power Juicer to blend raw vegetables and fruits and a Glamour Stretcher cord [made of rubber, the forerunner of today's stretch bands], and he sold exercise videos and fitness books. He invited women to join his health clubs and told the elderly and the disabled that they could exercise despite their limitations."[3]

The 10-inch record features Dave Bacal on organ. LaLanne occasionally hums along. Bacal played on the daily *Jack LaLanne Show*, and his peppy, carnival-like sound provides a stirring accompaniment for LaLanne's cheery and insistent instructions, Bacal, a veteran of the early television shows *Stump the Authors* and *The Jack Benny Show*, released what appears to be his sole album, *The Latin Touch of Dave Bacal*, in 1960. Here, he begins with a "wonderful march—keep your legs high!" LaLanne asks his listeners "to meet me halfway" and do the exercises every day. Alas, we have not been able to find a copy of *Glamour Stretcher Time* with the legendary glamour stretcher. The search continues.

KEEP FIT / BE HAPPY WITH BONNIE PRUDDEN remains a classic workout record, decades after its release. The album cover names her "America's No. 1 Expert on Physical Fitness." Prudden "was a fitness guru long before getting fit became fashionable, and her work has shaped the way Americans think about exercise."[4] She penned regular articles for *Sports Illustrated* as their fitness editor (and later appeared on the cover), was a regular guest on the *Today* show, and hosted several versions of *The Bonnie Prudden Show*. She also produced a television special, *The Flabby American*, in 1957. She's been called "one of the most visible postwar champions of physical fitness."[5]

An accomplished mountaineer and rock climber, Prudden began offering exercise instruction after being disappointed by her daughter's gym instruction.[6] After organizing

FIGURE 4.3

Jack LaLanne's Glamour Stretcher Time,
D R Sales, Inc., 1959.
Photograph was supplied by Befit Enterprises, Inc.
JackLaLanne.com.

fitness classes for neighborhood children and her daughters, she began publishing about fitness and its beneficial health effects, founding the Institute for Physical Fitness in White Plains, New York. At the invitation of President Eisenhower, she produced a report on "the shape of the nation" that called attention to the relatively low levels of fitness in American youth. Prudden's efforts contributed to the formation of the President's Council on Youth Fitness.

As her legacy website recounts, Prudden "wrote 13 books, countless manuals, set up pilot programs of every kind imaginable, designed fitness clothing and equipment for home and school, lectured nonstop throughout the country, brought out six records, two films, 1 film strip, established five day training workshops, wrote and taped 35 half hour TV shows."[7] She is also credited with creating one of the first rock climbing walls.

Prudden famously instructed her female audience to take a look in the mirror and ask if they were happy with their body.[8] *Keep Fit / Be Happy*'s notes continue the fetishistic focus on fat, with a list of "exercise facts," including, "Fat cannot accumulate on a well-exercised, sensibly-fed person." Side one, "set to exciting, vibrant music," helps listeners learn a basic set of exercises. Side 2 presents "patterns" of exercises, interspersed with music without instructions, so students can progress on their own. Studying voice, Janet's mom had done master classes with Prudden and often had the record on the home turntable. Prudden suggests that "the record never becomes obsolete or boring as the performance improves with use."

The cover photograph for *Keep Fit / Be Happy* and its sequel, *Keep Fit / Be Happy Number 2*, were taken by Charles H. Stewart. Generally known as Chuck, Stewart's voluminous photography "helped define the look and feel of jazz as it burst forth into the listening imagination of the American public,"[9] He shot over two thousand album covers, among them *The Ebullient Mr. Gillespie*, from Dizzy Gillespie (1959), *Sweet and Sassy*, by Sarah Vaughn (1963), and Alice Coltrane's *Journey in Satchidananda* (1971). (A recent online article reproduces a shot of Stewart, circa 1960, in front of a wall of his album cover work, including *Keep Fit / Be Happy*.)[10] Although the soundtrack for *Keep Fit / Be Happy* may lack some of the musical inspiration of Stewart's customary photographic subjects, the record stands up to repetitive play. Listeners may find themselves repeating Prudden's phrases, like "jump and push and bend and stretch" long after their workout session is over. After all, she promises, "this record is FUN . . . from start to finish."

KEEP FIT / BE HAPPY NUMBER 2, finds Bonnie Prudden delving deeper into the exercise arena, with more difficult exercises; she warns listeners (in capital letters) that if they run through the entire record, "you will be stiff the next day." She steps up the scrutiny, repeating her sobering suggestion: "one good honest look at yourself in a long mirror without benefit of clothing will tell you a great deal about the shape you are in and the shape of that shape." Further, "OBESITY . . . is always a bad sign whether it is general or in spots such as the spare tire or the heavy thigh." *Keep Fit / Be Happy Number 2* includes numerous photos of Prudden demonstrating each exercise, along with

FIGURE 4.4

Keep Fit / Be Happy,
Bonnie Prudden, Warner Bros. WS 1358;
cover photo by Charles H. Stewart,
exercise clothes by Danskin, 1959.

detailed notes ("Lie supine, bring bent legs to chest and force the spine to the floor") and encouraging missives ("You have started to build a fine body"). On the cover, an unnamed man, dressed for the office in long-sleeved shirt and tie, stiffly bends down—about half as far as Prudden. (We're sure his flexibility improved with her guidance.)

Music is by Otto Cesana, an Italian American composer, conductor, and teacher, whose pupils included such well-known musicians as Andre Kostelanetz, Charlie Barnet, and Alvino Rey. Cesana's own albums include the easy-listening meets classical with a taste of jazz *Ecstasy* (1952), *Sugar and Spice* (1953), and *Enchantment* (1970).

On **FITNESS FOR TEENS**, Prudden addresses the youthful listener. Following her exercise record has benefits: "You will be better looking. Everyone knows that boys look at girls. Not everyone knows that girls look at boys . . . really look." Her liner note advice on "How to Pick a Husband and a Wife" offers this nugget: "Convertibles wear out and make-up washes off. Check your future partner for something that won't do either . . . a good body."

Fitness for Teens finds Prudden returning to her original mission—to improve young people's fitness. On the cover, we see a small inset black-and-white photo of Prudden demonstrating the "v" position and two shots of the teenagers. In one, the gal holds books, while the letter-sweatered guy has a pair of track shoes casually slung over his shoulder. In another, he's doing a push-up as she beams—between exercises, we assume—at the camera. The back cover lists several books and records by Prudden, who by this time had launched a burgeoning product line, including her *Teenage Fitness* book from 1965. She charges young women with a dual responsibility. Along with keeping fit and slim themselves, they need to take care of their husbands and sons: "77% of our twenty year old boys already have gross evidence of arteriosclerosis . . . if you love him . . . watch his diet and see that he exercises." *Fitness for Teens* included a poster-sized insert filled with exercise photos by Joel Librizzi, a photojournalist whose work appeared in leading publications such as *Esquire*, *Newsweek*, and the *New York Times Magazine*.

Reading like a ski resort's promotional brochure, the notes for **FIT TO SKI** declare: "Skiing is for people who like people. Skiing is a sport for people in love. Skiing is for families." Prudden appears on the cover in a series of exuberant shots that show how to stretch with skis on. "Anybody can ski," she continues. "All it takes is good equipment, good sense, a good body and good preparation." Her trademark enclosed booklet, replete with more photos, continues that theme, with several shots of "exercises on skis," along with "warm-ups" and "chair exercises." On the record, her infectious enthusiasm got the authors psyched up for winter, vowing to become "fit to ski" before hitting the slopes. Prudden, an expert skier and mountain climber, was a patrol leader for the New York Ski Patrol, and worked with the US Olympic ski team. She had warmed up for this record by appearing in a 1957 *Sports Illustrated* article that demonstrated "ski exercises you can do at home."[11]

Prudden's **EXECUTIVE FITNESS** issues the (male) executive a frank warning: "The American executive faces a very serious problem and his mortality rate on the

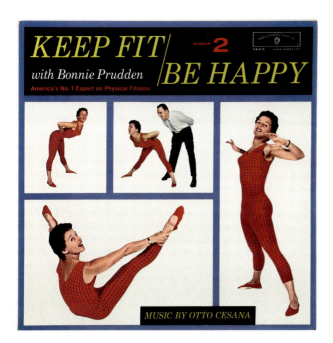

FIGURE 4.5

Keep Fit / Be Happy Number 2,
Bonnie Prudden, Warner Bros. BS 1445;
photo by Charles H. Stewart, 1962.

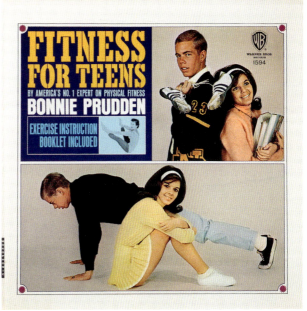

FIGURE 4.6

Fitness for Teens,
Bonnie Prudden, Warner Bros. W 1594;
exercise clothing for Bonnie Prudden Fitness Fashions, 1965.

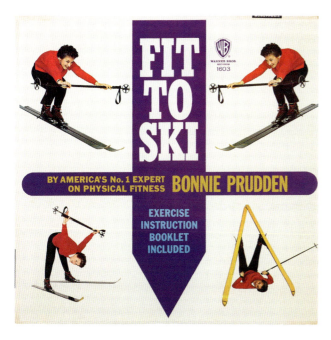

FIGURE 4.7

Fit to Ski,
Bonnie Prudden, Warner Bros. W 1603;
exercise clothing by Bonnie Prudden Fitness Fashions, 1965.

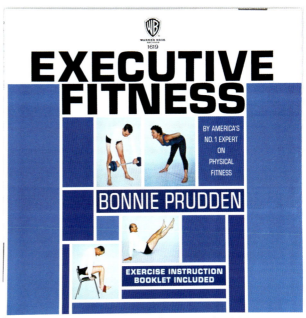

FIGURE 4.8

Executive Fitness,
Bonnie Prudden, Warner Bros. W 1619;
exercise clothing by Bonnie Prudden Fitness Fashions, 1966.

executive level shows that he hasn't begun to think about it." The cover's rectangles of energetic yet calming IBM-blue ground four color photos: Prudden's flexible bend and an exerting executive working on arm and core strength.

On this album, Prudden expands from physical health to mental and emotional well-being. Thus, the record includes "relaxation" sessions not unlike those found on hypnosis and yoga discs of the era. She cautions that the executive is "in danger": "He sweats, grinds his teeth, tenses neck and shoulder muscles, back and legs. His stomach knots, blood pressure shoots up and his heart revs alarmingly." Her counsel for men is just as strict as her well-known "Look in the mirror" advice for women: "Measure executive shape changes with a tape. Check neck, upper arms, chest, midriff, waist, abdominals, hips, thighs, and calves. Do this weekly." The infamous martini lunch? She queries: "How much and what do you drink?" She recommends: "Less is better. It doesn't cloud thinking or tamper with virility."

With a more rockin' soundtrack than her earlier efforts—no more easy jazz—*Executive Fitness* sounds "hip" and somehow masculine with its electric guitars and twisting rhythms. Tunes include amusing, bopping versions of "If I Had a Hammer" and "Peter Gunn." Prudden closes out her executive directives with a bit of existential rumination: "Running a business is not a sometime thing . . . neither is health vitality, virility . . . or the ability to enjoy life." Among the expected "executive diversions" for enjoying life? Gardening, golf, "love," hiking, skiing, swimming, and tennis. With Prudden's workout, you are prepared.

A striking scarlet human figure cutout stands in for a "T" on **FIFTEEN FOR FITNESS**, an album "designed especially for use in the 4th, 5th, and 6th grade classroom by pupils in their regular school clothing." Standing among rows of desks, a console television, and wintery wall decorations, girls in full skirt dresses and boys with tucked-in shirts and belted trousers work their way through "fifteen minutes of exercise set to music" from the President's Council on Youth Fitness. The children raise their arms in a back stretcher to the tune "Ain't We Got Fun," moving into jumping jacks to "Polly Wolly Doodle" and One Foot Balance to "Pop Goes the Weasel." An insert features "detailed exercise instructions" such as "Stand at attention," "Hop on left foot," and "Twist trunk to the right while bending forward." On the back cover, stick figure schematics depict each exercise. Repetitive gestures performed on a beat prepared young ones for uniform movement and following a leader. The voice on *Fifteen for Fitness*, Boyd Pexton, served four years as a navy lieutenant, later earning a doctorate in education from the University of Utah and becoming Salt Lake City School District supervisor for health and physical education.

"For family fitness fun," notes the cover of **EXERCISE WITH GLORIA AND HER SIX DAUGHTERS**, subtly distinguishing its message from the more marriage-maintenance-minded Debbie Drake. Gloria Roeder hosted a short-lived exercise program, *Exercise with Gloria*, in the mid-1960s. The notes hail her as "one of the top instructors at the

FIGURE 4.9

Fifteen for Fitness,
Windsor Records WLP 3 06, 1960.

FIGURE 4.10

Exercise with Gloria and Her Six Daughters,
Crown Album Corp., 1966.

nation's most reputable and fashionable salon in New York City" and remarks that "her 115 pound weight and proportions are the same today as when she attended college." One of Gloria's favorite sayings was "Be a doer, not a viewer"—watching her show excepted, of course. The LP, apparently her sole release, included a slim booklet, with cartoon-like drawings (no glossy photographs as with Drake's albums). She ends her notes with this tidbit: "And remember . . . practice that very important exercise . . . P-U-S-H yourself away from the table while still a bit hungry!!"

Accompanied by bouncy organ music, Gloria brisky moves through her set of exercises in a firm, singsong voice—"stretch and bend, to limber up the upper body." Gloria, as described in a 1964 *Chicago Tribune* article announcing her show, was "living proof that a mother of six daughters can maintain her girlish figure."[15] Her vision of exercise focused on "family first." On the cover, she poses with her six smiling daughters, Shirley, Gail, Karen, Michelle, Pam, and Donna, all in matching black leotards, some in black tights, the youngest girls in sleeveless tops. The notes remark: "The Roeders are probably one of the most un-sedentary families in America." The notes emphasize that she recorded *Exercise with Gloria* for families "who are unable to join her via television due to work, school, conflicting schedules, or for their weekend exercise treat (when her programs are not televised)." She underscores the flexibility of enjoying your own copy of her exercise record: "The time *you* choose to exercise should be at your convenience."

Revealing a preference for exclamation marks, FEEL GOOD! LOOK GREAT! EXERCISE ALONG WITH DEBBIE DRAKE boasts: "By exercising fifteen minutes a day you will discover the nearest thing to the fountain of youth!" The cover shows Drake on her hands and knees, dressed in her customary leotard, demonstrating a kick and extension move. She's exercising in front of a beautiful modern stereo console—playing, we assume, this record. It's a "decorator designed" Masterwork "custom stereophonic High Fidelity Console" model 1820-W, from Columbia Record Distributors, affectionately called the "baby grand."[12]

Drake, born Velda Louise Bellah, became a celebrity via her television show; a syndicated newspaper column, "Date with Debbie"; and regular releases of fitness books, including *Debbie Drake's Easy Way to a Perfect Figure* (1962), *Debbie Drake's Secrets of Perfect Figure Development* (1965), and *Dancercize* (1967). Sears even offered a Debbie Drake doll. Her popularity outgrew her core audience of women fitness followers: "The form-fitting leotard she regularly wore, as well as the fact that some stations broadcast her show at odd hours, meant an audience that extended beyond those interested in exercise."[13] Today, she would undoubtedly be called an influencer.

Feel Good! Look Great! comes complete with dieting guidelines and a "count your calories chart," as "the excess food you take in will bulge out in the wrong places." A glossy enclosed booklet includes a "weight and measurement guide for the average frame" (5′5″ women should weigh no more than 120 pounds; 5′10″ men, 165). Black-and-white photographs show Drake and an unnamed man going through her routine and include a few of Drake on a bicycle. Drake's message remains uplifting and inspiring, no doubt a key to her success: "If you follow these few tips, you'll find it easy and quite simple to keep trim, feel good and look great!" On record, her breathy voice exhorts listeners: "Up, hold, down, relax. Up, hold, down, relax." After a few selections, she starts to sound like one of those ASMR (auto sensory meridian response) videos, which apparently induce some listeners into euphoric, tingling sensations. Keeping her voice "soft and musical," Drake follows her own advice from her *How to Keep Your Husband Happy* record, released a few years after *Feel Good! Look Great!*

Jaunty and eminently listenable tunes, "twist and waltz among them," with curious titles like "Naughty Nellie," "Impudent Isla," and "Flip Flop Ferdi," accompany Drake's instructions. Music is by Noel Regney, a songwriter whose best-known number, "Do You Hear What I Hear?," was written as "a clear and plaintive plea for peace at the time of the Cuban missile crisis."[14] In the 1960s, he led the Noel Regney Singers, who released a beloved children's record, *Songs That Help You Learn French*. A prolific arranger, composer, and conductor for radio and television, Regney scored another hit with "Dominique," as performed by the Singing Nun.

A compact and portable baby-blue RCA Victor turntable provides the foundation for **MODERN SCREEN'S HOLLYWOOD METHOD** for reducing your weight and trimming your "shape." Photographer Carl Fisher, who studied at Cooper Union in New York City and worked in the 1960s with *Esquire* magazine's infamous designer George Lois, created a photomontage and delightful visual metaphor: clad in black leotard and tights, the model for "the world's finest movie magazine" demonstrates bends and stretches across the vinyl surface.[16]

The cover model for *Modern Screen's Hollywood Method* stars in the eight-page booklet that offers a word-for-word recording script and lays out small numbered photos of her movements that "many famous stars use to keep slim and trim." Each exercise addresses a potential beauty failure—"For Slim Waist and Flat Abdomen," "For a Lovely Bust Line," "For Slimmer Hips" with musical pairings, such as "Buttons and Bows" and "Little Brown Jug." The booklet's final page, with "cut" and "fold" on dotted-line instructions, transforms into "Your modern screen Hollywood method calorie-counter"—seven convenient purse-size reminders listing measurements and calories for vegetables, meats, dairy products and fruits, as well as sandwiches (an average cream cheese, jelly, and white bread has 370 calories) and soups (one serving of bouillon, 25).

BAZAAR'S SECRET FORMULA FOR A BEAUTIFUL NEW YOU promises a "wonderful new feeling of well-being." *Billboard* described the LP as part of an early 1960s "flirtation of national magazines with the record business."[17] With text and boxed features, the elaborate, gatefold sleeve album appears like a *Bazaar* magazine article (with the addition of the record). Much like today's "listicle" clickbait, the liner notes include several lists. First up, "9 Fashion Tips," including: "Intelligence, time, and vitality are

FIGURE 4.11

Feel Good! Look Great! Exercise Along with Debbie Drake,
Noel Regney and His Orchestra,
Epic BN 26034, 1963.

FIGURE 4.12

Modern Screen's Hollywood Method,
RCA Camden CAL 581;
photography by Carl Fischer, 1960.

essential in choosing clothes." Then, *Bazaar*'s "famous nine-day diet," with its promise that followers will lose nine pounds in nine days. The notes proclaim: "The right diet every day, the right kind of exercise every day are the two simple secrets of a healthy body." Side 1's "9 wonder exercises" offer "graceful hands," "supple feet," and "flat tummy." Side 2's "9 relaxing exercises" provide "a miracle cure for the tensions of the day." A chart of "desirable weights" is provided "for women age 25 and over (5′5″ small frame: 111–119). A calorie guide lists caloric content by major food groups (2 slices of bologna, 1/8″ thick, 220 calories; 1 wedge of chocolate cake, 2″, iced, 400).

Harper's Bazaar, which started publication in 1867, is considered the first fashion magazine in the United States. "The first and last word in fashion," *Harper's* is known for its influential art directors, editors, and photographers, including Alexey Brodovitch, Diana Vreeland, and Richard Avedon. Exercises on *Bazaar's Secret Formula for a Beautiful New You* were designed and the record narrated by "famous physical fitness authority" Nicholas Kounovsky, whose "sixomerty" method divided "the movements of the body into six basic factors of fitness—endurance, suppleness, balance, strength, speed and skill or coordination."[18] Lilting, waltzy tunes provide a dreamy, almost sleep-inducing soundtrack to what one commentator called "decidedly non-strenuous" exercises.[19]

Along with his still-appreciated books *Be Your Own Hair Stylist* (1950) and *Secrets of Hair Styling* (1954), the LP HEAR HOW TO LOOK YOUR LOVELIEST offers superstylist Victor Vito's advice for leaving long hours in beauty salons behind. Detailed discussion of hair types and scant photos demonstrating pinning and rolling techniques suggest a shift in beauty's labor. Vito's voice, sometimes referring to back cover illustrations, sounds confident and reassuring. More shampooing and a variety of pin curls frees the 1950s female to celebrate all face shapes and more naturally coiffed dos. Titles like these have been called records for "women who couldn't afford charm school."[20]

Long before the rise of health club classes in spin yoga, sweaty Bikram yoga, Kundalini yoga, power yoga, prenatal yoga, and "quick and easy" rocket yoga, Richard Hittleman—who focused on Hatha and Raja yoga—introduced the practice to a wide audience of Americans through his *Yoga for Life* TV program. His show, according to the notes, "inspired viewers everywhere to achieve a dynamic second youth through his stimulating and effective teaching techniques." His many books, which include bestsellers *Yoga at Home* (1962) and *Richard Hittleman's Yoga: 28 Day Exercise Plan* (1969), exposed even more Americans to what he called "the perfect method of cultivating and maintaining lifelong health."

The existence and popularity of yoga records is rarely mentioned in histories of yoga's commodification and popularization, which focus largely on books and TV programs. Hittleman's double album YOGA FOR LIFE asserts: "Twenty minutes of Yoga is worth hours of ordinary exercise." What sets yoga apart? "There is never any strain or loss of energy as in the quick strenuous movements of ordinary exercise of calisthenics."

CAPITOL FULL DIMENSIONAL STEREO

HARPER'S

BAZAAR'S

SECRET

FORMULA

FOR A

BEAUTIFUL

NEW YOU

9

Day Diet

Wonder Exercises

Relaxing Exercises

Exercises Set to Music

·

Tips by Bazaar's Editors

·

Calorie Count-Down

FIGURE 4.13

Bazaar's Secret Formula for a Beautiful New You,
Capitol SWAO 1522, 1961.

FIGURE 4.14

Hear How to Look Your Loveliest,
Carlton CHH 30, 1961.

FIGURE 4.15

Yoga for Life;
design/photography by Studio Five, 1961.

FIGURE 4.16

Yoga for Americans,
Indra Devi, Mace M10021, 1965.

On the cover, Hittleman looks placidly at the camera, dressed casually in khakis and polo shirt—no exotic attire here. *Time* magazine, which described *Yoga for Life* as "an antidote to the 'grunt-and-groan school,'" contrasted Hittleman's appearance with other male fitness gurus of the era: "No rippling triceps for him; lean as a leek, he eats only one meal a day."[21] His wife, Diane, clad in black fishnets—interesting choice of yoga attire—and blue leotard, demonstrates the "cobra" posture, the first pose on side 1. Like other fitness gurus of the era, Hittleman promised that with regular practice you could "rid yourself of flabbiness and excess weight" as you "develop poise, balance, grace and self-confidence." He hints at the sexual benefits of yoga, noting that Diane, "as the mother of our three children can extol the virtues of yoga for keeping things as they should be in the visceral area."[22]

Yoga for Life's enclosed booklet provides photographs and notes, with "postures demonstrated by Richard Hittleman and Diane." He suggests that "it is not always practical or necessary to refer to these while you are performing the exercise, but it will help you progress more quickly if you briefly study the figures of the techniques whenever possible." On the record, he marches through a sequence of poses in fairly quick succession, making it difficult to imagine a beginner following along. A few guitar flourishes serve to mark the end of the session. Throughout, Hittleman stresses the developmental aspects of yoga—unlike rote exercise, yoga encompassed a sense that Americans needed to learn as they went. But, along with more traditional fitness programs, yoga offered benefits beyond the body: "As you progress in Yoga, you will have a wonderful, positive change taking place in every aspect of your life."

On the cover of **YOGA FOR AMERICANS**, a deep red background frames pioneering yogi Indra Devi in a flowing sari. Notably, upon close inspection, one sees that her nail polish and lipstick are expertly applied. A black-and-white confetti pattern, reminiscent of many yoga mats, provides a subtle graphic touch. Below the title, demonstrations of three yoga poses featured in this "authentic course for home practice"; a tiny tie-in book floats in the lower right. Back cover notes gracefully rehearse Devi's credentials and accomplishments and her impact on the everyday: her relaxation technique was "introduced into several factories where the workers and the executives are now taking daily a five minute relaxation break following instructions from her record." Devi's manner is encouraging, but a bit impatient, as she conveys the positions and movements. The gatefold sleeve reveals basic photos of postures and exercises and a very general introduction to the history and purpose of yoga.

5

SUSTENANCE
EATING AND DRINKING

With a cover that recalls Bert Stern's photographs of Marilyn Monroe, a champagne glass obscuring her famous face, **ON WINE: HOW TO SELECT & SERVE** seems aimed at a modern wine drinker—a bit irreverent, not steeped in old-world traditions. Released in the 1960s, before the worldwide growth in wine drinking and appreciation, the album provides a crisp, useful introduction to fine wine. "Any wine goes with any meal, as long as it tastes good to you," reassures the terribly cultured continental voice of wine expert Peter M. F. Sichel, who obviously took pleasure in discussing "one of the truly sophisticated pleasures in life: the enjoyment of wine." However, his notes explain, "until now, wine has been so wrapped in tradition and ceremony that many people have shied away from it rather than risk breaking time-encrusted rules."

Sichel sounds like a character from James Bond's world. Born in Germany into a wine merchant family, he joined the CIA and ran their Berlin office in the 1950s. Back in the wine business by the 1980s, he introduced the world to Blue Nun, that ever-present Liebfraumilch, which may bring back bad memories for certain readers who overindulged in their youth. Since then (he was over one hundred at the time of this writing) "he has skillfully wheeled and dealed behind the scenes, getting out of Blue Nun as its sales slid; managing to sell the Bordeaux château he picked up along the way to the owners of Hermès; knowing who was who in all the big drinks companies and helping to place rising stars in them."[1]

On the record, Sichel enlists two apparently uncultured but enthusiastic American learners—in fact played by actors Kay Lande and Warren Moran—in lively conversation. Lande, a singer, released dozens of albums, mostly for children, such as *Let's Play School* and a Wonderland Read and Hear record, *The World of Color and Sound*. Moran was a broadcast personality, best known as an early announcer on the long-running TV series *To Tell the Truth*. (Sichel warns them to drink "in moderation.") Moran eagerly plays the role of beginning wine drinker, soaking up Sichel's extensive knowledge. At one point he gleefully gushes, "I can't wait to impress my friends with my abounding knowledge of wine." Side 2 offers a musical soundtrack to wine drinking—no more fast-paced, information-filled lecturing—aptly opening with Percy Faith's "Fascination" and closing with Sammy Kaye's "Wine, Women, and Song." As with wine, perhaps in music, too, "personal taste is most important."

Appropriately shaped glassware hold red (a Bordeaux blend?) and white (Sauvignon blanc?). A champagne tulip displays bubbles poured from a thick green champagne bottle. "This is a wine book on record," Bern Ramey declares on the first track of **BERN RAMEY ON WINE**. Indeed, more than most instructional albums we've reviewed, this one sounds like an audiobook. "There are no musical backgrounds," he continues, "no jokes, no vocals, just interesting, condensed wine information which will help you become a wine expert." But listening is not meant to be a chore, since he recommends imbibing while studying: "Drinking, of course, is the only way to really know wine." Appreciated advice.

Ramey "had a long career in many aspects of the wine field including those of winemaker, merchandising specialist, author, lecturer, educator, and sales executive."[2] He describes his goals for the record: "A tidal wave of increasing interest (and sales!) in wines, and therefore a thirst for basic wine knowledge, gave me the ideas for these records, which I hope present an easy and pleasant technique for learning the essentials." His approach is straightforward—much like a professor in Wine 101, or "Drink your way to an A." He warns listeners not to attempt to play all four sides of the double album in one setting: there's just too much information (and perhaps too much wine to drink to "listen" properly). He covers ten different wine topics, from "storing and serving" through "cognac and other brandies." He insists that "the more a person knows about a subject, the more he enjoys it" and promises "a mental trip to the wine country."

The album includes an extensive guide to wine pronunciation and terminology, including terms such as "jeroboam" and "Puligny-Montrachet"—each cross-referenced to the record track number. Color-coded illustrations map major wine regions of America and Europe in charming hues of lilac, tangerine, and sky blue. The back cover features a handy "wine cookery chart," with hints for cooking with wine (tongue, boiled, add a half cup burgundy per pound, pheasant, add a quarter cup sauterne, burgundy, or sherry per pound) and pairing wine and food. "There are no hard and fast rules," the notes encourage the wine student. "Don't be afraid to experiment." Although his enthusiasm for sherry may date this effort, overall the record holds up pretty well across decades of considerable change in the world of wine. We definitely found *Bern Ramey on Wine* to be "A Sound Education for the Greater Enjoyment of Wines." Please excuse us while we get back to our background research—which calls for some serious, well-informed wine drinking.

THE ART OF MIXING DRINKS & MUSIC provides an LP of "musical backgrounds by The Rhythm Makers." It's up to the listener to furnish what is missing from this Music Minus One package: not the piano line, sax solo, or drumbeat, but "The Drink." Decoratively housed in a special cutaway cover frame, *The Art of Mixing Drinks*—a small

FIGURE 5.1

On Wine: How to Select & Serve,
vol. 1, Columbia CSP 151,, c. 1964.

A SOUND EDUCATION FOR THE GREATER ENJOYMENT OF WINES

BERN RAMEY ON Wine

CONTENTS

FIGURE 5.2

Bern Ramey on Wine,
Wine Record Company;
photo by Wesley Bowman, 1964.

paperback based on "the famous Esquire Drink Book"—features inspiring glassware for your daiquiri, Irish coffee, and crème de menthe and contains 1001 cocktail recipes, including a chapter on favorite drinks of famous people, and "365 Excuses for a Party." April 20? That's Record Story Day! How about a Sunshade cocktail?

Striking scarlet and a selection of bar tools lure the listener into "adventures in good living." The music is "soft," allowing conversation, "yet rhythmic, for those who want to dance." Coming from the MMO team, this fine LP outclasses many "music for" easy listening records and finds its way onto our turntable often. Musicians include esteemed pianist Don Abney, legendary bassist and photographer Milt Hinton, bassist Wilbur Ware, guitarist Barry Galbraith, and drummers Osie Johnson and Bobby Donaldson. There's a definite bebop influence on "Poor Butterfly" with cellist and bassist Oscar Pettiford and Kenny Clarke's ride-cymbal timekeeping. Perfect for drinking, dancing, and discussion.

The Venetian Lagoon's purple and faded scarlet evening sky highlights a gondolier's blurred profile on **THE MUSIC & FOOD OF ITALY**, one of the Sounds and Tastes of Foreign Lands as well as the Gourmet series from Music Minus One. Just add "the Gourmet." That's *You*. This "adventure in good living" addresses multiple senses, providing not only music but also recipes from the land of the Bridge of Sighs. Maria Lo Pinto's cookbook, *The Art of Italian Cooking* (first published in 1948), displayed in an inset frame, forms the right side of the album cover, with a chianti bottle *e pane* vision of what is in store for the inspired chef. (Despite the northerly images, "Nonni's Kitchen" was in a village near Palermo.) Olive oil, Italian cheeses, and a wide variety of herbs create continuity among the sauces and meats. Apart from chianti, Asti Spumante, and grappa, the suggested liquor leans French.

The Renato Fantinni Orchestra de la Casa Europa provides a soundtrack that might generously be called entertaining: "Here is your passport to travel via the haunting folk songs, the popular music and soaring operatic arias of this land of history and high spirits, Italy." And of Mussolini and the Axis Powers—recent history when this record was released. Music, food, and iconic archeological sites provided diplomatic bridges, offering new alignments after World War II and hope of reestablished relationships between the diaspora, the homeland, and would-be world travelers. Other titles in the Gourmet record series include Jewish, French, and Oriental cookbooks. For example, *The Orient* (ca. 1967) includes a dizzying array of cuisines, gathered together by Myra Waldo, "food consultant for Pan American World Airways": Hawaii, Indonesia, Malaya, Thailand, and India. The soundtrack? "Vocal and instrumental treasures of Chinese music."

Notes suggest: "Exotic music and food are symbolic of the full, rich living—at home and away—that *Holiday* [magazine] inspires." Artist Will Dressler's staid sketch of a glass-clinking couple for the cover of **DINNER AND MUSIC IN THE PACIFIC** lacks his recognizable and often lurid bachelor-pad album art. He was, after all, responsible for the classic covers of Skip Martin's *Scheherajazz* (1959) and *The Sounds of Exotic*

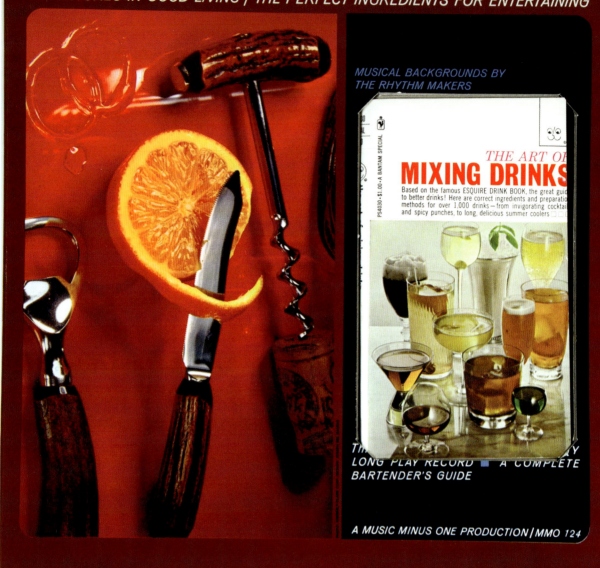

FIGURE 5.3

The Art of Mixing Drinks & Music,
the Rhythm Makers,
Music Minus One MMO 124, ca. 1969.

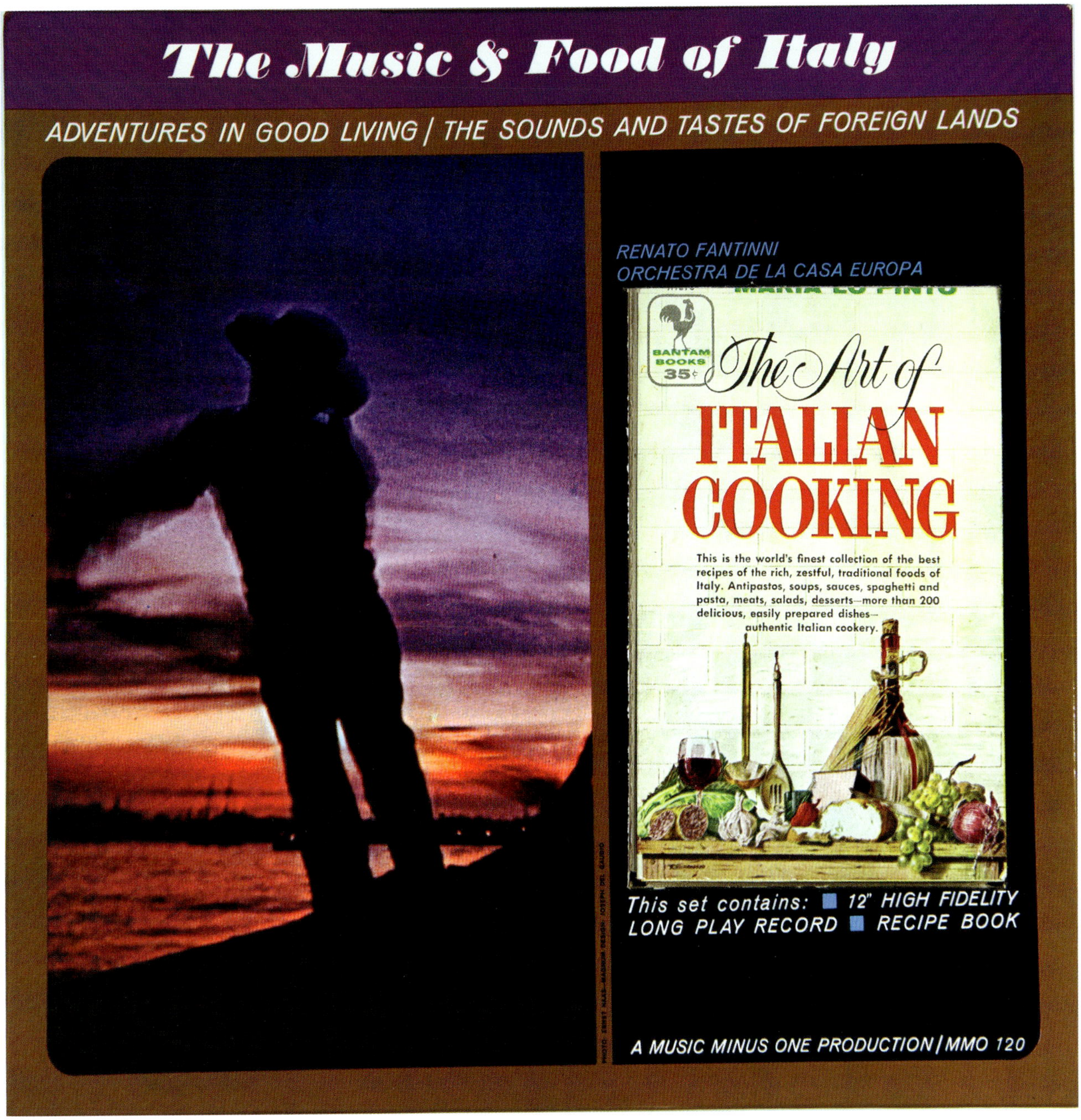

FIGURE 5.4

The Music & Food of Italy,
Renato Fantinni Orchestra De La Casa Europa,
Music Minus One MMO 120, ca. 1960.

Island (1960) by the Surfmen. Yet the monochrome pen and ink drawing creates contrast to the glowing green avocados, fuchsia hibiscus blossoms, and flaming tiki torch of the gatefold sleeve photo shoot within, where giant clamshells serve up a vibrant tomato, artichoke, and olive salad and a watery brown "Hilo Punch"—cloves, cinnamon, ginger ale, rum.

An extensive menu, complete with recipes, presents Koala Kabobs (broiled chicken livers), Papeete Shrimp Curry, and Ono Ono Chicken served in pineapple boats. The "exotic" food and schmaltzy slide guitar interrupted occasionally by staccato chants and wavery operatic voices are "designed to bring Pacific magic into your home, creating a mood of enjoyment much as *Holiday* does each month in the homes of 900,000 active, affluent, and pleasure-loving families." A numbered schematic diagram identifies the dishes displayed in colorful buffet. The series also includes albums from other "places of excitement": Spain, San Francisco, Brazil, and Scandinavia.

A white gardenia, champagne coupes, diamond necklace, and black tie attire evoke the glamour of **DINNER IN RIO**. The unfussy open capital font outlined in tropical ocean blue give "Rio" a festive focus and suggests a dinner party in varied rhythm. Photographer Mitchell Bliss, who also shot the tinted black-and-white covers of RCA's classic *Dinner in Havana* (1954) and *Dinner in Buenos Aires* (1957), features clasped hands—right ring fingers communicating commitment—against a light tablecloth. The woman's *mantilla* veils her shoulders: the chaste lace, slipped from her dark hair, now suggests elegant couture for a night out in the big city.

According to the travel guide–like notes, "Although Brazil's urban culture, like its language, is predominantly Portuguese, Rio's swankiest supper clubs are more in the French-Continental style." Meia Noite (housed in the Copacabana Palace Hotel) "features pink and white satin streamers, light wood furniture in the French provincial style, mirror topped tables and a lush carpeted floor." On the menu? The simplistically described "native specialty, *picadinho*, a typical Brazilian dish composed of chopped meat, olives and eggs, served with fried rice." Nearby *Perroquet* was apparently an early tropical forest theme restaurant, where "foliage, murals and colorful props simulate the natural richness of Brazil's inland regions." In Gavea, the club Monte Carlo "features a lavish floor show" and looks down upon Rio's beaches from an old castle, and on Praia Vermelha, the "tasteful, unostentatious" club Casablanca.

RCA's stylish Dinner In LPs often include a back cover recipe, offering a regional dish to cook at home. Ocean and palm tree memories reanimate as "shrimp with hearts of palm and coconut milk" simmer on suburban stovetops. Unlike many midcentury record menus, this one sounded palatable, so we confidently invited guests, put on the provided soundtrack, and pulled out our vintage red Dansk Kobenstyle pot. Tomatoes, onion, and garlic sautéed in butter, topped off with a cup of unsweetened coconut milk, form the foundation for lemon-marinated shrimp. Adjusting the recipe, we added the shrimp last to avoid overcooking. Our diners found the dish lacking in spice, but, served with basmati rice, nevertheless delicious. The musical numbers including "Mama Eu

Dinner And Music*

IN
THE PACIFIC

inspired by the colorful pages of

HOLIDAY

HERE IS
AN EVENING OF
UNIQUE
ENTERTAINMENT

*

Bring the
romance of Pacific Islands
into your home
for an evening—
any time you choose!
Set your table as it would
appear in one of the
beauty spots of the world!
Serve a dinner typical of
that same locality!
Listen to the music
that has made that
area famous!

*

This Dinner
and Music Album contains
everything you need for
a gracious evening
of entertainment.
Here are recommended table
settings and suggestions
you can follow,
a wonderful and unusual
Dinner Menu to serve,
and, of course,
the recipes you will need
for preparing such a dinner,
complete with a top quality
long playing record of the
music that you would hear
if you were visiting
that area

LONG PLAY
33⅓

HIGH FIDELITY

* trademark

FIGURE 5.5

Dinner and Music in the Pacific,
RCA Custom LO7P 2074;
package design by Heintz & Company,
cover art by Will Dressler, ca. 1960.

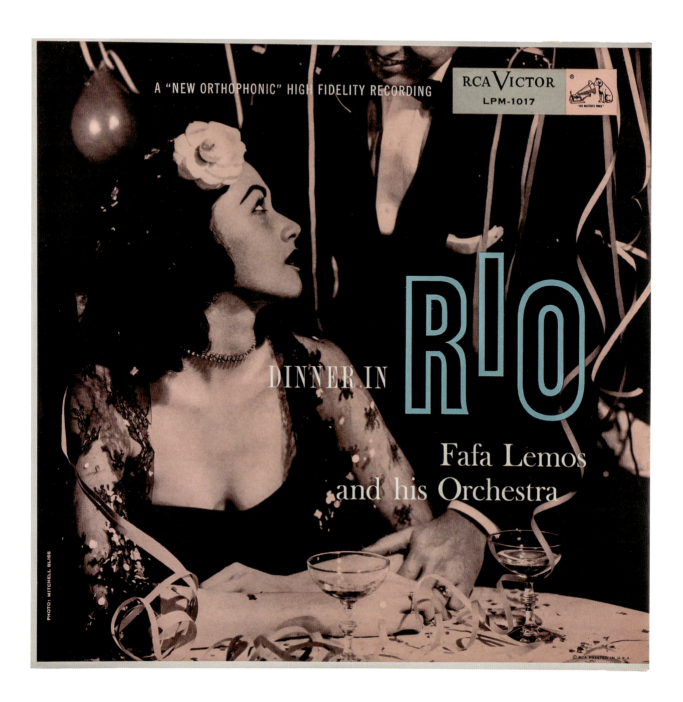

FIGURE 5.6

Dinner in Rio,
Fafa Lemos and His Orchestra,
RCA Victor LPM 1017;
photo by Mitchell Bliss, 1954.

FIGURE 5.7

À la Carte: Music for Cooking with Gas,
Harry Fields, His Piano and Orchestra,
Capitol Custom PB 2914, 1956.

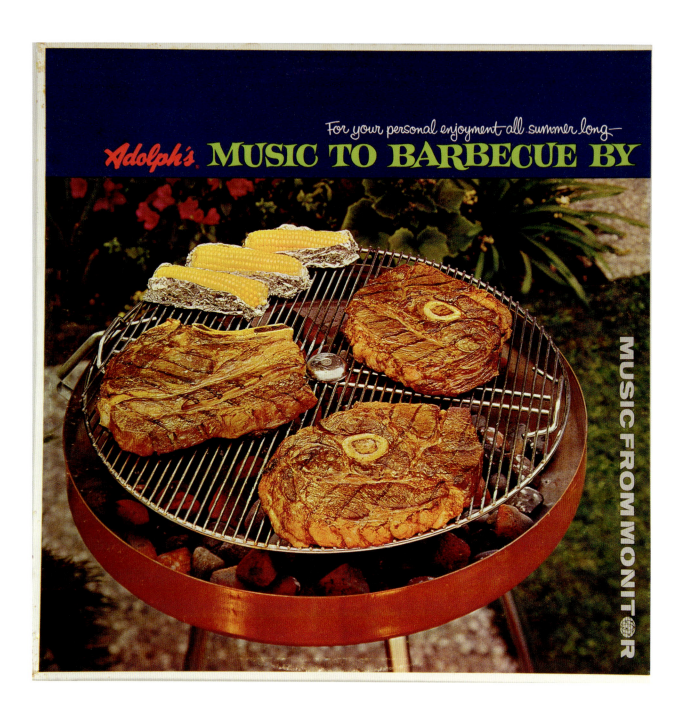

FIGURE 5.8

Adolph's Music to Barbecue By,
Adolph's, 1963.

Quero," "Baia," and "Gracioso," from Rio-born violinist and orchestra leader Fafa Lemos, lean mostly toward Baiao and Samba easy listening and provided soothing background for a successful vinyl-inspired dinner party.

Medium pink and raw red typography on À LA CARTE: MUSIC FOR COOKING WITH GAS welcomes listeners to a meaty meal of "music that's rare and well done!" Mastering that perfect sear on a steak implies the magic of new culinary methods and equipment styles, and Caloric "offers the very finest in gas ranges to insure complete flexibility in kitchen design." Keeping up with consumer demand, the company offered an á la carte menu of colors, sizes, and oven and cooktop arrangements to suit individual tastes and needs "when you dream of a new kitchen." A thin red line sets off the album's titles against the cover's white background, echoing print advertisements of the era. Below it, vibrant illustrations of Caloric appliances pair with detailed insets presenting tempting outputs: cakes, cookies, steaks, and ham in homey, flower-bedecked arrangements. The "ultramatic" countertop range's sleek wooden handle provides a distinctly modernist design touch.

Easy listening is on the menu with Harry Fields and His Orchestra and a, yes, á la carte selection "featuring a unique instrumental blend and smooth, melodic arrangements." (We assume the new Caloric stove came with a manual along with this LP.) "Green Dolphin Street" ("an interesting bossa nova beat that still maintains the jazz idiom") and "Gravy Waltz" ("delightfully set to jazz") set a sparkling mood for the chef, and "Habanera Samba" adds a touch of spice. No recipes or explicit instructions here— just the subtle suggestion for acquiring a hi-fi set for the kitchen.

"For your personal enjoyment all summer long," promises the bright cover of ADOLPH'S MUSIC TO BARBECUE BY. Three Flintstone size steaks dominate a suspiciously shiny grill, along with some shucked corn ears, nestled in similarly shiny aluminum foil. A promotional record from the leading brand of meat tenderizer, *Music to Barbecue By* includes menus for "3 Great Barbecue Meals" from Jeannette Frank, "author of the *Modern Meat Cookbook*" (1958). Frankly, the recipes sound tempting: Barbecue Chuck Steak ("an elegant barbecue party meal 'alla Italiana'"), Barbecue Family Steak ("an exciting outdoor dinner with an Indonesian flair"), Barbecue Kabobs with side dishes ("green peppers, cherry tomatoes and bacon strips"), and chilled relish tray with garlic-cheese dip (olives-onions-mushrooms-celery-zucchini). Hungry yet?

Music to Barbecue By was linked to NBC Radio's *Monitor* program, which ran from 1955 to 1975. The album's notes effuse: "*Monitor*: NBC's exciting weekend radio show! A fast paced varied format of News, Special Events, Sports, Comedy, Music—all designed to entertain all members of the family wherever they are—whatever they're doing." (Adolph's was a prominent advertiser.) On the disc, the selections include numbers guaranteed not to give guests indigestion, including "A Swingin' Safari," from Bert Kaempfert, Nelson Riddle's version of "Bonanza," and Percy Faith's "Jamaican Rhumba."

The record's promotional possibilities become clear when reading the liner notes: "Light a Fire under Sales with Adolph's." Upon close inspection, one finds "Limited Edition—Not for Sale" printed on the label. So this item was a giveaway; perhaps when customers bought enough steak they garnered a free record. Adolph's Meat Tenderizer, promoted today as "the perfect match for tough cuts of beef, pork, or poultry," includes enzyme powders that help break down meat fibers, resulting in a more tender steak.[3] As the inner label chimes: "Adolph's Meat Tenderizers—Great for Outdoor Cooking." Let's get grilling!

6

FAMILY FIDELITY
THE HARMONIOUS MARRIAGE AND
WELL-ADJUSTED CHILDREN

"Life is luscious when you're a girl, and the most luscious part of all is loving a man," coos Helen Gurley Brown on **LESSONS IN LOVE**. This "Adults Only" record presents "How to Love a Girl" on one side and "How to Love a Man" on the other. The cover photo of Brown was shot by Peter James Samerjan. Known for his pin-ups and so-called glamour photography, Samerjan "helped to introduce the use of nude glamour into the field of advertising photography in the 1950s."[1]

Lessons in Love capitalized on Brown's spectacular success with her landmark book *Sex and the Single Girl* (1962), which "shocked early-1960s America with the news that unmarried women not only had sex but thoroughly enjoyed it."[2] In 1965, Brown was hired as editor in chief at *Cosmopolitan* and reigned supreme there until 1997, revolutionizing women's magazines along the way. On *Lessons in Love*, she "got to say hundreds of things I didn't get to say in the book."

Brown remains a divisive figure, scorned by conservatives and feminists alike, while championed by others as a trailblazing pioneer and promoter of female sexual empowerment. Unlike proponents of the mainstream feminist movement, she emphasized the individual, not the collective.[3] Her *New York Times* obituary remarked: "In retrospect, Ms. Brown's work seems strikingly apolitical, beholden mostly to the politics of personal advancement."[4]

With spoken tracks such as "Capturing a Man if You Aren't Pretty" and "How to Behave at Home When You're Misbehaving" (for the male listener who's having an affair), *Lessons in Love* offers free associations about dating and relationships that are familiar to anyone who's ever glanced at *Cosmopolitan*. For men, rules abound: "Take time to court her," "Laugh at her jokes," and "Act confident, even if you aren't" (in bed). For women, "the luckiest of sexes," she offers advice: "It's easy to say 'Yes' to a man, but there are times you need to say 'No,'" "Appeal to his bad taste sometimes" by wearing sexy lingerie, and "Humor your husband and his sudden impulses." It's an odd mix of candid counsel and sexist stereotypes, and there's that basic discrepancy of he, the Man, and her, the Girl.

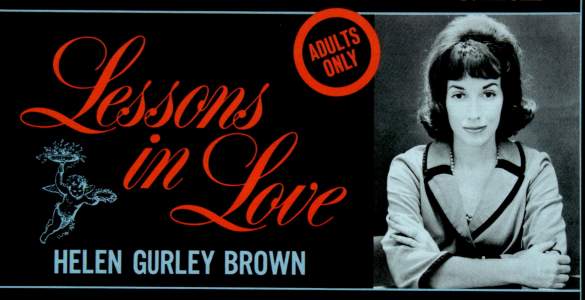

FIGURE 6.1

Lessons in Love,
Helen Gurley Brown, Crescendo GNP 604;
photo by Peter James Samerjan, 1962.

Billed as "Authentic! Entertaining! Non-Technical!," **WHAT YOU CAN LEARN FROM THE KINSEY REPORT** was "recorded as given before actual audiences of various service, social and civic groups." On the cover, a woman, wearing a prim, buttoned-up white blouse, looks shocked—apparently at what she learned from the report. The record captures Dr. Murray Banks, "the most sought after speaker on the most talked about subject in America today." Banks released several albums during the 1950s, including *Anyone Who Goes to a Psychiatrist Should Have His Head Examined!* (1965) and *How to Quit Smoking in Six Days or Drop Dead in Seven!* (1965).

Banks, billed as a clinical psychologist, sounds a bit like a borscht-belt comedian. He peppers his pronouncements on coitus and orgasms with jokes, asides, and nonsequiturs like "I thought homosexual meant that you do it at home" that elicit uproarious, nervous laughter from the audience. He jumps from topic to topic, only occasionally mentioning Kinsey Report findings. He does echo Kinsey's progressive views about sex and declares that "our minds are filled with lies, distortions and stupid beliefs" that hinder sexual relations. Early on, Banks proclaims that Kinsey has "taken sex out of the cellar, out of the darkness, and brought it out into the open where we can sit down and discuss it intelligently." Sadly, despite the promising title, listening to this "personal interpretation of essential sex factors" presented in Banks's "unique and dynamic style" (translation: stilted comedic approach) wasn't that enjoyable or edifying.

What You Can Learn from the Kinsey Report represents an aspect of the widespread media attention paid to the Kinsey Reports, based on the work of Alfred Kinsey, which revolutionized the scientific study of human sexuality. Kinsey, armed with a PhD in biology from Harvard University, utilized confidential personal interviews to conduct one of the first large-scale studies of human sexual behavior. His landmark book *The Sexual Behavior of the Human Male* (1948), which became an unlikely bestseller, remained in the news for several years. His follow-up, *The Sexual Behavior of the Human Female* (1953) was less popular, but perhaps more groundbreaking, as it challenged a number of myths about female sexuality. Together, these two books are known as the Kinsey Reports.

Although his research remains controversial, Kinsey "was the major factor in changing attitudes about sex in the twentieth century. He changed the nature of sexual studies, forced a reexamination of public attitudes toward sex, challenged the medical and psychiatric establishment to reassess its own views, influenced both the feminist movement and the gay and lesbian movement, and built a library and an institution devoted to sex research."[5] Today, the Kinsey Institute continues his work and sums up their goals this way: "Kinsey Institute researchers and affiliates have explored the what, how, and why of sexuality, gender, relationships, and reproduction to learn how we live our sexual lives—with others and ourselves."[6]

DR. JOYCE BROTHERS DISCUSSES LOVE-MARRIAGE-SEX presents "the ten basic problems dealing with love, marriage, and sex about which she is often asked for advice" such as "how to make friends," "pre-marital sex," "in-laws." No problems in these

FIGURE 6.2

What You Can Learn from the Kinsey Report,
Dr. Murray Banks,
Audio Masterworks LPA 1210, 1956.

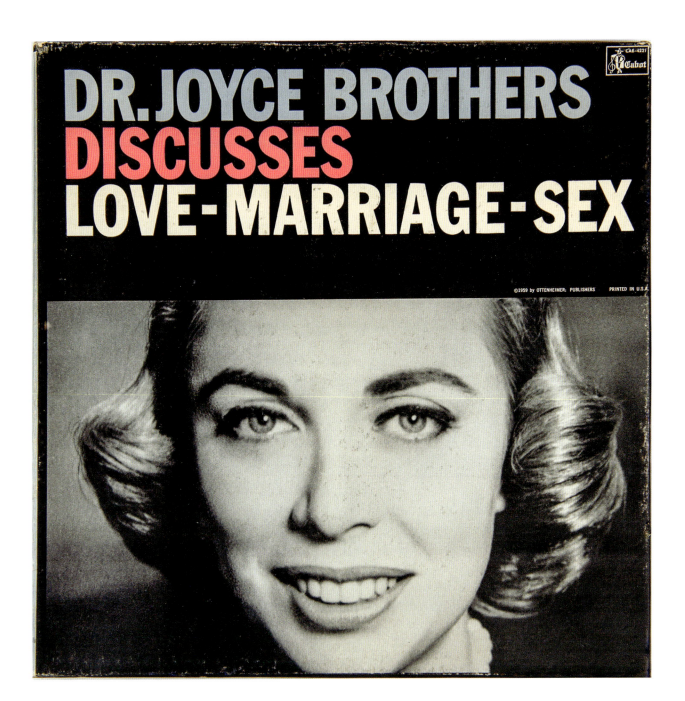

FIGURE 6.3

Dr. Joyce Brothers Discusses Love-Marriage-Sex,
Cabot CAB 4221, 1959.

areas? No worries! "Even if you need no help in these matters, you will enjoy listening to the manner in which Dr. Brothers handles these problems." We could all probably use a little more exposure to a level-headed expert like Brothers. On the record, she jumps into giving her advice on marriage, relationships, and success. Like any good psychologist, she starts with childhood: children make friends as a way to think about meeting potential marriage partners later in life. She encourages listeners to "make relationships with people in your immediate neighborhood," not in "greener pastures" in "faraway cities." How to do this? For one, "take an active part in community activities." Brothers offers straightforward advice, relatively free of outdated notions, though she warns without critical reflection that when choosing a marriage partner, there are many issues that "make racial intermarriage difficult."

Brothers shot to fame by winning the popular television game show *The $64,000 Question*—by answering questions on boxing. With her winning public persona and a doctorate in psychology from Columbia University, she launched the pioneering *The Dr. Joyce Brothers Show* in 1958. The program's themes included sexual satisfaction (for women) and menopause, which were "considered taboo subjects to discuss on television and radio during the 1960s, yet Brothers' ability to leverage her traditionally feminine demeanor while imparting scientific knowledge about such topics made her popular among audiences."[7] She discussed psychological perspectives on children, love, marriage, and sex and showed a "willingness to publicly address what were then borderline taboo subjects, such as sexual fulfillment and infidelity."[8] She wrote a syndicated advice column that appeared in hundreds of newspapers and appeared often on television and, occasionally, in films into the 2000s. Thus, she made "the unlikely journey from housewife to celebrity quiz show contestant to the nation's best-known media psychologist."[9]

Brothers kept her era-appropriate female roles foregrounded and managed to break new ground in public discussions of sex and marriage: "Conforming in many ways to the dominant image of women in the 1950s and early 1960s, Brothers described herself as a mother, wife, and psychologist last."[10] The liner notes reassure the listener that, despite her busy schedule, "Dr. Brothers manages to keep house more than successfully for her husband and daughter." With her toothy smile, eyes stylishly made up, and flawless complexion lending her a glamorous appearance, the black-and-white album cover photo depicts Brothers like an actress or a model. This album has aged better than most of the midcentury marital harmony records we've heard.

The pale azure of the walls, echoed in chair stripes, comics, doll's dress, and dad's socks, provides the backdrop to THE FAMILY ALL TOGETHER. Adoring expressions and matching beige dresses unite mother and daughter as they clasp the baby doll in blue. Heavy upholstered furniture, decorative fireplace millwork of rosettes and columns, and father and son in cuffed trousers and brown leather shoes: this living room gathering maintains a formal air. Adults readjusting to the return from war and youth experiencing cultural clashes—with the generation gap looming—must have found this

FIGURE 6.4

The Family All Together,
Boston Pops Orchestra • Arthur Fiedler,
RCA Victor LM 1879, 1955.

album a strange intervention, hearkening back to a past already fading by the mid-1950s. The cover art, signed "Wilson Smith," resonates with *Saturday Evening Post* and Norman Rockwell visions. Liner note author Alice Thompson Beaton remains hopeful about a nostalgic return: "America has rediscovered that great institution, the happy family . . . the family that does things together, shares its good times, likes to be with one another. Mother and Dad, big and little brothers and sisters are learning that it's fun to be a family, to enjoy interludes when differences of ages, of personalities are forgotten in the warmth of togetherness."[11]

Unsurprising gender differences order the cover painting, as well as the description of the siblings' response to the music. Brother "Jimmy" has "learned to love the haunting beat," "the grandeur," the "skillful arrangement" of the musical selections. Older "sis," knitting "a new pair of argyles, . . . has learned to follow the wistful sweetness of Debussy's *Claire de lune*" and now hums "to herself the tender melody *Intermezzo*." No emotional Jim and boisterous Betsy in this midcentury household. Family listeners are asked to discuss the music with one another, to take a vote on "Enjoyed" or "Not for Me." This album moves beyond music appreciation: "It is an unpretentious but effective venture into a living experience . . . of discovering more about those we love . . . of finding a wider world than the narrow confines of our own personalities." Gershwin's "Porgy and Bess (A Symphonic Synthesis)," Voelcker's "A Hunt in the Black Forest," and the nursery song "Pop Goes the Weasel" offer an optimistic sonic atmosphere in which "differences, great as they may seem, need not always divide people."

While working for Simon & Schuster, publisher of the wildly successful Little Golden Books, Arthur Shimkin proposed a new line of records "after reading comment cards from frazzled parents who wished they did not have to read Golden Books so repeatedly."[12] He went on to produce over three thousand Golden records, including a Grammy-winning *Peter and the Wolf* from Leonard Bernstein (1960). Sold at popular department stores like Montgomery Ward and Sears, many had tie-ins to popular television shows such as *Captain Kangaroo*, *The Munsters*, and *Romper Room*. Golden Records, as a 1965 ad gushed, was "the fastest-selling, most complete line of children's records in the world."[13]

Initially released with full-color sleeves and pressed on bright red or orange vinyl, "the records were perfect for young children. They were very durable, could be tossed around the room without being broken and still remain playable."[14] (Horrors!) Marketed along with Golden Books and Golden Encyclopedias, the Golden Book and Record series retailed for sixty-nine cents in the mid-1960s, helping "children learn to read as they hear the sound and follow the story and pictures."[15]

HELP YOUR CHILD LEARN TO READ—"a special long-playing record"—includes six perennially popular Little Golden Book stories, along with the illustrations. A "beep," so familiar from film strips, indicates when to turn the page. Bright, cheery voices, including those of Danny Kaye, "Kari," and "Rita," provide lively readings, lightly accompanied by a range of instruments. Hearing *The Little Engine That Could* still inspires ("I think I can. I think I can. I think I can").

FIGURE 6.5

Help Your Child Learn to Read,
Golden Records GST 12;
produced by Ralph Stein, 1972.

From the cover of **TEACHING YOUR SECOND GRADERS**, it's difficult to discern that a more accurate title would be *Teaching Your Second Graders Bible Lessons*.[16] As a young girl points out something on an easel, a group of other second-graders (we assume) look on, boys dressed in dark shoes, suits, and ties (one favors brightly striped socks), girls wearing long-sleeved blouses, pinafores, and black Mary Janes. A teacher, in somewhat surprisingly fashionable high heels and a flower-print dress, supervises. Upon closer inspection, the fact that each student holds a leather-bound bible provides a big hint: the record "is a second-grade class in bible teaching," released by Gospel Light Publications. In small print, the cover indicates "A How to Teach Record," and the inner label clarifies: "A How-to-Teach Sunday School Record." On the cover's top left corner, a neat graphic logo, featuring a simplified record player, identifies Teach Records, 33⅓ LP.

Teaching Your Second Graders presents a custom-made Sunday school class. "First the child learns the facts from God's Word. Then these facts are applied to his life." The liner notes further explain: "This is a record with a fourfold impact: Education/ Inspiration/Drama/and Entertaining, too." As for "entertaining": "What can be more delightfully entertaining that an unstaged, unrehearsed, uninhibited group of children and a teacher teaching.?" (Hmm, we wonder how uninhibited Sunday School teachers want their pupils to be . . .) The record includes instruction, classroom examples, and commentary: "This recording is not a class per se. It is taken apart and analyzed for you step by step, so that your listening is guided. This is indeed a teaching record." A list of tasks for "as you listen" are provided, with commentary such as "The teacher turns to the Bible after she is sure they thoroughly understand the story" and "how the children are taught to pray–individually with a little encouragement."

Teaching Your Second Graders features teacher Frances Blankenbaker, who went on to write *What the Bible Is All About: Bible Handbook for Kids* (2016). On the recording, we are told that second-graders are "concerned about God's place in the world." By second grade, therefore, "we can teach him to trust and obey God." Thus, the teacher is offered a "Bible lesson developed for a child to match his particular age." After a brief introduction from Ethel Barrett, a well-known Christian author and educator, we listen in on "a real Sunday School class." A helpful narrator keeps us informed about the lessons, which include "points of contacts"—parable-like stories about moral behavior—and the use of visual aids that apparently depict Bible stories. The children dutifully speak up, and make tentative connections to what they know about the Bible. Listeners are told to "notice the inflection" in the teacher's voice, "how she creates a change of mood." Regrettably, she talks so fast, and in so many run-on sentences, that it's hard to understand her. At times it seems as if she were trying to fit the entire Old Testament onto the record.

Two blond girls in short dress coats and white knee socks grasp giant theme books. Wearing dark slacks and collared shirts, two taller boys sport military-short haircuts. Paired boy/girl and holding hands, the children stand behind a uniformed, white-gloved

FIGURE 6.6

Teaching Your Second Graders,
Teach Records R-P2, 1962.

crossing guard as a station wagon whizzes through the small-town traffic light. Different children may have different safety and health concerns, as well as diverse ways of engaging appropriately in their societies, but all are born needing guidance, from understanding the danger of scalding water to caring for newly emerging teeth.

SONGS OF SAFETY, MANNERS CAN BE FUN, HEALTH CAN BE FUN presents settings and scenarios assumed familiar to those who grew up in the midcentury United States: going to the dentist, riding bicycles, putting away toys, drinking milk—all with unremarked acceptance of authority and expertise. Dozens of songs implore young listeners to pick up wet towels, say "Please" and "Thank you," ask to be excused from the dinner table, eat healthy food, wash hands, and know that "The Doctor Is Your Friend." Urban cowboy and country singer Frank Luther sets a solid midwestern tone to his cheery lessons on how "we" behave, aimed at achieving harmony in the family home ("Causing work for others is completely wrong, so we put our towels and clothes where they belong") and meeting an array of social expectations ("It's fun to use good manners!"). Alternative title? Maybe *Fit In and Get Ahead with Good Teeth and Pleasing Manners*. Maybe not so fun, though.

"NOW WE KNOW" (SONGS TO LEARN BY) is part of a series of "wonderful and exciting" extended-play albums "for children and perhaps their parents." Presented by folk singer Tom Glazer and television host Paul Tripp, the set is billed as "an exciting and delightfully new adventure in education and entertainment." Bright orange, yellow, turquoise, and purple blocks of background color feature light-hearted drawings of molecules, a radar system, and an atom's path.

Glazer, a versatile songwriter who had a hit record in 1963 with "On Top of Spaghetti," was "best known for his whimsical children's songs."[17] Aside from the Now We Know records, he released numerous educational titles, such as *Building a City* (1948) and *Let's Play Zoo* (1951), with the Young People's Records subscription service.[18] Glazer went on to record several titles in the Ballad for the Age of Science series, which "introduce scientific concepts and terms, using catchy, easily learned words and music."[19] Tripp hosted *Mr. I Magination*, an early children's TV program that introduced young audiences to careers via travel to "Imagination Land." The music is by Hy Zaret and Lou Singer, who wrote dozens of songs together, including the progressive collection *Little Songs on Big Subjects* (1947), which popularized their jingle-like melodies.[20] (Two of their clever children's numbers were later covered by the quirky alternative rock band They Might Be Giants.)

Several Now We Know titles appeared on *Billboard*'s Best-Selling Children's Record charts during the 1950s. *Billboard* called the Now We Know records "a remarkable series of entertaining educational songs" that "will probably sell steadily for a long, long time. Schools should be a sure-fire market for it, too."[21]

The songs are fun. On album 1, for ages nine through thirteen, each track answers a basic question, as if posed by a child: "How Does Radar Work" and "What Is an Atom?"

FIGURE 6.7

Songs of Safety: Manners Can Be Fun, Health Can Be Fun,
Frank Luther, Vocalion VL 73683, 1963.

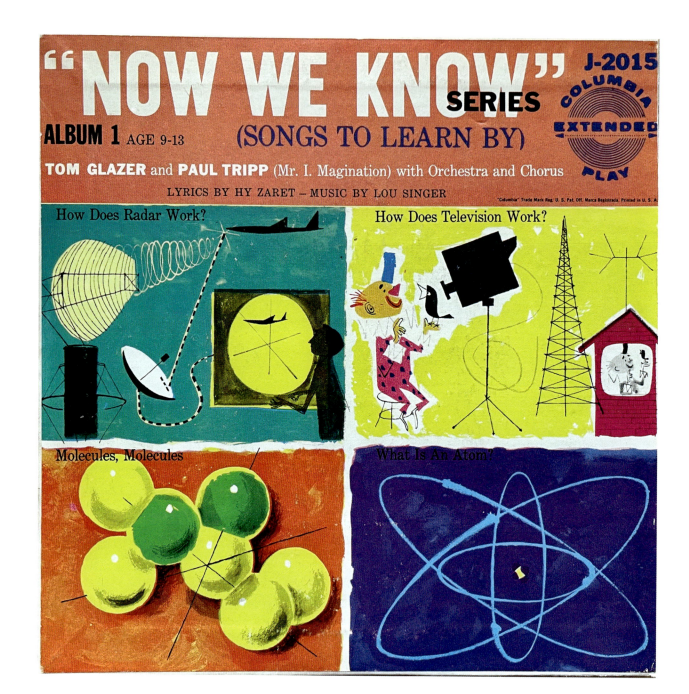

FIGURE 6.8

"Now We Know" (Songs to Learn By),
album 1, ages 9–13,
Tom Glazer and Paul Tripp,
Columbia J 2015, 1955.

(the specter of nuclear war was clearly on young minds in 1955). After hearing "Molecules, Molecules," listeners may find themselves singing along to complicated—yet somehow catchy—phrases like "Everything everywhere in the world is made up of moving molecules." As the notes affirm, "No one is too young to sing and no one is too old to learn."

Two black-and-white, sex-and-gender-divided photos set the stage for **HEAR HOW TO TELL YOUR CHILDREN THE FACTS OF LIFE**. Green and black accents and grid lines resemble the no-nonsense layout of a nature guidebook. Forthright Dad and puzzled Junior have a serious talk over a low round table with childhood pictures from more innocent years, travel souvenirs (a burdened donkey and an open lotus), and an Ikebana plant arrangement. Button-down shirts and dark pants, ties, and shoes set a ceremonial tone for reviewing the "male sex anatomy." (Is Dad describing something about size?) Near a multidialed stereo cabinet, Mom, with full accompaniment of jewelry, shows a wedding band and shapely legs. Ponytailed Missy, enveloped in a boxy, belted, high-necked dress, displays her engagement ring and a sedate smile. (The record's segments on "The Male Reproductive System" and "Preparation for Marriage" offer a heady combination.)

The spoken-word script by pediatrician and marriage and family counselor Dr. Rebecca Liswood suggests a formal lecture, not helpful advice for parents, and she ultimately provides little guidance for that dreaded talk about the birds and the bees. Rather, concerns about male puberty earn her greatest attention. Her comments to young females are dominated by dating ideas far removed from physical intimacy and resulting marriage and children, not necessarily in that order. More than once the doctor warns that a boy forced to marry a pregnant girl will feel "trapped" and resent her and the baby, leading to a troubled future.

Dr. Liswood, bless her, had a career that brought her face to face with children damaged by abusive households and oppressive social norms. On this recording, she tries to dispense with negative beliefs around menstruation and male masturbation (not a concern for girls, apparently). Talk turns to positive values of marital "intimacy," but not a whisper about pleasure—and certainly not female pleasure. Not surprisingly, she maintains typical-for-the-time notions about sexual relations outside of marriage and a "respectful" but patronizing attitude toward homosexuality. Some of her misguided mid-century mainstream "wisdom" can still be heard haunting public health and sex education policy in the current era. As such, *Hear How to Tell Your Children the Facts of Life* provides a disturbingly apt record of entrenched perspectives about family, gender, and sex.

Bold yellow and red capital letters reach toward three-dimensionality with white graphic shadowing that suggests emergent foundations and potential revelations resonating through directive function symbols, such as those for union, disjoint, and proper subset. Part of The New Math: A Guide for Puzzled Parents series, the album **SETS, THE LANGUAGE OF MATHEMATICS** offers hope to moms and dads intending to help with the evening's math homework.

HEAR HOW **TO TELL YOUR CHILDREN THE FACTS OF LIFE**

CARLTON **HEAR HOW** SERIES
CHH/29

DR. REBECCA LISWOOD, Exec. Director of the Marriage Counseling Service of Greater New York outlines the correct methods for sex discussions with teen-agers.

FIGURE 6.9

Hear How to Tell Your Children the Facts of Life,
Dr. Rebecca Liswood,
Carlton CHH 29, 1961.

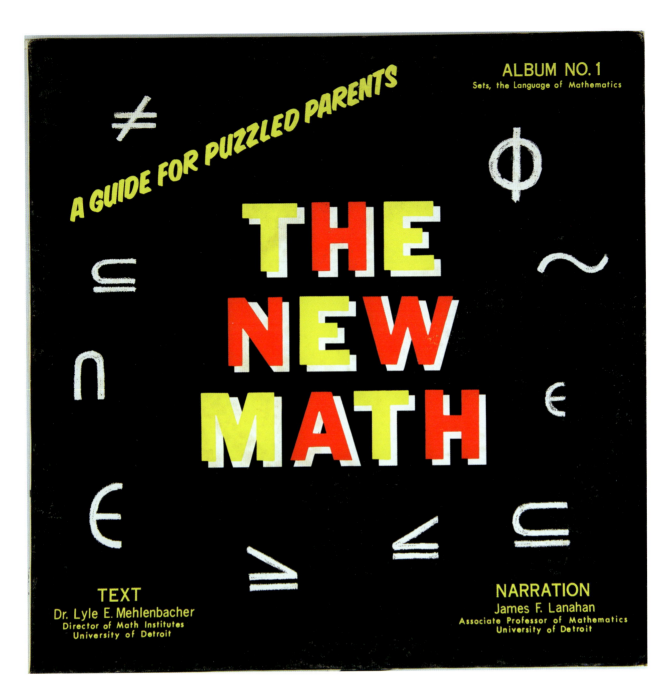

FIGURE 6.10

Sets, the Language of Mathematics,
New Math Records TNM 101, 1966.

Mathematicians and educators, the coauthors received advanced degrees from the University of Michigan and held faculty positions at the University of Detroit. The liner notes reproduce their spoken script, which justifies the need for "new math," describes basic notation, and provides useful definitions, such as the null set and the intersection and union of sets. Later volumes such as *Signed Numbers and Their Ordered Relations* (1967) and rereleases were picked up by RCA Victor.

With new math, *why* questions become more important than *how* questions—for example, why is division performed the way it is?, rather than, how is division done? "Numerical concepts are introduced using sets" and represented within set theory. Emphasis falls on the creation of a "well defined set": Is an object or number a member of a set or not? Is it in or is it out? "If we can't determine individual members, we're not interested," declares the narrator, making notions of "on a spectrum" difficult to capture, as well as "uninteresting." The real-world cultural impact of set theory? The resulting strong binaries do resonate broadly with rigid roles and boundaries—is X in or out?—present in midcentury notions of gender and are key for formalizing and articulating racial and other exclusions. Set theory mathematics made possible various innovations in statistics and probability theory, and, of course, computer science. More recent formulations in data science apparently have opened modes of dealing with messy data that set theory could not attain. Is there a vinyl record for that?

A serious black-and-white geometric cover with brick-brown typewriter font opens the gates for GETTING INTO COLLEGE TODAY. Ivy-covered Gothic architecture, dormers, and chimneys communicate the desired scholastic status. In their youthful, yearning voices, college hopefuls Ronny and Carol provide an introduction, focused on the difficulty "these days" of negotiating competitive college entrance requirements. Next, a roundtable of experts addresses basic questions of who should go to college (not everyone), if class rank matters (it does), and whether entrance exam scores offer a better predictor of success than the high school record (generally not).

Parents are admonished not to "sacrifice their children on the altar of their own prestige." In other words, not every Junior can attend Daddy's alma mater, and that's OK. Given that female undergraduates were not accepted into the elite set of eight Ivy League schools until the late 1960s, and Harvard didn't admit the females of Radcliffe College fully into Harvard until 1977, this 1961 album's emphasis on male students isn't surprising.[22]

Guidance counselors from the Taft School and Sandusky (Ohio) High School align their strategies with admissions officers from the University of Michigan, the University of Toledo, Yale University, and Mills College—all under the auspices of the Association of College Admissions Counselors. Clearly, beyond helping high-schoolers along their career paths, there were plans in the making for the professionalization of the "college counselor." *Getting into College Today* offers a quaint reminder of the era, before the widespread availability of entrance exam prep courses and coaches, application essay editors, and college entrance consultants.

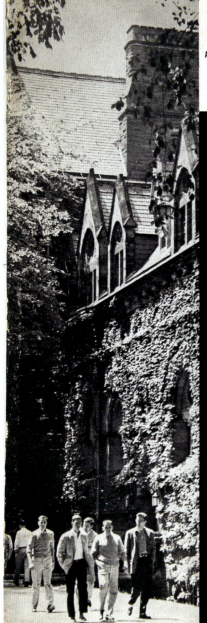

AN ASSOCIATION OF COLLEGE ADMISSIONS COUNSELORS—GUIDANCE ASSOCIATES PRODUCTION

getting into College today

Volume 1

FIGURE 6.11

Getting into College Today,
Globe Albums GA Vol. 1, 1961.

The kids are off to college. The newly empty nest may cause couples to turn their attention to each other. They may realize they aren't as happy as they'd like to be.

Fitness guru Debbie Drake offers some advice. "There is nothing more unattractive than fat thighs," Drake declares on her album HOW TO KEEP YOUR HUSBAND HAPPY. The cover provides guidance in tidy, chipper script font: "Look Slim! Keep Trim! Exercise Along with Debbie Drake." Drake offers a clear message: "It is the obligation of every woman to bring out her best features." Her notes begin: "Right after life and liberty, the Declaration of Independence lists 'the pursuit of happiness.' For most everyone, happiness means health and love. Do you know that overweight is a threat to the happiest of marriages? The obese wife knows that she is a disappointment to her husband. It is dangerous to family contentment and security when Mamma is the best advertisement for her own cooking." Ouch! Needless to say, "an attractive bust line is something you must work on all the time."

Her "Checklist for Keeping Your Husband Happy" beckons beyond the realm of mere fitness: "Firm and graceful body. Clothes, sexy—for your evenings home. Nice voice (keep it soft and musical; also a pretty laugh)." And remember: "Men need constant attention and affection." On the album cover, Mrs. Drake occupies her seafoam-green-cardiganed hubby's mind completely as festive orange and pink highlight her slimming moves and happy-husband mood.

The record intersperses "light" classical music—think dreamy harp glissandos and staccato violin scales—with Drake's upbeat instructions. It's a far cry from today's beat-thumping club workouts. *How to Keep Your Husband Happy* was produced by Bobby Gregg, a drummer with a fascinating career. He played with a who's who of 1960s and 1970s musicians, including Bob Dylan (he played drums on *Bringing It All Back Home* and *Highway 61 Revisited*, both released in 1965); Peter, Paul, and Mary; and Simon and Garfunkel (he can be heard on the remixed version of "The Sound of Silence," which launched the duo's international success). He produced albums by a variety of musicians, including Sun Ra, and released an instructional record, *Drums the Easy Way* (1967). The photographs are by Henry Parker, who shot dozens of album covers, mostly for Columbia and Epic, ranging widely over the musical genres. Notable Parker efforts include *TV Sing Along with Mitch* from Mitch Miller and the Gang (1961), the Dave Clark Five's *I Like It Like That* (1965), and *Aretha Franklin—Yeah!!!* (1965).

Drake, whose measurements were reportedly 38½–22½–36 on her 113-pound frame, found that her time in the television spotlight didn't last as long as LaLanne's or Prudden's.[23] As one observer opined: "Drake was giving too many women in her audience a guilty conscience and new grounds to feel sorry for themselves. After all, how many viewers could realistically aspire to even a small reflection of her sexiness?"[24]

BOB'S MARRIAGE REPAIR KIT features the colorful Baptist minister Bob Harrington, a.k.a. the Chaplain of Bourbon Street, "America's most exciting evangelist." At the height of Bob's popularity, he appeared on *The Phil Donahue Show*, *The Merv Griffin Show*, and *The Tonight Show*. His obituary summed him up: "Harrington's street

FIGURE 6.12

How to Keep Your Husband Happy,
Debbie Drake, Epic BN 26102 PE 26102;
photography by Henry Parker, 1964.

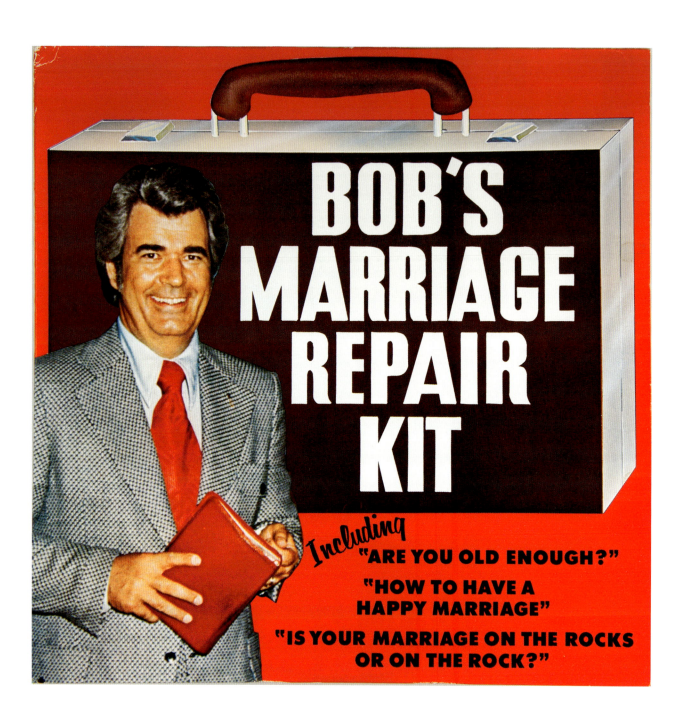

FIGURE 6.13

Bob's Marriage Repair Kit,
World Records R 5, 1974.

ministry message was bold and simple. 'God loves you just as you are. He knows you are a sinner and wants to save you. Don't figure it out. Faith it out!'"[25] He released over thirty albums, including gold records *Laughter, Truth, and Music* and *Chaplain of Bourbon Street* (1972), as well as *Slop Bucket Repentance* (ca. 1975) and *It's Fun Being Saved* (ca. 1975).

In the liner notes, entitled "A Lie at the Altar," Bob tells listeners, "Adultery knocks one day like an uninvited guest. Yet, long before the event, two out of three, if not all three people, stood at a wedding altar, one day and lied. If people could be legally convicted of perjury at a wedding altar, the jails would be flooded with newly-weds." His insights include this slice-of-life wisdom: "Marriage is not a pie eating contest." He reflects: "Since the number one cause of divorce today is marriage—bad marriages— then we ought to spend time discussing what good marriages are supposed to be and how they can be that way." Several photographs of Bob in action grace the rear cover, with useful captions such as "He believes that 90% of his success today, other than the Lord in his life, is his marriage success." Harrington was married three times, and his first divorce led to his stepping down from his ministry at First Baptist Church of New Orleans. He was reported to have frequently said: "I want my tombstone to read: 'Born the first time—September 2, 1927 in Cox Heath, Ala. Born again—April 15, 1958. Died—He didn't. Transferred to heaven.'"[26]

Apparently recorded in front of a live audience, *Bob's Marriage Repair Kit* finds Harrington riffing on his (first) marriage. He addresses the following topics: if you are old enough to be married, how to be happily married, and how to repair instead of re-place your husband or wife. He quips: "Most marriages today are hellish, because they are not based on holiness." When you said "I do," you said it to God, he screams, revival style. "Let God direct you" he insists, and avoid nonbelievers: "You can never be happily married with a nonbeliever."

Details about exactly how to repair your marriage are a bit muddled—mostly he encourages married couples to include God in their marriage. Peppered with 1970s-era phrases like "This is where it's at," "Freaked out," and "Marriage is a 100–100 thing" (not a 50–50 thing), much of his advice is aimed at wives, whom he prompts to have a "right attitude toward sex." Throughout his discussion about sex, he cracks jokes, meanly mimics women, and screams at the top of his lungs—all encouraged by a loudly laughing audience.

Listening to this gem today, it's difficult to discern any practical marriage tips, other than that both husband and wife should be "working toward God's will." Our copy of *Bob's Marriage Repair Kit* was still sealed—unfortunately, this record didn't help any-one repair an on-the-rocks marriage.

The oldest is off to college. The second marriage is fairly harmonious; all those advice records have helped. Now—time to relax and enjoy home life. **LET'S ALL SING BY THE FIRESIDE** finds a family, sheet music in hand, bathed in mauve, gathered near the veined marble hearth's glowing coals and a turntable console, vinyl disc poised on

FIGURE 6.14

Let's All Sing by the Fireside,
Hugo and Luigi with Their Family Singers,
Mercury MG 20153, 1956.

spindle awaiting its drop onto the platter. "This is an age of 'Do-It-Yourself' not only for novice carpenters, plumbers and Sunday painters. For millions of music-minded moderns, tired of being drenched by store-bought'n, factory-made music, which gushed out of the radio and the television set, it is an age of Sing-It-Yourself."

Presented here with lyrics for singing along, the selections "Grandfather's Clock," "I'll Take You Home Again, Kathleen," and a medley of "Daisy and the Band Played On" offer a songfest of warbling, wobbling sopranos and an emphatic organ "as healthy and nourishing as the big Sunday dinner at Grandma's." Fireplace-mantel plants in brass containers with centered mirror, wood paneling, sofa and stacked metallic table lamp, and four family members: these exact photographic elements also grace the cover of Mercury Records' *Music to Live By* (ca. 1956), a sampler of popular and jazz tunes and "classical excerpts" discussed in our book *Designed for Hi-Fi Living*. Probably part of the same photo shoot, here Dad has dispensed with formal dark suit coat and Junior his gray vest; Sis has traded black capris and hair band for high-waisted skirt and soft bob, and Mom's prim neckline reveals less—no trace of fireside modernism, just "old-fashioned family style." *Let's All Sing by the Fireside* was one of a number of similar titles from producing duo Hugo Peretti and Luigi Creatore, including *The Sound of Children* (1960) and *Sing-a-Long* (1960) from the Sing-a-Long-ers.

7

MIND ALTERING
EXPANDING YOUR MIND FOR GREATER SUCCESS

HOW TO THINK is one of those records that initially struck us as unusual and possibly a bit goofy. But, on listening, we came to appreciate its sincerity and seriousness. The recording includes detailed information about how the brain works, along with rules about how to use it, all interspersed with musical refrains about the brain. Writer and narrator Steve Allen's liner notes include two sections: "A Word to Children" ("Once you learn how to think better you'll want to do it every single day for the whole rest of your life") and "A Word to *Parents* and *Teachers*" ("Our educational processes are devoted almost entirely to teaching us *what* to think and rarely give us formal instruction in *how* to think").

Allen, known for hosting the first installment of the long-running *The Tonight Show*, was an accomplished author, composer, and musician. He released dozens of recordings and won a Best Original Jazz Composition Grammy Award for his song "Gravy Waltz." He "believed that everyone had a 'silly center' and that no one should try to suppress it."[1] *How to Think* provides evidence that he certainly didn't suppress his own silly center. Jayne Meadows, who was married to Allen, adds her voice, along with their son Bill Allen. Pianist Paul Smith, who worked with jazz luminaries such as Tommy Dorsey, Dizzy Gillespie, and Ella Fitzgerald and served as music director for *The Steve Allen Comedy Hour*, conducts the orchestra.

Hearing *How to Think* was enjoyable—even over fifty years after its release. It's a winning combination of catchy, clever, and creative. We found ourselves singing the wacky refrains from the fourteen songs that liven up the spoken narration. For example, a bouncy nursery-rhyme-style piece includes such lines as "Thank goodness you've got a cerebellum. If they ask you just what is it, well, you tell them, if you didn't have one, you would surely lie there, till the buzzards came and said, 'Oh, hi there!'" A guitar-driven number with an upbeat rock sound contains the refrain "The thalamus does a marvelous thing. Sees objects move and hears bells ring. It tells if things are cold or hot." (It sounds better than it reads, trust us. A little searching on YouTube produces recordings of a few songs from the LP.) Side 2 lays down nine rules for how to think—a progressive and provocative list that includes lessons in language use, lying, and racial stereotyping.

A small graphic ribbon on the cover bears the "GCN Seal of Excellence," referring to the *Gifted Child Newsletter*, "for the parents of children with great promise." James Alvino, author of *Parents' Guide to Raising a Gifted Child: Recognizing and Developing Your Child's Potential* (1985) adds to the notes: "Whether played in the home or the classroom, *How to Think* can increase a child's ability to reason logically." Alvino believed that "most children can handle more intellectually than they're given credit for, that this expectation of them must begin in the elementary grades and that many activities and approaches reserved for gifted learners can have application with all learners."[2]

While we're not sure *How to Think* lives up to its claim that it will become "a collectors' item . . . a treasured addition to any home or school record library," it offers a thought-provoking glimpse of midcentury discussions about educating gifted children and about improving one's ability to think. Not so goofy, after all.

If ever an album cover called out to be an altarpiece, the **CONCENTRATION & MEDITATION** album by Indra Devi appears ready for contemplation. Devi's prayerful hands, halo-like aura, and serene mien appear saintly in the portrait by Dallas-based society and celebrity painter Dmitri Vail. White Legende font against an azure background signals an airy Easternness for Devi, "the world's foremost authority on yoga." Born Eugenie Peterson in 1899, in the Russian Empire, Devi's familiarity with Western modes of expertise and dissemination elevated her reputation. As the notes pinpoint, a timely concern for mastering the mind—"almost the sole source of our successes and failures"—heralded Devi's resonance with the midcentury self-improvement zeitgeist, as did her emphasis on the notion that "meditation does not interfere or conflict with any religious beliefs or practices." Secularizing the sacred appears in many moments of mass marketization, even as such a move attempts to open various opportunities for those previously excluded. Devi's own story of migration and entrepreneurship prefigures the tsunami of so-called yoga and associated practices in the United States.

CALM NERVES FOR SELF-CONFIDENCE urges listeners to "relax your body . . . uninhibit your mind . . . release your powers . . . be self-confident!" From the Self-Power series produced by Emile Franchel, a "registered psychologist . . . in the forefront in the fields of mental science," the album offers "an answer to indecision, inhibition, irresolution and feelings of inferiority, insecurity and inability." In the 1950s, British-born Franchel, who considered himself a psychologist who specialized in hypnotism, hosted a television show, *Adventures in Hypnotism*, and produced several books, including the hypnotically titled *254 Questions and Answers on Practical Hypnotism and Auto-Suggestion plus Glossary* (1957). In the back cover photograph, he bears some resemblance to Peter Sellers in *Dr. Strangelove* (1964). Franchel appeared as himself in the obscure but memorable 1959 film *Horrors of the Black Museum*. In a video trailer available online, he breathlessly announces that the film was produced

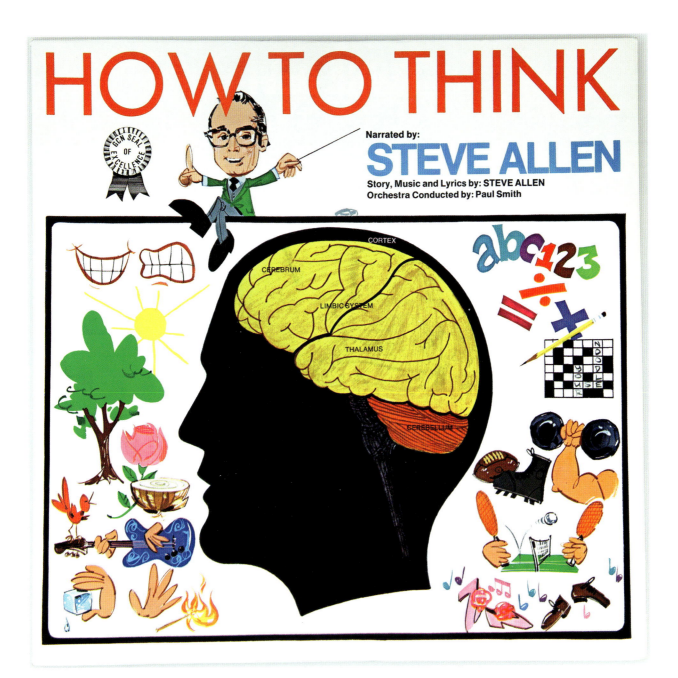

FIGURE 7.1

How to Think,
Steve Allen, Meadowlane LP 010, 1972.

FIGURE 7.3

Calm Nerves for Self-Confidence,
Psychoscope Record #4 R 1365;
cover design by Russell-Greene, 1958.

FIGURE 7.4

Reduce Tensions and Sleep Deeply,
Psychoscope Record #3 R 1359;
cover design by Russell/Greene,
photography by Emil Cuhel, 1958.

for lighter daytime relaxation." In a bit of cross-promotion, listeners are urged to collect a full set of Self-Power titles: "Play the *Relaxation* record and other recordings of your choice—saving *Sleep Deeply* to be played last of all." Upon listening to *Sleep Deeply*, the last thing we heard was, "Your arms are growing heavy. Very heavy. You are going deeper, even more deeply asleep."

The cover of **MUSIC TO HELP YOU STOP SMOKING** features a woman's bejeweled hand in the act of stubbing out a cigarette, its smoke swirling up from a metallic ashtray. A cocktail glass filled with cigarettes and some matches sit nearby under a modern wooden lamp. The "Living Strings" logo, complete with two graphic violins, hovers over her hand. If you bought *Music to Help You Stop Smoking* hoping for tips and techniques, you would have been disappointed—the record features the Living Strings playing a selection of standards and classical piano music.

The Living Strings were a creation of RCA producer Ethel Gabriel. They released dozens of easy-listening albums, usually based on a particular theme, such as *Living Strings Play South of the Border* (1962) and *I'm a Believer and Other Monkees Hits* (1967).[4] The liner notes provide the sole hint of the album's message: "Only will power will help you stop smoking. But this music will help your will power." The numbers include "Autumn Leaves," "Clair de Lune," and Chopin's "Polonaise in A-Flat." The notes promise the listener that the music "is so entertaining and the songs are presented in so fascinating a way that it will relax you, make you feel good, and keep your hand from groping toward a pack of cigarettes." Perhaps the record exemplifies RCA's belief in the power of music—or it may represent just another way to repackage easy-listening discs.

You've set out on a personal journey, into the wilderness, to the top of the rocky mountain, where the air is clear, the stars shine brightly, and only a few pines dot the summit, seeking visions for personal realization and success. But that first step, the setting out—how to muster the will to make the climb? To crest the highest height, walking stick in hand? **MUSIC FOR COURAGE AND CONFIDENCE** offers musical motivation to send you on your way. (Mike Eitzel from the indie band American Music Club released a covers album entitled *Music for Courage and Confidence* in 2002—we're focusing on the vintage RCA Victor LP.)

For RCA Victor's Moods in Music series, the Melachrino Strings provided soothing accompaniment for many an accomplishment and desired states of mind—relaxation, reading, dining, faith. Here, with only the pulchritudinous plucking of harp for percussion, tunes such as "You'll Never Walk Alone," "Ah! Sweet Mystery of Life," and "Pennies from Heaven" fill out two sides of hopeful positivity. The back cover features inspirational quotes from Henry David Thoreau, Seneca, and Robert Louis Stevenson. Henry Wadsworth Longfellow's "A Psalm of Life" appears in full: "Be a hero in the strife!" and "Learn to labor and to wait," the poet exhorts. Just the sort of writing to provide calm and solace for the road ahead. As historian Jill Lepore points out, Longfellow "loved writing poems that everyone would read, poems that everyone could read, poems in

FIGURE 7.5

Music to Help You Stop Smoking,
Living Strings, RCA Camden CAL 821, 1964.

FIGURE 7.6

Music for Courage and Confidence,
The Melachrino Strings,
RCA Victor LPM 1005, 1954.

which people, unsophisticated people, even little people, might find pleasure and so-lace."[5] Ah, easy reading with easy listening.

Threatening storm clouds transform into a dramatic golden sunset in the transition FROM DEPRESSED, MELANCHOLY, TRAGIC, SAD TO GAY, HAPPY, BRIGHT, JOYOUS on the first record in the Affect Your Emotions through Music series from Westminster. Also mapping this shift: a pallid Pepto-Bismol pink compact font glides toward expansive, bright red, yellow, and purple lettering. Jules Maidoff, a successful commercial illustrator who later founded an art school in Italy, designed the covers. (A thorough typographic analysis of the series can be found on the Fonts in Use web-site.[6]) The cover's "iso/vect" symbol, a curved arrow vector rising thorough a small graph, suggests a scientific background, and the technical liner notes do not disappoint, touting "accurate and systematic observations" and introducing two principles: "The ISO proposition, or the matching of mood to music; and the VEC(TOR) principle, the change in direction and magnitude of that music toward the desired level of affect or mood." Not to be confused with easy-listening genres, "the groupings, dimensions and goals of this ISO/VECT series must be completely divorced from the commonly heard 'mood music,' as for example 'music to read by' or 'to drive by' or 'to swim by.'"

"Affect your emotions through music," urge the liner notes. As ISO/VECT pro-moter and liner note author Leo Shatin PhD, states, "Music has been increasingly em-ployed for psychological purposes since World War I, and especially since World War II." (Shatkin's own writings include 1954's "A Study of the Relationship Between Music and Post-Electroshock Awakening.") On side 1, music evoking a damped-down melan-choly mood—low, plodding requiem strings swelling into meaningful pauses and long tones dominated by brass, flute, and reed—evolves toward scurrying notes of all kinds building through Bolero-like tension to crashing cymbals and a slam-bang finish. Side 2 includes quick step rhythms, floating flute, cascading piano, and quirky percussion instruments to "maintain joyous mood." If not quite joyous, certainly bright.

The enthusiastic and often capitalized liner notes for THE BURGESS METHOD: DEVELOPING YOUR ESP POWERS, begin: "Can you read minds? Predict the future? Find lost articles? Russ Burgess, parapsychologist, hypnotist, suggestologist and lec-turer strongly believes it is possible." Burgess, we are told, "has come to the conclusion that ESP (extrasensory perception) is more an art form than a science." Hedging his bets, perhaps, he also calls upon "the science of Suggestology," to develop his listen-ers' psychic abilities. How? "The Burgess Method is a new, revolutionary system of fusing physiological and psychological factors by rejuvenating the entire system with controlled, rhythmic Yoga Breathing, a Head Roll exercise plus employing the science of suggestology."

What in the world is "suggestology"? One commentator suggests, "Maybe a sug-gestologist is someone who makes money by suggesting that you can develop non-existent powers by listening to what sounds suspiciously like a hypno-relaxation

FIGURE 7.7

*From depressed, melancholy, tragic, sad to gay,
happy, bright, joyous*,
Westminster WIV S1;
cover design by Jules Maidoff, ca. 1958.

record."[7] Whatever it is, Burgess says, "it's better than hypnosis." Burgess was a popular entertainer, er, psychic who, in his heyday, performed at county fairs, medical conventions, and universities, as well as on *The Ed Sullivan Show* and *Captain Kangaroo*. He also reportedly taught stress management and meditation at Northeastern University.[8]

The Burgess Method features an impressionistic cover by Lee-Myles Associates, a New York–based advertising and design firm that promoted Folkways records to mainstream media. The package contained three mimeographed inserts—"The Burgess Method: What Is It? How Can It Help Me?," "Stop Smoking Today" on "Russ Burgess Parapsychologist, Hypnotist" stationery, and "Instructions for Breathing Exercise." Included are "some recent comments," such as "I feel that your method is truly one of greatness. My wife and I have had much success with it. Mr. Leroy Banger—Oregon." Other Burgess records include *Lose Weight and Keep it Off* (1972), *Meditation for Western Man* (1973), and *Stop Smoking Today* (1972), available at the time for three dollars, from Burgess himself.

The record begins with Russ insisting, in a slightly nasal voice, "If you have a sincere desire to manifest psychic experiences," the recording will "open the door to a more exciting and fruitful life." He promises that his method will bring forth your "latent psychic abilities." He informs the listener, "The process on this record has taken many years of experimentation and it has assisted many to more exciting and fascinating experiences. . . . You are not engaging in the realm of the occult, witchcraft, black magic, or voodoo," Burgess reassures. "ESP is a form of creativity." *Developing Your ESP Powers* was also released on ABP Records, which evolved into American Program Bureau, a speaker agency featuring such notables as Ellen DeGeneres, Cornel West, and Sophia—the world's very first humanoid celebrity.

The cover of **PSYCHO-CYBERNETICS** features the book of that title, by Maxwell Maltz, MD, with its blurb: "The greatest adventure in living; getting to know yourself." Psycho-cybernetics—a term coined by Maltz—"is a remarkable discovery that will help you to escape life's dull, monotonous routine. It will make you look younger, feel healthier, and be more successful." Psycho-cybernetics "heralded a transition in popular culture from the Norman Vincent Peale version of positive thinking in the 1950s, to the secular, selfist psychologies of the following two decades."[9] Maltz was "one of the world's most widely-known and highly regarded plastic surgeons"—at least according to the album's notes. His classic book *Psycho-Cybernetics*, published in 1960, remains an influential entry in the self-help pantheon.

What's the connection between plastic surgery and self-help, one wonders? The notes provide the "hook": "He proved that personalities can be changed for the better by eradicating 'emotional scars,' just as plastic surgery removes outer scars." *Psycho-Cybernetics*, the album, "marks the first of his works to take on the additional dimension of sound." A printed script is included in the package, to foster the "double sensory method of absorbing information." Selections include "Why Not Imagine Yourself Successful," "How to Unlock Your Real Personality," and "How to Develop

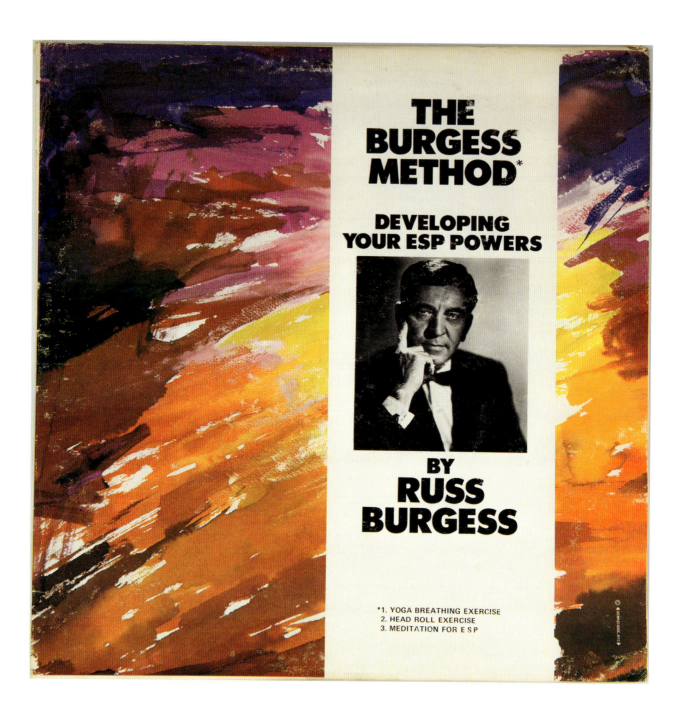

FIGURE 7.8

The Burgess Method: Developing Your ESP Powers,
Russ Burgess, RJB 105;
album cover by Lee-Myles Assoc. N.Y.C., 1972.

FIGURE 7.9

Psycho-Cybernetics,
Success Motivation Institute SMI 1348, 1965.

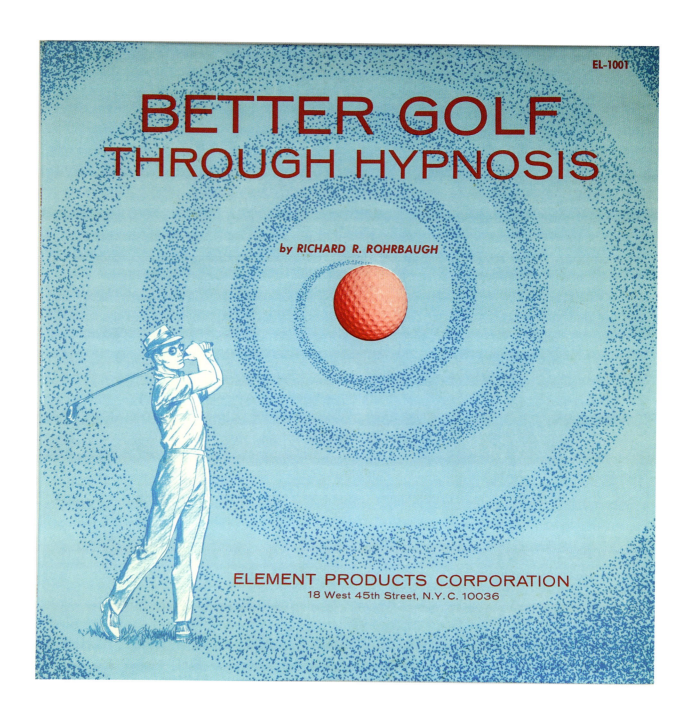

FIGURE 7.10

Better Golf through Hypnosis,
Mirrosonic Records, LTD. EL 1001, 1966.

That 'Winning Feeling.'" Scientific terms abound—"servo-mechanism," "self image psychology," and "automatic guidance system." All, no doubt, useful in achieving your goals: "You can succeed."

Vibrant blue particles swirl against a pale turquoise background on the album cover of **BETTER GOLF THROUGH HYPNOSIS**, spiraling into the red-hued golf ball's atomic center. A golfer, decked out in sunglasses, trilby, and kiltie loafers, follows through on his stroke. The liner notes claim that listening to the recording will allow "virtually untapped capabilities inside of you" to come to the surface, and that "new confidence, self-assurance, self-control and pure concentration will become yours." The recording consists of Richard R. Rohrbaugh's droning, repetitive exhortations to become "loose, limp, and relaxed." Rohrbaugh's expertise reportedly arose from a desire to improve his own golf game by applying a decade's work in hypnosis (and also, possibly, from his experience playing on the Marines' golf team at Camp Pendleton, California).

The method works as the listener, "receptive and sensitized" to suggestion, masters their muscles by "letting go": "Each suggestion will become absorbed into the subconscious mind to be recalled automatically and at will when needed on the golf course." Free from doubt and fear, and with unshakeable mental control, the modern US populace primes for peak performance. Aha! The reference for the LP's cover illustration: "The mind must sink itself into the deepest possible state of concentration where all thoughts are merged into one, as particles drawn to an irresistible magnet"—or a golf ball. (This thought may remind some readers of Chevy Chase's character Ty Webb repeating the mantra "Be the ball" in the 1980 movie *Caddyshack*.)

AT LEISURE

Leisure pursuits, too, caught the scent of success, and the recording industry promoted listening as an essential leisure activity. Records for learning to play an instrument, to dance, and to develop music appreciation were a natural fit. Additionally, a staggeringly wide variety taught and tempted the listener to create a better self at leisure. Many instructional titles encouraged recreational learning, relaxed accomplishment, and outdoor activity. It's fun to speak another language! Practice your ukulele! Train your dog! These records often reflect transcendentalist beliefs in the inspirational and transformative power of nature. So, relax, listen, and take the time to get out and do more.

There's always something new to try—a mental block to unlock, an aspect of yourself to improve. Suddenly, for many, at midcentury, there was more time to do so: "Following the war, a boom in economy resulted in expanded leisure opportunities inside and outside the home. Manifestations of this change include the commodification of leisure activity and an increased emphasis on self-fulfillment and self-gratification."[1] Designer Henry Dreyfuss pondered the growth in leisure time: "To what use is this leisure being put? Is it making its recipients happier, better equipped to live a full life, to realize their full potential of personal development?"[2] If instructional records are any indication, midcentury leisure was busy.

Without doubt, instructional and self-improvement records blurred boundaries between labor and leisure, imploring listeners to bring their lessons home and pore over study guides in private. While presented as enjoyable or relaxing, efforts to improve oneself resonate with a pedagogy of comparison, competition, and the fear of falling behind. In other words, learning at home to get ahead on the job, as well as in a broader social sphere, brings work demands into the household. Instructional records also encroach upon so-called leisure or family time, even if "dynamic" learning methods promise improvement without conscious awareness.

As one midcentury language instruction record enthused: "No classes to attend, no tiresome studies." Learn at home when you want, as often as you want. This focus on individualized study under personal control in the privacy of a domestic wonderland sounds familiar. "Friends and family" might be included in this learning journey, but strangers meeting and mingling in a classroom are definitely not in the picture. While the emphasis is on learning "pleasantly," the more honest instructional manuals admit that "some application is necessary." Useful to know, as foreign language LPs often contain inexplicable lapses and leaps. "Where are you from? I'm Italian. It's made of wood." Pronouncing page after page of words that are meant as new vocabulary to be memorized soon triggers a kind of panic: beyond rote repetition and three or four word declarations (*Buon giorno! Sì, io parlo italiano*), every single word of the new language remains to be learned. *Aiuto!*

Before the advent of language learning computer programs, apps, and e-learning platforms, language instruction records proliferated. Such recordings fit into an interesting niche, often promoted to tourists and other travelers who hoped for a bit of conversation with a country's people. After World War II, however, a new era of linguistic flow and fluency clearly connected to continued military concerns around the globe. Language learning methods were often developed to meet such concerns, adding a whisper of intrigue and spy-inflected glamour to evenings spent at home with a glass of ouzo or vodka, a fat phrase book, and an instructional record.

Using methods taught in the US Army, Living Language, starting in 1946, released dozens of language learning records, as well as *Living Method Touch Typing* and *Reduce in Record Time.* Most Living Language albums included four ten-inch LPs and retailed for $9.95 in the 1950s—replacing the $25 shellac set sold previously through Columbia Records.[3] David Stevenson, president of the Children's Record Guild, which sold the Living Language series, heralded language leaning as a necessity: "We have not even begun to scratch the surface of the many ways to use records in as teaching aids. The jet age, greater tourism, etc., are all helping make polylingualism more necessary."[4] Living Language records were extravagantly promoted with a $50,000 for "January Alone" ad campaign, with ads in major national magazines, including *Esquire,* the *New Yorker, Harper's, Atlantic Monthly,* and *Popular Mechanics,* and newspapers such as the *New York Times, New York Herald Tribune,* and *San Francisco Chronicle.*[5]

Living Language lives on as a line of Random House self-study courses. We've included several examples of their midcentury record sets. The recorded content is similar to today's offerings, and the nostalgic, romantic view of native speakers—a whiff of potential romance in the air—endures as a mainstay in foreign language training promotion.

Although only a few language albums were big sellers, these records lured customers into record shops. According to Cy Leslie, head of Instant Learning Records, instructional records "bring a new and more serious kind of customer into the record store and once this traffic is created, an alert salesman can usually move his regular disks as well."[6] Language records were seasonally popular: "The language records have been found to have special appeal in the summer when buyers contemplating European tours want a quick brush-up on their high school French, Spanish, Italian and German, etc. This idea is regarded as virtually a sure thing from summer to summer since for most people high school language learning is a dim memory by the time they can afford the Continental junket."[7]

Records also offered a convenient way to learn to play musical instruments. A typical learn-to-play album included musical tracks that left one instrument out, so that the listener could "fill in"—by playing guitar or saxophone, for example, along with a band. Music Minus One emerged as a leader for such "play-along" albums, releasing hundreds of titles that provide "a unique way to study, rehearse and perform with professional ensembles in the comfort of your own home."[8] During its early days, Music Minus One had a few competitors, including Young Violinists' Editions from Remington Records, a short-lived label that nonetheless benefited from covers designed by Alex Steinweiss.[9] Columbia Records introduced "Add-a-Part" records in the 1940s, but didn't continue the line after the LP was introduced. Savoy Records released a Jazz Laboratory series of *Do-It-Yourself Jazz* records featuring pianist Duke Jordan, with a quartet playing on side 1, and the same songs without the saxophone, on side 2.[10] Jamey Aebersold's Play-A-Long albums are still available, but only on compact disc.

A host of records offer instructions for appreciating and understanding music—especially classical and jazz. Appreciation comes with a sense of watching, listening, and learning, and perhaps also a certain passivity. Sit back and enjoy the latest popular hits, unfamiliar melodies of foreign lands, symphonies improved through stereo, secrets of jazz revealed! Of course, participation can deepen appreciation, not to mention cognitive and physical integration and development, deepening in turn a sense of accomplishment.

For example, NBC-TV aired *The Subject Is Jazz*, a thirteen-part educational program that promised "no long-hair talkfests." The show presented performances by Duke Ellington and Benny Goodman and offered "a serious profile of the history, development and growth of jazz in all its forms."[11] Celebrated conductor Leonard Bernstein made his first television appearance in 1954 on CBS's *Omnibus*, a high-culture program featuring classical music. He "made the subject seem vivid and vital through his clear, unpretentious writing and clever metaphors."[12] Bernstein released many recordings in this vein; we feature his 1963 effort *Leonard Bernstein Conducts for Young People* in the Learning to Listen: Music Appreciation chapter.

In researching the *Adventures in Rhythm* and *A Child's Introduction to Rhythm* records, we found ourselves wondering about the distinction between appreciation and participation. Should the rhythm LPs be in the music appreciation chapter, in the sense that recognizing and becoming conscious of a rhythm helps to explicate and comprehend a piece of music? Or should we place both records in the "Joining In" chapter—with the teacher's encouragement to pick up rhythm sticks, clap your hands, beat the drum, and think about the connection to dance movement?

Active participation in music and dance can take many forms: attempting to follow precisely or imitate, repeating and mimicking, even mocking. Sometimes unwittingly, such participatory actions can be controversial, especially if learning and embodying a certain step or instrument creates a benefit to, or attributes innovation to, someone other than the originating culture or person and leads to profit. Participation can lead to accusations of appropriation—dancing other people's steps, embodying the other—and stealing.

Dance instruction was an early success story for the recording industry. As listeners acquired their first record player, learning to dance was promoted as a socially useful practice. Dozens of dance record labels sprang up, and many small record companies supplied records for dance studios. By midcentury, both RCA and Capitol Records capitalized on the learn-to-dance market, introducing Fred Astaire and Arthur Murray instructional record series.[13] Social etiquette included knowing your way around a dance floor.

In *Esquire* magazine's etiquette guidebook from 1953, "sports etiquette" appears along with "business etiquette" and "social etiquette." (Our copy bears the inscription: "To Bill, on your 18th birthday. With love, Mother.") Their "primer for good sportsmen" warns about the "unwritten laws" that the up-and-coming businessman is likely to encounter when participating in golf, tennis, yachting, horseback riding, skiing, shooting, and fishing. The stakes are high: "When a man trespasses against the sportsman's code of knowledgeable conduct in and around a particular sports-passion, that man is mentally written off as a wrong guy—or, at the very best, as a good guy not to ask back."[14] Thus, sports-related instructional records advise not only how-to but also how-not-to. For example, the Hear How series from Carlton Records tailored their leisure instruction records accordingly, providing advice on what to avoid as well as how to accomplish success.

According to *Billboard,* Carlton's Hear How series "blossomed against the company's expectations."[15] Carried in discount stores like Grand Union, Korvettes, and Woolworths, supermarket chains A&P and Food Fair, and drug stores such as Polk and Sun-Ray, Hear How records were also featured in mail order catalogs from Montgomery Ward and Sears, Roebuck.[16] In addition to these retail outlets, Carlton marketed Hear How titles in nontraditional locations—for example, *Hear How to Be a Better Bowler* record was sold in bowling alleys, and *Hear How to Improve Your Fishing* was stocked in tackle shops.

At-leisure instructional records can be seen against the backdrop of a burgeoning postwar interest in sports and recreation, as well as continued Cold War efforts to "contain" the Soviets. As sport came to be promoted as an avenue for self-improvement, the aspiration for improved physical performance mirrored the quest for improved mental, occupational, and domestic accomplishment. The rise of a rational regime for athletic training during the late nineteenth century offers a "central metaphor for improvement in general—as we can see, for example, in the aspects of 'management training' or 'training of social skills.'"[17] Leisure, as documented on instructional records, drew Americans out of the house—to dance, attend concerts, play golf, hunt, and perhaps travel out of the country to speak a newly learned language.

LEISURE AND SPORT

PERSONAL GOLF INSTRUCTIONS FROM DRIVER THRU PUTTER came in a deluxe gatefold package, now coveted by sports memorabilia collectors. The album contained two LPs, a "step by step with Arnold Palmer" guide "to the instructions spoken on these records," a brief biography of Palmer, and a list of his "most outstanding championship victories." The bio proclaims: "With bulldog tenacity, which has made Palmer a colorful and exciting player, he comes from behind time and time again to grab a major title." Interestingly, there's also a full-page color advertisement for a Mercury Monterey automobile.

On the glossy cover, the "handsome and charming" (as his *New York Times* obituary described him) Palmer is photographed selecting the proper club from his golf bag.[1] A graphic golf ball announcing "2 record album" hovers over a dark square with further details, lending the image an advertisement-like appearance. *Personal Golf Instructions* was released on the Sports Champions label, which specialized in seven-inch flexidiscs from baseball greats such as Mickey Mantle, Frank Robinson, and Al Kaline. The records are narrated by sports announcer Chris Schenkel, well known for broadcasting major league sports, tennis, boxing, the Olympics, and, of course, golf. Palmer, "the champion golfer whose full-bore style of play, thrilling tournament victories and magnetic personality inspired an American golf boom, attracted a following known as Arnie's Army and made him one of the most popular athletes in the world."[2]

Side 1 opens with some ambient noise from the practice tee. Then Schenkel describes how the record will help you learn golf "in the comfort of your own living room." The two-page booklet's black-and-white photographs are essential to the lessons and frequently referenced, as the record pauses, giving the listener time to peruse them. Listeners are told to "open your booklet to page 2," as Palmer provides pithy pronouncements. On the golf club grip: "The left hand is closed on the shaft with the thumb in such a way that there is a distinct groove formed between the thumb and the back of the hand." Skip around, the record encourages; "simply open the booklet to that part of your game that is giving you trouble." Palmer provides tips for practicing, even in the office (squeeze a ball or use a cut off golf club grip to strengthen hands), Schenkel asks, "What the key is to hitting that long ball?" Palmer warns golfers against a "wide stance." Overall, his advice boils down to "Practice a lot."

The liner notes for **LEARN TENNIS WITH ARTHUR ASHE** console the eager athlete-in-training: "Don't be discouraged at first if your strokes are not working as well as you would like. Tennis takes time and practice." The record blandly promises "Beginners and Advanced Players" that they can "Learn How to Play Tennis" by listening. Each band focuses on a single stroke, from forehand to overhead. An enclosed booklet serves as a handy introduction, with a glossary of tennis terms ("Ace—an untouchable service") and instructions on "how to score," in addition to dozens of black-and-white photos of Ashe in action. The notes exclaim, "'Mr. Cool' as he's known on the court, Arthur possesses one of the most effective games in the history of tennis." He looks great, of course, but we're not sure that merely viewing these shots would be all that helpful in improving your game. More useful are the clear and patient recorded instructions on the disc. Ashe begins on an upbeat note: playing tennis "keeps your body in great shape and it's a lot of fun as well. . . . Good luck to all of you."

In addition to his achievements on the court, Ashe has been heralded as an activist, an educator, and a role model.[3] The liner notes foreshadow his later stature, describing him as "a thoughtful, concerned and socially committed young man with an easygoing manner." Ashe went on to help found the Association of Tennis Professionals, the organization that unionized the professional tour and that protects the interests of its players.[4]

In an interesting coincidence, in 2022, right as we were writing about the album, African American tennis pro Leslie Allen produced an online video that featured *Learn Tennis with Arthur Ashe*. Her insights about the record, and about how tennis has changed in the ensuing decades, are fascinating. For example, she links Ashe's efforts to teach tennis to a wide audience during the 1970s, and the "big boom" of interest in the game, to his experience of entering the affluent, mostly white world of elite tennis.[5] She contrasts the traditional way that people were taught to play—in posh country clubs or with private instructors—with Ashe's instructional record: "For a few bucks, you can buy an album, put it on your turntable, and learn how to play the sport." (In the video, she carefully demonstrates how to play the record, perhaps for younger viewers.) She finds *Learn Tennis with Arthur Ashe* inspiring—almost fifty years after it was released.

What a beautiful day for a swim! The cover of **SWIMMING FOR FUN AND FITNESS**, produced by Cascade Pools "in Cooperation with President Kennedy's Physical Fitness Program," showcases a modern suburban house's alluring backyard pool—a few palm trees dotting the indoor/outdoor living landscape. Judging by the "Pools of Tomorrow" pamphlet inside the LP, the scene shows Cascade's Capri model, which "complements any home with eye-catching elegance. A heavenly pool—priced down to earth!" Patriotic pink, white, and blue typography enhances the illustration's mod aqua, yellow,

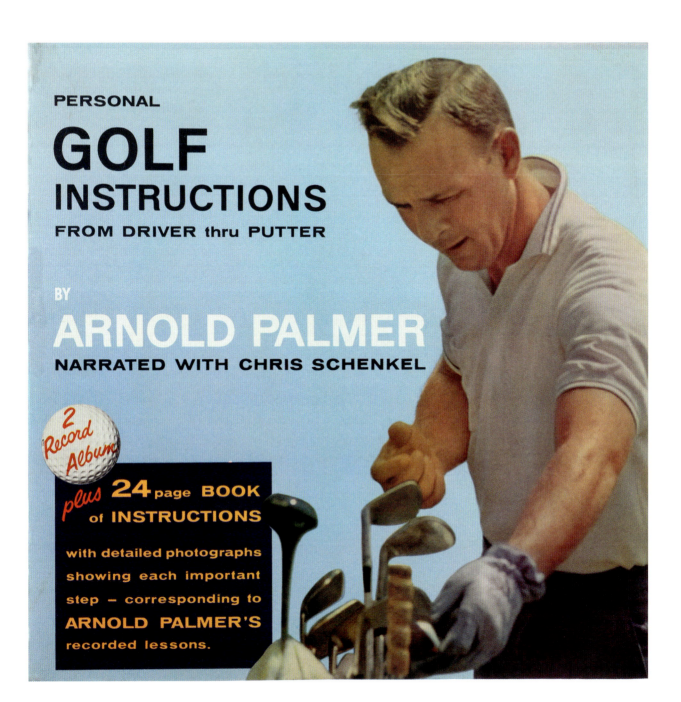

FIGURE 8.1

Personal Golf Instructions from Driver thru Putter,
Arnold Palmer, Sports Champions SCI 32,
pressed by Decca; art director, Kae Jones;
photographer, Hank Chachowski, 1962.

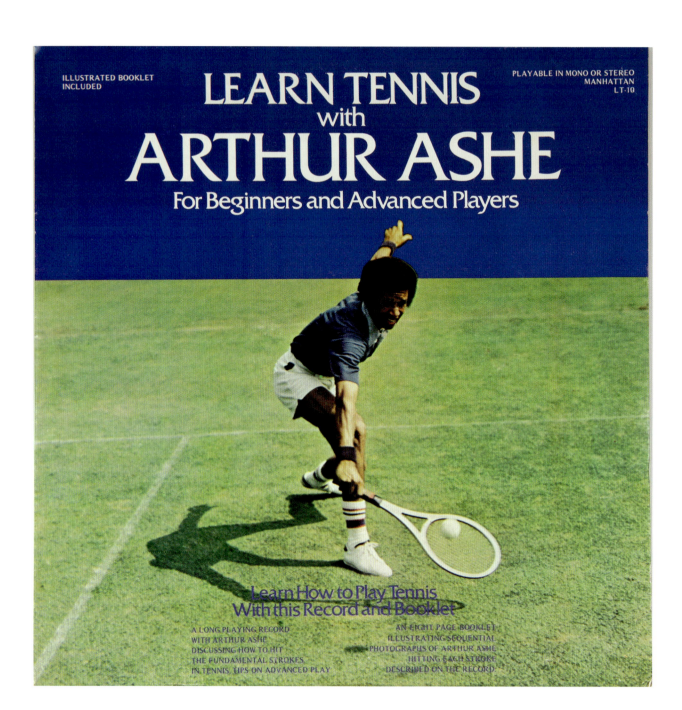

FIGURE 8.2

Learn Tennis with Arthur Ashe,
Manhattan Recording Company, LT-10, 1974.

and tan tones. An inset sepia-toned photo, "Presenting Buster Crabbe," hovers over the pool's deep end (8⅔ feet, according to the catalog).

Crabbe won a gold medal in the four-hundred-meter freestyle at the 1932 Los Angeles Olympics and went on to enjoy a successful film and television career. He specialized in heroes—he played a terrific trio of Tarzan, Flash Gordon, and Buck Rogers. In the illustration, a well-muscled cartoon man emerges from the pool, positioned similarly to Crabbe's inset photo. His beaming, slender, bikini-clad wife is seated at an outdoor table, sipping a cold drink, shaded by a red-and-white umbrella. (Where's his drink? His chair? Perhaps this guy is a friendly neighbor, trying out the Capri model he's had his eye on—or the pool boy, testing the chlorine levels).

Crabbe's dedication reads: swimming "gives you a wonderful feeling of relaxation and well-being, and at the same time, it tones up all the important muscles of your body. Some exercising is work. Swimming is fun! Learning to enjoy swimming, both for pleasure and good health, is important to you and your family." Crabbe proclaims that "the secret to good swimming is learning to r-e-l-a-x in the water." The liner notes include small graphics depicting the Dead Man's Float, Dog Paddle, and the American Crawl.

Part 1, "Learn to Swim," opens up with a stagey spoken-word scenario, as if the listener is eavesdropping on a pool party at Crabbe's home. One couple remarks, "Ever since we got our Cascade pool, we've had a ball at our house. We got so popular, we're never alone to argue anymore." The rest of the side presents Crabbe's earnest yet sophisticated instructions, interspersed with commentary from his "students" and with gushing accolades about pool-owning benefits: "A Cascade pool makes a house a home!" and "What could be better than having the children at home with their friends?" Part 2, "Music to Swim By," provides an easy-listening soundtrack, clearly not meant for either teenage pool parties or Olympic record-setting.

A shiny black bowling ball dominates the cover of **7 DAYS TO BETTER BOWLING**, with ten pins looming and a neighboring lane's pins shown at the moment of impact. Graphically, the ball splits the cover into two parts: the photographic depiction of the wooden lane paired with an emotionally evocative red with uneven, subtly animated typography. Together these express the record's focus—the physical and mental aspects of bowling: "The degree to which you master the 'mental side' will determine whether your score is higher or lower than bowlers of equal mechanical ability." The $5.95 price is prominently featured, along with a caution: "This recording is for right handed bowlers only. It is unique in its field, and should be not be played until you have read the instructions carefully on the reversed side of the jacket."

The album promises "A new approach to the 'mental side' of Bowling which improves your game by developing • relaxation • confidence • concentration • coordination." The deadly serious liner notes suggest "acquiring the proper mental attitude, overcoming distractions, concentration upon the immediate target, and the coordination of all the mechanical or functional elements of the game." Strict instructions are provided: "Listen to the record in solitude or free from distraction." No time during

FIGURE 8.3

Swimming for Fun and Fitness,
Artrec SLP 63/7000, ca. 1964.

the day? No problem, as "this recording has been specifically designed to adapt to the schedule of the busy executive or career woman: Listen for one hour at bedtime. Make certain your record player is set to repeat." What if I fall asleep, you wonder? Don't worry—"should you be fortunate enough to relax to the point of drowsiness or sleep, you will receive even more rapid benefit from this recording than those who merely relax, since the instruction is directed primarily to your sub-conscious mind."

Contrary to the cover title, the record's label states "Dynamic Bowling"—side 1 for daytime listening, and side 2 "for listening upon retiring." The recording employs "auto suggestion," which apparently works "without any conscious effort on the part of the listener." Bowlers need to relax: "Since tension is the enemy of coordination, the first portion of the recording is devoted to teaching you the art of controlled relaxation." A soothing, emotionless male voice assures listeners that "all of us have been conditioned to respond automatically to key words," and "dynamic bowling employs two key words—merely repeating the key words to yourself at the proper time is all that is necessary." *7 Days to Better Bowling*'s two key words are "relax" and "bowl." This treasure resembles the current fad for ASMR videos that purport to lull listeners into a calm state and to trigger pleasant, tingling sensations. Few seem to focus on bowling, however.

The cover of **HOW TO SKI (A LIVING-ROOM GUIDE FOR BEGINNERS)** features a comfortably seated Skeeter Werner, leaning back against a beautiful hi-fi cabinet—the kind that midcentury furniture fans drool over. She's wearing stretch ski pants, a wooly off-white ski sweater, and lace-up ski boots. Her nearby snow skis feature the then-state-of-the-art cable bindings called "bear traps."

Werner was a blazing star of the US National Ski Team who competed in the 1956 Olympics, finishing a disappointing tenth place in the downhill. She retired soon after and opened a ski school in Steamboat Springs, Colorado. At the peak of her fame, she appeared on the cover of *Sports Illustrated*—not in skiing gear, but wearing "candy-striped Duofold ski underwear," demonstrating exercises for preseason conditioning. The accompanying article called her "one of the country's prettiest skiers."[6] Although such clothing may seem tame today, her appearance in close-fitting long underwear marked a departure from the male-dominated covers of *Sports Illustrated*'s early years, perhaps helping inspire the magazine's celebrated—and criticized—"swimsuit issue," which made its debut in 1964.

Liner notes provide detailed guidance about boots, including a mention of socks: "Wear one heavy pair over a lighter pair." Then on to bindings, skis, poles, and clothing. On "Selection of Equipment," Werner jumps in with an admonition to not buy cheap gear, while suggesting that "expensive clothes don't make the skier." The rest of side 1 offers tips for preseason conditioning and a set of "Ski Exercises." Side 2 moves on to the slopes, starting with "Walking on Skis" and concluding with "Turning on Skis." A handy guide to ski terms, such as "edges," "fall line," and "powder snow" is included.

How to Ski was released during the midcentury boom in downhill skiing that was fueled by postwar growth, advances in equipment, ski lift technology, and snow-making

FIGURE 8.4

7 Days to Better Bowling,
Audio-Dynamics Corp ADC SS 61 2 RH, 1961.

capacity, as well as by media coverage of glamorous ski racing champions such as Stein Ericksen and Andrea Mead Lawrence—both gold medalists at the 1952 Winter Olympics—and Skeeter Werner.[7] Werner's experience as a fashion model seems to inform her sartorial advice: "You can avoid being called a ski bunny by keeping your socks on the inside of your ski pants." Thanks to her, you, too, can "become one of the thousands who consider skiing 'a way of life.'"

Cerulean blue evokes sea and sky on HEAR HOW TO IMPROVE YOUR FISHING. Small black-and-white action shots capture deep sea, surf, lake, and fly fishing, displaying diverse rods and reels and styles of handling. A woman in waders, standing midstream, proves that this is not just a man's domain. Reasons for fishing? Companionship, spending time outside, and "getting away from the grind."

World Professional Casting champion John Dieckman "tells how to improve your luck" by "planning your equipment," learning "different types of casting," and most crucially—as any old salt will tell you—"fooling the fish." Dieckman worked as a consultant for a fishing equipment manufacturer and wrote books including *Target Fishing* (1956) and *Horse Sense Catches Fish* (1959).[8] The spoken instruction is detailed and complex, but, luckily, a two-page booklet offers drawings to guide spin casting: positioning arms and feet, holding line, feathering line, and adjusting the drag.

"So pull up a record player," encourage the notes. "It's like having a private session with an old scout, as he takes you aside and gives you the lowdown." Our copy of *Hear How to Improve Your Fishing* came with an attached "Fishing Calendar for 1965" that mysteriously rated fishing conditions for each day of the year ("best, good, fair, poor") based on "fishing experience over many years."

Ahoy skippers! Welcome aboard! The blue-tinted photo on OUTBOARD MOTOR BOATING finds a family, safely seated and creating little wake, plying the waters of the Tennessee River in what looks like a Larson runabout. It promises, "Here's your nautical educational record for fun and safety afloat." Safety is important: anyone might buy and operate a water craft. Those who own or drive a boat may have no prior knowledge or experience of boating. Generally, at least in the US, no license is required to drive a pleasure boat.

This LP, distributed by boating clubs, was intended to help new motorboat owners avoid tragedy and practice "common sense afloat." Writer and producer Jerry Landrum was a photographer in the Muscle Shoals area who served in the Coast Guard Auxiliary on the Tennessee River during World War II and hosted a radio series, *Cruising down the River*. Radio show skipper Al West narrates the nautical lessons on vinyl, including "What Alert Skippers Should Know," "Language of Boatmen" ("say, 'lines,' not 'rope'"), and "Capsizing." The two greatest causes for boating accidents? Overloading and overpowering a boat—meaning too many people or too much weight aboard and too large an engine for the boat size. To the rescue, *Outboard Motor Boating*'s enclosed booklet pledges: "This nautical record, when played frequently, can be a tremendous aid in

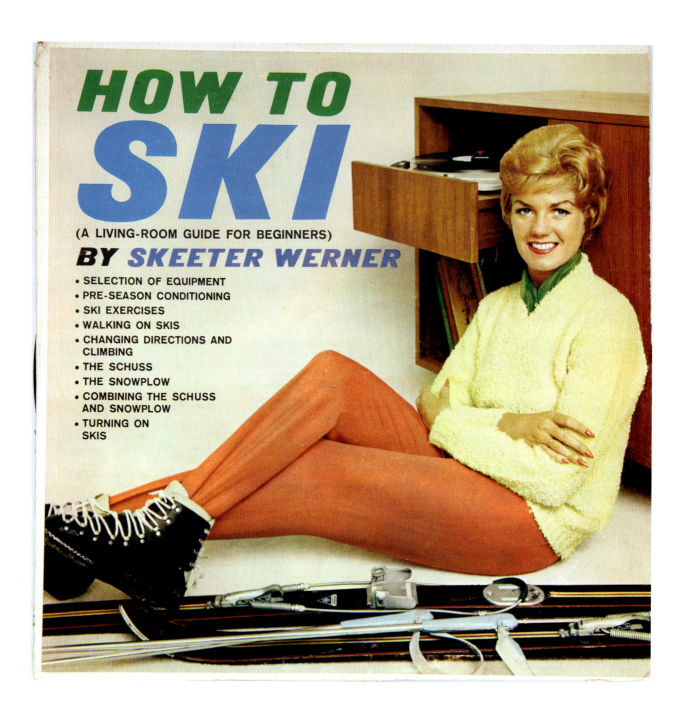

FIGURE 8.5

How to Ski (A Living-Room Guide for Beginners),
Skeeter Werner, Skico XTV 60733, ca. 1957

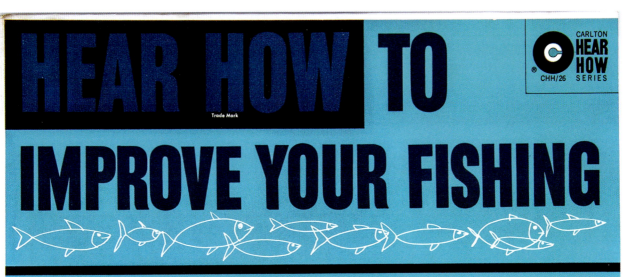

FIGURE 8.6

Hear How to Improve Your Fishing,
John Dieckman, Carlton CHH 26, 1961.

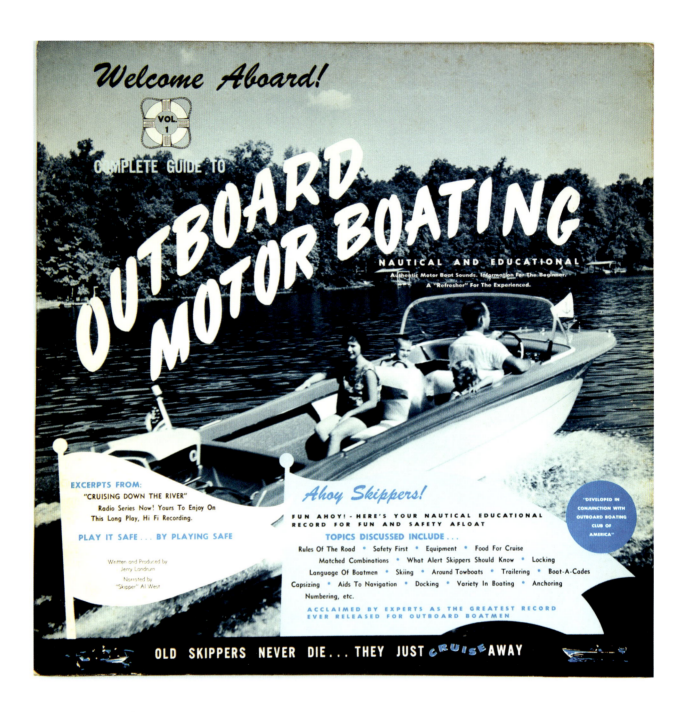

FIGURE 8.7

Outboard Motor Boating,
Outboard Motor Boating Records SO: A101, ca. 1960.

learning the fundamentals of safe boating." We wish more boaters would take heed of these helpful hints and respect the rules of the river, lake, and sea.

Threatening thunderheads emit frenzied lightning bolts on INSTRUMENT FLIGHT . . . . as a maroon Cessna 310D with white stripe detail confidently navigates the stormy skies. The notes complain: "Entirely too many pilots lose valuable time and money when they are forced to sit on the ground." A gray antenna atop the plane provides the solution: trading visual flight for instrument flight with a Motorola NAVCOM 100 system.

This recording package, which came with an illustrated booklet, attempts to dispel the "air of complexity" around "flying the gauges" as it promotes "air progress through education." From filing a flight plan and mastering Air Traffic Communications to a glossary of terms and back cover photo schematic identifying eighteen gauges, indicators, and gyros, "never before has any medium been used to illustrate an actual instrument flight in such a basic and realistic manner." Side 1 begins with pilot Paul Blackman calling in for weather "sequence reports" for his trip from Santa Monica to San Francisco. Blackman (flying Cessna "33Golf") and air traffic control radio back and forth, negotiating altitudes, locations, and times, resulting in a successful landing as side 2 closes. *Instrument Flight . . .* marks one of the most ambitious instructional records we've heard.

On HEAR HOW TO TAKE BETTER PHOTOGRAPHS, "one of the great magazine photographers gives you a private lesson in the art of picture-taking." The notes brag: "You couldn't find a more qualified tutor than Ralph Morse." Morse's subjects ranged widely, but he was especially well known for his war photographs and his shots of NASA's space program. He enjoyed a long, lauded career: "For nearly 50 years as a photojournalist, his vivid, inventively captured images of major world events peppered the glossy pages of *Life* and *Time* magazines."[9] To Morse, "a camera is as familiar as the back of his hand. After listening to him on this record, you'll be on the road to that happy state yourself." (Although when he retired, in his mid-eighties, he got rid of all his cameras, saying, "If I had a camera, everybody and his brother would say: 'Gee, would you take my wedding? Would you do this for the condo?' I don't own a camera, so I can't do it.")[10]

On the cover, an illustrated camera's cable release bisects bright green and blue graphics. Below, two photographs, one of a submarine taken from above and the other of Morse with his "prize-winning photo of the USS Nautilus." Notes include a list of filter corrections for color films, such as Kodachrome and Ektachrome, along with a chart of "color film filter correction for flashbulbs and electronic flash." Morse's inspirational instructions begin: "There is no such thing as a limit to your expression," as he touches upon "daylight photography, analyzing your mistakes, scenic and night photography, and traveling with your camera." He gets a bit bogged down in a myriad of details about the varieties of cameras available, but, generally, *Hear How to Take Better Pictures* successfully blends basic instructions with beneficial advice: how to translate what you see in your imagination into a photograph.

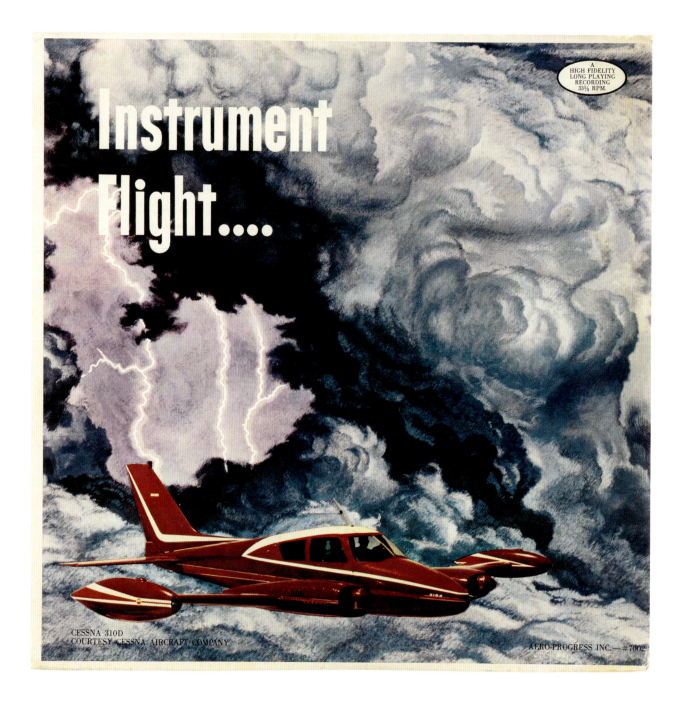

FIGURE 8.8

Instrument Flight . . . ,
Jeppesen Records RIF 2; by RCA Custom,
cover art "courtesy of Cessna Aircraft Company," 1960.
© Boeing Digital Solutions, Inc., 2023.
For reference only—not for navigational use.

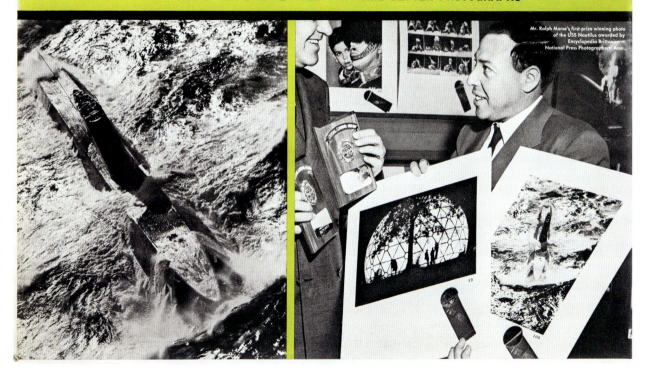

FIGURE 8.9

Hear How to Take Better Photographs,
Ralph Morse, Carlton CHH 18, 1961.

"America's Foremost Bridge Authority" Oswald Jacoby offers "all you need to know about bidding" on HEAR HOW TO PLAY WINNING BRIDGE. Bidding? Isn't this a record about bridge? As the notes explain, Jacoby "serves as your private tutor" in the intricacies of contract bidding, the system that revolutionized bridge playing in the twentieth century. The notes point out that "many players feel that hearing the instructions imbeds them in the mind more than reading them." Further, "the album proceeds logically from the basics, such as the point count, upward and onward." The notes include a glossary of bridge terms, including "trump–the suit in which the contract must be played," and "jump shift–a jump bid in a different suit or no trump."

Bridge was once one of America's most popular pastimes, hailed as "an elegant game, full of strategy and tactics."[11] Bridge tournaments attracted widespread media attention and were held throughout the country in university unions, church basements, and glamorous hotel ballrooms. Books about bridge were bestsellers. Popular films such as *Shadow of the Thin Man* (1941) and *Sunset Boulevard* (1950) included scenes of bridge playing. Champion players like Charles Goren and Oswald Jacoby appeared on national magazine covers. During the 1940s, almost half of American households included a bridge player.

What happened? Some blame television, while others point to a growing appetite for leisure outside the home. The rise of working women might have contributed, too—as women worked more outside the home, they had less time for daytime bridge clubs.[12] Bridge was a relatively slow game to play. It took a long time to learn. It had arcane and complex rules and became associated with older players—a "grandmother's game." Bridge has enjoyed a mild resurgence in recent years, fueled by online opportunities to play and, of course, apps, such as FunBridge and Bridge by NeuralPlay.

Jacoby was a natural choice to present *Hear How to Play Winning Bridge*. He was "among the best-known gamesters in the world—poker, backgammon, canasta, whist, chess, pinochle, craps, gin rummy, you name it. With fiendish computational ability, a phenomenal memory and seemingly limitless energy, he could belly up to a green baize table and take you to the cleaners."[13] Aside from winning games, Jacoby wrote voluminously: he published books on backgammon, canasta, contract bridge, gambling and probability, gin rummy, and poker, including *What's New in Bridge?* (1954) and *Mathematics for Pleasure* (1962). For decades he produced a nationally syndicated bridge column, "Jacoby on Bridge." He often claimed, perhaps rightfully so, "I am the best player of all games in the world today." We don't think Jacoby is the world's best instructor, however—he jumps into the finer points of contract bidding, point counting, and four-card suits without providing much background or an overview of the game's basic aspects. Listeners hear how to play *advanced* bridge.

LEARN PALETTE KNIFE PAINTING FROM THE ARTIST AND INSTRUCTOR JERRY JOLLEY is "one of a series of ten records on floral painting" (although we've never seen any others) that include "visual instruction *plus* the voice of the artist." The cover suggests: "For Beginners Preferably." Palette knife painting instructor Geraldine

FIGURE 8.10

Hear How to Play Winning Bridge,
Oswald Jacoby, Carlton CHH 10;
produced by Dick Kleiner, 1961.

Hazel Jolley was born in Rochester, New York, and studied art at the Rochester Institute of Technology. She designed displays for Rochester department store Sibley, Lindsay & Curr and then moved to San Francisco, where she recorded this album in 1965 (no mention of 1960s California flower power). A brief back cover biography states that she had "numerous one-man shows." A key to her faith in this audio-only instructional package: she "creates paintings 'in Reflection,' a term she uses, meaning from the mind's eye." Aha! So students don't need to "see" what they paint—they can learn by listening.

Learn Palette Knife Painting begins with Jolley pronouncing: "There are golden moments when art and music speak in one single theme." Speaking over a somewhat distracting acoustic guitar—which must be the "background music produced especially" for this record—she intones, "The object of this course is to teach you to be more sensitive." On side 2, she urges her students to "get into the rhythm of the music." Close-up photos of "positions of hand and knife on canvas for the Jerry Jolley palette knife strokes" present the "dob stroke, paint on tip of knife," "the line stroke, use pressure and start with the tip of the blade," and "the feather stroke, gentle touch."

Instructions include:

1. Listen to the complete record.
2. Set up your equipment and start painting with the record playing—<u>Stop it at any part until you catch up.</u>
3. Place the Visual Aid (The Album) in front of you at all times.

With a slightly wooden delivery, Jolley leads aspiring artists through the technique of palette knife painting. Her methods are based on the mantra "Observe, Absorb, and Produce," or, as she rephrases it, "Look, Think, and Paint."

Once she begins to describe the techniques, she warms to the lessons, sounding like a competent and patient instructor. She offers straightforward advice on how to mix paint and how to compose a painting, stressing details, such as "Position your loaded palette knife on the very edge of the knife" to paint the daisy's stem. "You do not have to copy," she informs her students. "In fact, I wish you would not copy. . . . I would rather you be creative yourself." She continues, "I would suggest you work about three hours at a time" and then "rest your eyes."

The liner notes provide an extensive list of materials "recommended by Jerry Jolley™," including a range of paints, palette, palette knife, and "plenty of old clean soft rags or paper toweling and paper bags." A coupon was enclosed for ordering a 20″ by 26″ "litho kit" that provided color figures of a palette, the palette knife strokes found inside the gatefold sleeve, and the daisy painting on the album cover—total price, $5.00, California residents add 4 percent sales tax. Our copy of the coupon was never used.

Like many instructional records, LET YOUR PARAKEET TEACH HIMSELF TO TALK encourages repeated listenings. "Easy to use," the notes assure the listener; "just play the record on your phonograph and let your bird perch near the speaker." Pet owners

FIGURE 8.11

Learn Palette Knife Painting from the Artist and Instructor Jerry Jolley,
Fine Art Record Company 1, 1965.

should "let your bird listen on his own" with the "repeat mechanism if your phonograph is so equipped." Apparently, this record is just the beginning of parakeet learning, as words and phrases learned here prepare for "his further training."

Records like this one—and, for any collectors out there, there are several—followed popular midcentury radio programs that featured canaries and other "talking" birds, often heard "singing along" to music. Hartz, which released *Let Your Parakeet Teach Himself to Talk*, sponsored *The American Radio Warblers* from 1937 to 1952.[14] The notes point out that "you will get better results from this training record if you make sure your parakeet is in the best of condition—healthy, happy and contented." Odd. No such declarations appear on the children's training records we've reviewed.

After a brief introduction for the human listener, which describes the record's "scientific, new method," the parakeet priming begins. Over and over, a woman's voice repeats: "Hello. Hello. Hello, baby. Hello, baby." She finally moves on to "Hello, baby. Want a kiss? Hello, baby. Want a kiss?" The last track presents an actual parakeet, so listeners can "hear how a parakeet should sound." Unfortunately, our research budget did not allow us to acquire a parakeet to try out the record. But we found ourselves repeating "Hello, baby, hello, baby" for days after listening.

Framed dog portraits worthy of a hunt club or a nostalgic, proto–man cave, tinged with hunting season's colorful leaves set against forest green painted wood paneling: *Sports Afield* magazine presents TRAINING YOUR DOG TO HUNT, POINT, RETRIEVE. In the upper right corner, the words "Sports-In-Sound" splay out along the bottom edge of a black vinyl disc on spindle, reinforcing records' role in carrying lessons for outdoor life into the living room. As pronounced in the binocular lenses just below, "Bring the expert into your home." Included with the LP, a "free illustrated chart showing hunting breeds," allowing us to identify the cover models: beagles, a pointer, an American fox hound, and a Labrador retriever. The four-page pamphlet features appealing drawings of "field and water" dogs, including Gordon setter and flat-coated retriever, and "hounds" such as basset and saluki.

Henry P. Davis, "sporting dogs editor" for *Sports Afield*'s Gun Dogs of America Series speaks sincerely and knowledgeably. He covers the early African environment–dependent development of dogs hunting by scent versus dogs hunting by sight, canine intelligence, and bringing a new puppy into the home. No "music for hunting" here—rather, detailed and thoughtful instruction on how to mold retrievers, springers, and hounds into hunting dogs. "Never nag at a dog." "Never tease a dog." "Never lend your dog to anyone, or they won't be a friend for long." "Never bring your dog into bad company." Sound advice.

The aptly named Fred Bear, "America's No.1 Bowhunter," outfitted in green camouflage shirt and beige fedora, and Curt Gowdy, *American Sportsman* television show host, in a black-and-red check wool zipper jacket with matching hat, sit around "camp" sharing the SECRETS OF HUNTING. A bow (a Fred Bear Grizzly Recurve?) and full quiver

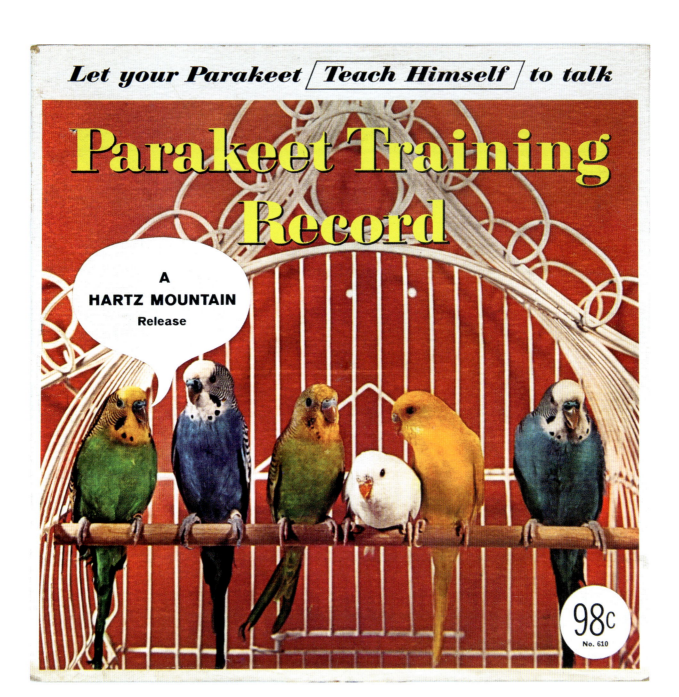

FIGURE 8.12

Let Your Parakeet Teach Himself to Talk,
distributed by Hartz Mountain Products Corporation, ca. 1955.

FIGURE 8.13

Training Your Dog to Hunt, Point, Retrieve,
Henry P. Davis, Sports-in-Sound L.E. 901, 1960.

FIGURE 8.14

Secrets of Hunting,
Fred Bear, Henry Russell Recording Studio W4RM 3967;
produced by Dick Lattimer, album design by Lee Bleifield,
photo by Jim Pond, rifle courtesy of Winchester-Western, 1968.

FIGURE 8.15

Music for Big Dame Hunters,
the Sounds of a Thousand Strings, Crown CLP 5173;
cover design by Hobco Arts,
photo by Joseph Tauber, cover model Irish McCulla [*sic*], 1960.

lean against a tree stump. A combination of sans serif capitals and Buffalo Western font (highlighting pale green) signals contemporary outdoorsman and connection to the natural world.

The black-and-white through-the-lens—or through-the-sight—shots on the back cover display some of "Fred's long list of big game trophies," among them an elk, an elephant, a kudu, a polar bear, and a warthog. Still, says Bear, more important than the kill and the trophies is the "companionship, talks around the campfire," and the imperative for a father to take his sons out "to observe nature." Discussion around the fire ranges over gathering white-tail deer intelligence, getting to know the territory, and acquiring the correct equipment, as well as "valuable tips on tracking" and building blinds. "You'll want to play the record several times, and then review it before each hunting season." Advice for "young thrill seekers"? Go out into the woods and "tangle" with a grizzly.

What is a book about midcentury records without Irish McCalla? The pinup model turned *Sheena, Queen of the Jungle* turned artist lifts the mood on several of the era's albums. In our book *Designed for Dancing*, we featured her beachfront pose in a tropical-hued *traje der rumbera* on *Latin Twist* (1959). McCalla was the inspiration for the Ramones' "Sheena Is a Punk Rocker." Her direct gaze, in this instance, indeed suggests more roar than romance.

Bringing the bachelor-pad animal-print rug back into the rugged wilderness, this photo offers a cautionary tale. The "prey" displays her own arrow-pierced trophies: French tropical pith helmet, wide-brimmed fedora safari hat, plaid button-down shirt. MUSIC FOR BIG DAME HUNTERS clearly braves territory beyond the country club sippers, even if the "uniform of the evening" described in the liner notes misses the mark: for males, an "Ivy-League suit, thin rep-stripe tie, button-down-collar shirt, and Italian shoes." (Survival requires something more intrepid, we'd think.) Still, the stakes are raised: "Who is stalking whom can never be easily answered. But one fact stands out. The right atmosphere is an absolute necessity for victory. Moonlight helps. But music can turn the tide of a seemingly disastrous defeat." The Sounds of a Thousand Strings make a game effort to lure in the quarry with tunes such as "When the Lights Go On Again," "I Hear a Rhapsody," and "Till Dawn."

9

JOINING IN
PLAY AN INSTRUMENT!
LEARN TO DANCE!

On the cover for **A CHILD'S INTRODUCTION TO RHYTHM**, well-groomed and attentive rosy-cheeked smiling youngsters follow a youthful conductor's lead. Everyday noise-making items—keys, cooking pot, cereal box—lay down the beat. The cover collage mixes blocks of primary colors and naive illustration (dots for eyes, lines for mouths) with individually photographed objects such as spoons, a knife, a saucer. The notes announce: "This is a 'do-it-yourself' rhythm record for the youngster." Self-expression is encouraged "through the language of rhythm in response to the music he hears." Tongue clicking in 2/4 time conjures up crickets in "The Land of Forest Music" section. For the "Country Carol," the kids are rocking with rhythm instruments in 3/4 time. The "Land of Folk Songs" section includes hammering, galloping, and "work rhythms—planting, milking, and churning butter in 3/4 time" to the song "Billy Barlow." The *New York Times* called *A Child's Introduction to Rhythm* "a fine record that can be recommended for the child's musical education."[1]

On the cover of **ADVENTURES IN RHYTHM** from Ella Jenkins and her Rhythm Workshop, a monochrome photograph drenched with orange presents an ensemble of African American students playing cowbell and rhythm sticks. The tambourine in a young woman's hands glows an icy pale blue, as if hit by a spotlight. A sweater's diamond motif evokes rhythmic movement noted in the jazz-influenced pattern of the 1920s. An older group of people—perhaps parents—look on.

The included pamphlet describes Jenkins as "a rhythm specialist, folk singer, and interpreter of primitive music." She leads the listener and rhythm-stick-wielder through a series of increasingly complex beats, beginning with "and 1 and 2" through "1234 <u>hold</u>," then combines these for a multiple rhythm song, "Zum Gali Gali." Next, Jenkins introduces rhythms and right hand/left hand exercises with a drum, starting with "RLRL hold" and advancing through beats such as "RLRLR <u>LRL.</u>"

One of her earliest efforts, *Adventures in Rhythm* marks the beginning of Jenkins's singularly successful musical career. She has been called the First Lady of children's music: "Few musicians have made such an indelible impact on the development of

FIGURE 9.1

A Child's Introduction to Rhythm,
Golden Records LP 99, 1963.

young people as Ella Jenkins."[2] She released over forty albums, including *African-American Folk Rhythms* (1960) and *A Long Time to Freedom* (1969). She put out *Camp Songs with Ella Jenkins & Friends* in 2017, when she was in her nineties. Folkways has described her as "the first 'folk' performer to teach fun, interactive music in schools and preschools, incorporating world cultures, the joy of music, and the basic skills every child needs."[3] Jenkins received a Grammy Lifetime Achievement Award in 2004.

Bright blue and warm red, orange and yellow enliven the dark wood pictured on the cover of FOLK SONG KIT. An acoustic guitar casts a sharp shadow within a rustic, multishelf display case shared with a well-played banjo and a black vinyl record. The "kit" was created by Jac Holzman, founder of and producer for Elektra Records. The spare, evocative cover was shot by photographer and filmmaker George Pickow—husband of folk singer Jean Ritchie—who photographed a range of album covers, including folk classics like Ritchie's *A Time for Singing* (1965) and Josh White's *Chain Gang Songs* (1958), as well as *Fastest Balalaika in the West* (1962), *Music to Watch Girls By* (1967), and *Hits for a Truck Driving Man* (1976).

Released to capitalize on the 1950s folk flowering, Elektra's *Folk Song Kit* "is designed to give the beginner a grasp of the fundamentals of folk guitar playing"—all that is missing is a scruffy beard, a peasant skirt, and a certain practiced righteousness. Open the *Folk Song Kit*'s box to find an LP, an instruction booklet, recommendations for folk records and folk music clubs and shops, basic musical settings for several folk standards (such as "Red River Valley"), and a guitar chord chart. The thoughtful booklet features a cover photograph of New York's Washington Square Park, where "folk enthusiasts gather," and includes lyrics and chords for each song, a brief informational note, as well as an introductory essay, "The Folk Song Bridge," by Lee Hays of the Weavers. Side 1 consists of guitar lessons—"If you are adept and have musical training of some sort you might master this course in a week"—from virtuoso guitarist and banjo player Billy Faier, publisher of the folk music magazine *Caravan*.[4] Side 2 includes twenty folk songs, "arranged in the probable order of difficultly, taking into consideration the chords used and the strums," sung by Milt Okun, an influential arranger, producer, and conductor who went on to work with Peter, Paul and Mary, Miriam Makeba, and John Denver.

Folk Song Kit received *Billboard*'s top score of four stars (very strong sales potential—essential inventory). Their upbeat review concluded: "An imaginative production, which should find a good market, particularly as a gift item."[5] Despite folk music's anti-commercial rhetoric, the music industry—including instrument makers, sheet music publishers, and record companies—helped create a thriving market for folk music materials.[6] A look at folk music magazines and records like *Folk Song Kit* show that "even the most anti-commercial and anti-mass culture movement negotiated with commercialism and sought for ways to live with its principles as well as the commercialism necessary for the success of the folk music revival."[7] In folk-friendly publications such as *Sing Out!* magazine, Elektra promoted *Folk Song Kit* as "beautifully boxed."

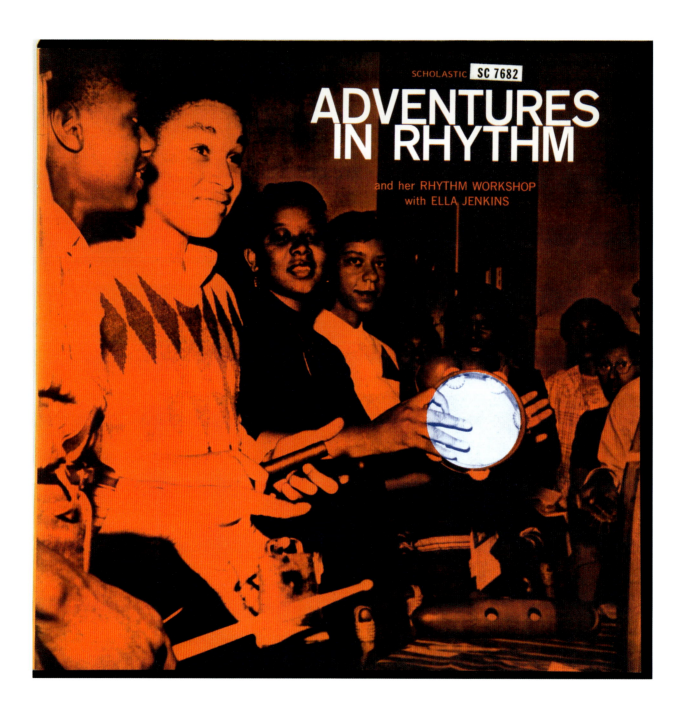

FIGURE 9.2

Adventures in Rhythm,
Ella Jenkins and Her Rhythm Workshop,
Scholastic SC 7682;
cover design Rosenhouse, 1960.

FIGURE 9.3

Folk Song Kit,
created by Jac Holzman, Electra EKL KIT;
design by W. S. Harvey,
photo by 3 Lions–Pickow, 1959.

We hauled out Janet's dad's vintage Gibson guitar, followed the tuning instructions, and started strumming and singing. We made progress after several listenings. As yet, though, we lack the confidence to check out the scene in Greenwich Village. Maybe we'll go electric.

Promising "the nearest approach to personal instruction yet devised," **PLAY THE UKULELE: AN INTRODUCTION TO UKULELE PLAYING BY SYDNEY NESBITT** deviates from the typical Music Minus One play-along format. Here, we find Sydney Nesbitt, a popular entertainer who specialized in the ukulele, attempting to teach the diminutive, often-underestimated instrument by playing and singing, much like an introductory music lesson. The great-sounding record opens with Nesbitt earnestly enumerating the parts of the ukulele, reading from the enclosed booklet. He moves on to tuning the ukulele and points out how the ukulele should be held, referring to several photos in the booklet. Finally, on track three, Nesbitt starts to play a selection of tunes, including "Jingle Bells," "Red River Valley," and "Good Night, Ladies," singing along in a pleasant baritone. A noteworthy inclusion is "Be Kind to Your Web-Footed Friends," a popular novelty song set to the tune of John Philip Sousa's "The Stars and Stripes Forever."

The informative, easy-to-follow booklet echoes a mantra that Nesbitt repeats on the record: "Remember—practice makes perfect." And the notes provide some ukulele boosterism: "The ukulele has come into its own as a musical instrument and is featured in numerous recordings, on the radio, TV, and in the movies." The rise of radio coincided with the popularity of the ukulele: "The speed with which the 'ukulele became a staple of radio entertainment helped complete its transformation from an exotic novelty to a staple of popular culture. No longer was it regarded chiefly as a Hawaiian instrument played by Hawaiian musicians performing Hawaiian music."[8] (We found a listing for "Sydney Nesbitt and His Ukulele" on the BBC from March 12, 1926, along with "A Short Concert of New Gramophone Records" and "Dance Music.")

The ukulele was primarily promoted to children during the 1950s and 1960s, which fostered an impression that the ukulele was a toy. As the century progressed, the adaptable instrument assumed new roles: "The ukulele—marketed as easy to play and effortlessly portable in an era of easy prosperity and automotive mobility—was an ideal tool of adolescent self-expression."[9] Countless musicians took up the ukulele as a stepping stone to the guitar, including Joan Baez, Jimi Hendrix, and Neil Young. And we can't leave out Tiny Tim, whose warbling, ukulele-fueled "Tiptoe through the Tulips" was an unlikely hit in 1968. Recently, the ukulele has emerged as a signal of authenticity in indie pop.[10] As Fender's How to Play Ukulele website explains: "Small, portable, relatively inexpensive, and fun to play, the ukulele is a great instrument for beginners to pick up and deepen their love of music."[11]

Playing the ukulele, Nesbitt suggests, provides many benefits and "will give the player an added stature among his friends and social acquaintances; even help him in a business way by developing 'personality' and 'confidence' . . . facing a crowd." Perhaps there is a *Better Selling with Your Ukulele* record?

LET ME TEACH YOU TO
**play
the
UKULELE**

An Introduction to Ukulele Playing
by Sydney Nesbitt,
World Famed Performer and Teacher

- *The nearest approach to personal instruction yet devised.*
- *Learn to accompany yourself and others in a matter of minutes.*
- *12″ LP with 8 page instruction book and 16 popular songs.*

COMPLETE: $3.98

Music Minus One MMO 150

FIGURE 9.4

*Play the Ukulele: An Introduction to Ukulele Playing
by Sydney Nesbitt,*
Music Minus One, MMO 150, 1961.

"Entertain at Parties! Be Popular! Pick Your Way to Success on the Guitar," promises PLAY GUITAR, VOLUME 1: SOUNDS OF TODAY. Yep. There's just something about playing a guitar. Countless bands seemed to have formed to make the members more attractive—usually to girls. (Jonathan has painful memories of Janet falling for a guitarist back in high school. He's just about over it today.) "Strum your way to success and popularity with this self-teaching course" seems to be the key message. Granted, there's an unexpected nod to gender equity, as the illustration depicts two guitarists: a guy with an electric guitar, modeling an early Beach Boy look, and a gal with an acoustic model, embracing sorority cool with her sweater, coiffed hair, and necklace, playing to a small crowd of beaming listeners. But it's clear who's playing lead.

"I will teach those who have failed before!" insists Gene Leis, the promoter behind the album, which includes an elaborate insert with chord charts, photos, instructions and suggestions, such as: "Probably the most important aspect of your new project of learning to play the guitar is <u>you</u>." Leis developed a mail order self-taught guitar course and then recorded a series of Play Guitar LPs in the early 1960s. Much of this two-LP set promotes Leis's Nexsus method, a package that consisted of five records, a 132-page instruction book, and a "wall-size" chord map.

The album is infused with a do-it-yourself ethic reflected in Leis's copyright note: "Research, theory, art-work, lay-out, composition, procedure, arrangement, recording engineering, solo guitar, narrated, edited, produced and published by Gene Leis." (It's unclear if he provided the cover illustration.) The notes strongly promote practice: as a student of Leis recalled: "If you wanted to advance but didn't want to work at it, he'd say, 'He wants to go to heaven without dyin'."[12] And what are the "sounds of today"? "A blues pattern with an up-tempo, a touch of the twist, a bit of 'rock and roll' with a swinging, rocking sensation, that makes you feel young at heart"—and maybe like a rock god.

THE EASY, NEW COLOR-MATIC SYSTEM TO PLAY THE ELECTRIC GUITAR, a box set with a "giant 36-page" instruction booklet and two LPs, offers another way "to quickly and easily learn the latest basic guitar techniques, entirely on your own!" The record set begins with the basics: "Sitting down, with your legs crossed, place the guitar in a horizontal position." Instructions for tuning the guitar, holding the guitar pick, and strumming follow. Each lesson is supplemented by instructions and illustrations in an enclosed booklet.

The narrator's voice conveys patience, authority, and optimism, as if he's taught many guitar-god wannabes before. Oddly, though, he refers to the record as *Play the Electric Guitar the Easy Way* throughout, without referring to the "Color-Matic system," which consists of a set of stickers, with "dots" that map on to chords when placed on the guitar frets. The notes explain: "The Color-Matic system is designed to do two things: teach you how to play chords on the guitar immediately, and provide you with a sound musical foundation so that you can learn more about music and the guitar without having to unlearn bad habits that 'jiffy' methods often give you."

The cover conveys the seductive suggestion that strapping on an electric guitar clearly comes with benefits: an audience of appreciative, go-go-booted female fans

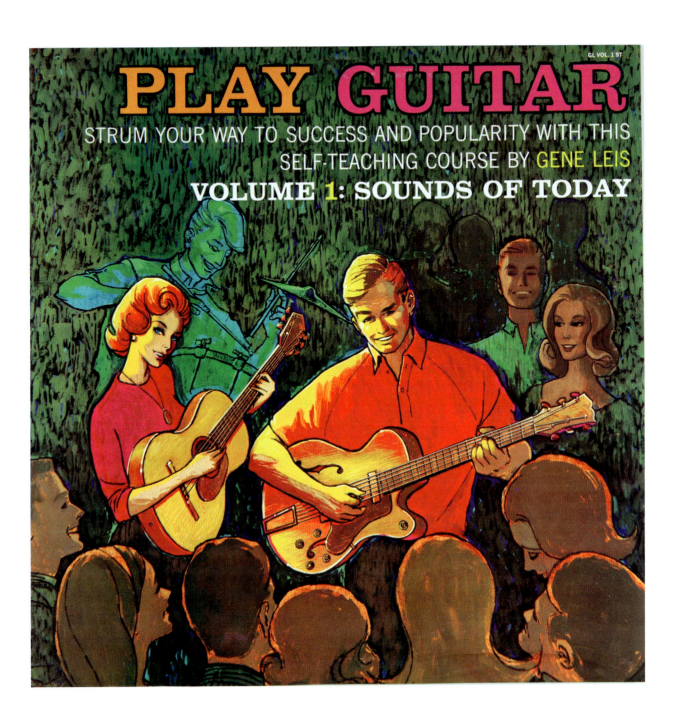

FIGURE 9.5

Play Guitar,
GL Vol. 1 Gene Leis Studios, ST, 1962.

dance and smile. One gal rocks a Mondrian dress, its modern blocks of color clearly signaling that she's dancing to contemporary sounds. The sixties set list includes "It's Not Unusual," a chart topper for Welsh wonder Tom Jones; "My Love," an international hit for Petula Clark; and another Clark gem, "Downtown." Each song appears on the record in both slow versions (for learning), and up-tempo, regular versions. The slow version of "It's Not Unusual," with its languid, twangy guitar, sounds a bit like an easy-listening parody, as if someone played a 45 at 33. Fun once. The regular version rocks out, with a skilled but unnamed lead guitarist offering a Ventures-like instrumental sound. We miss Tom Jones, though.

"The Ventures Show You How to Play by Ear!" exclaims the cover of **PLAY ELEC-TRIC BASS WITH THE VENTURES**. Two photographers are listed: Ivan Nagy and Peter Whorf. Nagy was a colorful character: photographer, film and television director, and convicted bookmaker, linked to the notorious "Hollywood Madam" scandal in the 1990s. He produced many album covers, including several for Martin Denny, Sandy Denny, and the Ventures. Whorf shot one of the all-time classic (and perennially copied and parodied) record covers, Herb Alpert's Tijuana Brass *Whipped Cream & Other Delights* (1965).

Volume 4 of the Play Guitar with the Ventures series, the record endorses the "Guitar Phonics" system, "a new, exciting technique to learn songs" without spending "long hours learning to read music." Side 1 is narrated by a man in classic instructional style, familiar from radio advertising and instructional films. Step by step, he methodically introduces the Guitar Phonics system, progressing from notes and basic chords to well-known tunes "La Bamba" and "Red River Valley." Side 2 encourages playing along with contemporary pop songs like "Shotgun" and "I Hear a Symphony." A bonus for collectors, *Play Electric Bass* includes four songs that the Ventures had not previously recorded and released, including an exceptional version of James Brown's "Papa's Got a Brand New Bag." Our narrator points out that, "on the second time through, the bass is missing," and the rest is up to you.

Wilbur Savidge created the Guitar Phonics system and collaborated with Liberty Records to release seven records on their Dolton label, including four with the Ventures as well as *Play Guitar with Chet Atkins* (1967). The first release, *Play Guitar with the Ventures* from 1965, is one of the few best-selling instructional records—charting at number 96 on the Billboard Top 100. The Ventures, known as the most successful instrumental rock band ever, had a string of hits during the 1960s, including "Walk, Don't Run," "Pipeline," and "Hawaii Five-O." Their guitar sound was tremendously influential, with its fuzzy distortions, reverse tracking, and protopsychedelic special effects.

Savidge's Guitar Phonics website reports that over six hundred thousand Play Guitar albums were sold. Don Wilson from the Ventures remembers the records' popularity: "For the next forty-five years, people from all over this continent and Japan have been bringing us those albums to be autographed after our concerts, and they always thank us for helping them learn to play. If they looked a little closer at the album covers, they

FIGURE 9.6

The Easy, New Color-matic System to Play the Electric Guitar,
Columbia RSC 0202, ca. 1967.

FIGURE 9.7

Play Electric Bass with the Ventures,
Dolton 17504;
cover photography by Peter Whorf and Ivan Nagy,
design by Woody Woodward,
booklet design by Ed Francis, 1966.

would see that they should be grateful to Mr. Savidge."[13] The enclosed booklet offers detailed diagrams, photos that show how to hold the bass, and a short section on "Tuning the Electric Bass." In a nod to accessibility, the notes also provide instructions on "How to Play Bass Patterns on the Standard Guitar." Much cheaper than music lessons, and gets around that guilty feeling when your instructor realizes you have not practiced since your last session.

YOU CAN PLAY . . . SONNY ROLLINS features a black-and-white photograph of the legendary jazz saxophonist superimposed over a spare graphic brick wall. Rollins, who continues to release records into his nineties, famously played with Charlie Parker, Thelonious Monk, Miles Davis, and John Coltrane. The cover's homespun appearance belies this jazz instruction record's extraordinary execution. An "Aebersold Play-A-Long," the disc is volume 8 of "A New Approach to Jazz Improvisation."

Released at $8.95 for both the book and the record, the album was aimed at "intermediate/advanced" players. The vinyl record is still available on the Aebersold website: "Even if you don't own a turntable, they make attractive musical tributes to another era and they are a great way to decorate your studio/practice room."[14] Side 1 begins with a B-flat tuning note played on piano, followed by a voice (Jamey Aebersold's presumably) counting out 1, 2, 1, 2, 3, 4.

Aebersold, a talented musician, produced over a hundred Play-A-Long albums. He also presides over Jazzbooks, which continues to distribute them, as well as other offerings like the Music Minus One series of music instruction records. As recounted on the informative music website Plays Well with Others: "Based on his belief that 'anyone can improvise,' Aebersold launched the business with a $500 loan from his parents, and a tiny classified ad in *DownBeat*. A half-century later, 133 Aebersold Play-A-Long titles (now available as CDs and streaming online) have sold over five million copies worldwide.[15] Aebersold recounts his early marketing efforts: "I took my record player and I took the LP with me and I demonstrated to people how you could practice the scales and build a solo."[16]

Aebersold's records, which were fundamental for many musicians, offered a way to learn jazz away from metropolitan centers, nightclubs, and music schools. The records have aged well: "In an era of advanced digital recording technology, it is difficult to fathom how well these recordings have stood the test of time, despite the fact that they were made in Aebersold's basement."[17] Jazz great Randy Brecker was also influenced by them: "That is, in a nutshell, the way I learned to play, and developed my ears and phrasing."[18] Inspiring.

The cover for LEARN-PLAY BONGOS WITH "MR BONGO" shows a beaming Jack Costanzo happily playing along with the target consumers for the album: Mom, Dad, Sis, and Junior, all energetically taking up the bongos.[19] Costanzo—a.k.a. "Mr Bongo"— helped to popularize bongos, playing enthusiastically into his ninety-eighth year. The liner notes boast, with only a little exaggeration, "the country's leading bongo player,

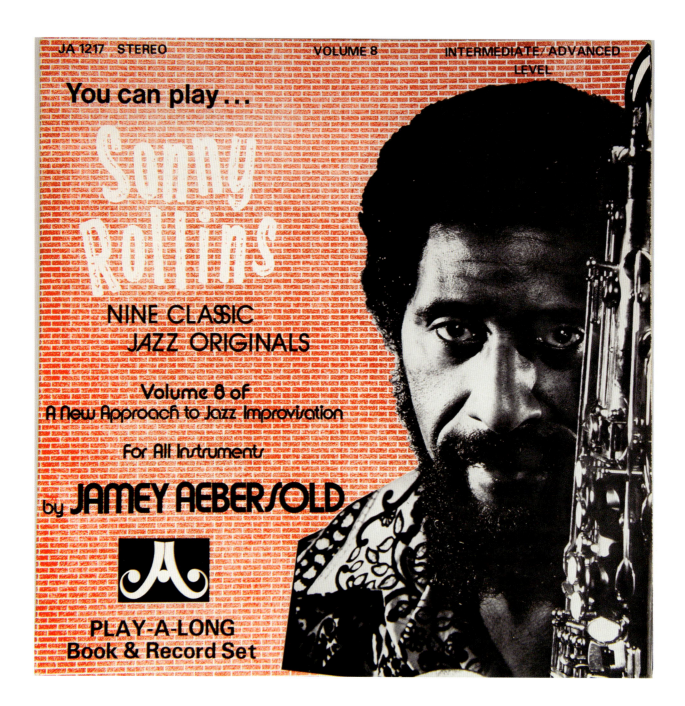

FIGURE 9.8

You Can Play . . . Sonny Rollins,
Jamey Aebersold, JA 1217;
cover by Pete Gearhart,
cover photo courtesy of Milestone Records, 1976.

Jack Costanzo is, more than any individual, responsible for the bongo's acceptance and great popularity in the United States."

Costanzo claimed to have started playing bongos as a teenager on a set he made from wooden butter tubs.[20] As an obituary noted: "He also had the charisma and debonair good looks of some the Hollywood stars he collaborated with in the 1950s and '60s—whether on screen or as a percussion teacher—including Marlon Brando, James Dean, and Gary Cooper. His many other collaborators included Betty Grable, Yma Sumac and Patti Page."[21] He played with bandleaders Stan Kenton and Nat King Cole and went on to record dozens of albums, several listing him as Mr. Bongo. Costanzo also appeared in several movies, including *Harum Scarum* (1965), starring Elvis Presley, where he played a "bongo-beating Middle Eastern slave Julna."[22]

The cover design credits go to Pate/Francis and Associates, who designed classic covers for Si Zentner and His Orchestra's *A Thinking Man's Band* (1959) and Martin Denny's *The Enchanted Sea* (1959). Photography is by Garrett-Howard, who worked with Pate/Francis, and formed design firm Group Five with Leo Monahan in the early 1960s.[23] Group Five produced hundreds of album covers and were influential in shaping the look of pop music. In the memorable words of graphic designer Art Chantry, "Almost by accident, they invented so many style genres that they may be the single greatest pop culture innovators of all time. and nobody knows who they are."[24]

Costanzo's liner notes provide steady, sober guidance for the beginning bongo player: "Slow and relaxed. That's the way to learn the bongos." Exercises include "variations off the Afro-Cuban basic beat." "Pitfalls and warnings" offer advice: "Practice slowly! Build up speed gradually. Never let nails touch the drumhead. This may damage your instrument." The notes conclude: "It's Easy. It's Fun. It's Exciting. Great fun at the beach, at parties, forming an orchestra or playing for your own amusement." The LP is expertly narrated by Ira Cook, "one of Los Angeles' leading personality disk jockeys." We're not sure it will make us Mr. and Mrs. Bongo, but *Learn-Play Bongos* is one of the most straightforward and doable learn-to-play records we've acquired.

An extraordinary album, the elaborately packaged ETHNIC DANCES OF BLACK PEOPLE AROUND THE WORLD includes two LPs and a thirty-six-page booklet filled with historical notes, pedagogical instructions, and simple drawings. An extensive catalog of physical education records from Kimbo fills the inside of the gatefold sleeve. Titles such as *Authentic Afro-Rhythms*, *Authentic Indian Dances and Folklore*, and *Modern American Square Dance Music* clearly reflect an often-contested desire for students to dance "other peoples' dances" as a way of cultural understanding.[25]

The brainchild of dancer, choreographer, and teacher Marie Brooks, the album was intended for dance and cultural instruction from elementary school to college. Unlike many dance instruction records, *Ethnic Dances of Black People around the World* eschews choreographed dance diagrams. Instead, Brooks points out that "the dance method utilized on this album presents an opportunity for one to move freely

FIGURE 9.9

Learn-Play Bongos with "Mr. Bongo,"
Jack Costanzo, Liberty LRP 3177;
design by Pate/Francis & Associates,
photography by Garrett-Howard, 1960.

and naturally without being distracted by counting steps and losing the essence of the inner feeling motivated by the percussion."

Brooks opens the extensive notes with her rationale: "The most needed element in our educational institutions today is communication—dance is a communicating force." Born in Guadeloupe, she grew up in Trinidad, where she became interested in Caribbean dance. She studied in New York with famed choreographer Katherine Dunham and went on to dance and teach internationally. Brooks founded and directed a number of dance companies, including the Marie Brooks Children's Dance Research Theater. Her teaching philosophy might be summed up in a single quote: "Dance is too creative to be art just for entertainment."[26] Brooks "was known best for her unselfish sharing of dance with children, and the children will always be remembered for their special understanding of the dances they learned and their very colorful and voluminous, twirling skirts."[27]

Side A features dance from the Ibo tribes of Nigeria. The notes provide a brief overview of the Ibo tribe, and how African rhythms "were transplanted to Haiti in voodoo songs." Side B focuses on Calypso, "the singing newspaper of the people." She describes Calypso as "a social dance, and can be done alone, as an exhibition dance, or with a partner." Shango occupies side C—"a sacred dance . . . dedicated to African gods." God of thunder and lightning, Shango "is one of the distinct Afro-Religious, Yoruba cults in Trinidad." Side D begins with Maracatu, influenced by the enslaved Angolans who were of royal heritage. Maracatu dancers "parade through the street with the King and lesser royalties, all regally attired." The album closes with the Samba, or "Batuque" ("the name of a very old dance in Brazil"). Her notes include inspiring moves like "the Samba Hop" and "Umbligada."

Brooks offers these insights: "These dances reach out into other parts of the curriculum. They relate to social science and history classes. They are the expressions of the life style, customs and religion." For her, "to understand and know people you must first understand their culture." Listening to *Ethnic Dances of Black People around the World* made us want to get up from our computer keyboards and move!

The record presents Brooks's precise, uplifting narration, with an occasional outburst of joyous singsong. She's accompanied by basic drumbeats and patterns. The drums, so essential for dance, are performed "under the direction of Montego Joe." Born Roger Sanders in Jamaica, Montego Joe played with a stellar cast of musicians during his long and varied career, including Art Blakey, Max Roach, George Benson, and Dizzy Gillespie. He released the acclaimed record *Arriba! Con Montego Joe* (1965) on the Prestige label. He worked with Harlem Youth United (Har-You), who recorded *Har-You Percussion Group: Sounds of the Ghetto Youth* in 1967 under his direction. That record was recently described as a forgotten treasure, "an exquisite mix of funky Latin tracks that has a feel only youthful optimism can generate."[28] Along with *Ethnic Dances*, it's well worth seeking out.

"You'll learn how men should lead, women should follow" on Betty White's **HOW TO WALTZ**. White (not the famous actor who died in 2021) released a series of Betty White

FIGURE 9.11

How to Waltz,
Conversa-phone D 102, 1960.

FIGURE 9.12

Arthur Murray Favorites: Rhumbas,
Chuy Reyes and His Orchestra, Capitol T 1369, 1960.

tag on the back cover—$2.97. Arthur Murray Favorites were promoted by Capitol Records as the "all-time best selling albums of dance music, all beautifully repackaged for added sales."[30] The series featured updated, photographed covers, replacing the color illustrations of the 1950s editions.

Against a copper backdrop, footstep schematics depict the female and male dancer roles using stylized prints of high heels and flat shoes. This modern map of steps guides an enthusiastic couple. His brown suit takes formality down a notch. Her full-skirted spaghetti-strapped dress with bright blossoms match pink pointed pumps, and a long strand of pearls has shifted from her bends and sways.

The Rhumba emerged as a US dance floor favorite in the 1930s and remains popular today. As a midcentury dance manual explains: "Like all modern social dances, the Rumba had gone through a period of extensive development and change before it came to the American dance floor. As danced today in this country, the Rumba is a popular favorite, distinguished by smooth and supple movement of the hips and a short, rather heavy walking step."[31]

The notes don't include much information on the musicians and leave out the talented vocalists altogether. Listeners must be content with rather generic praise: "Chuy Reyes and his Orchestra rank high as one the genuine exponents of Cuban and South American rhythms. His music is colorful, exciting, delightful for dancing—and lots of fun even if you sit it out!" One number, "Jack, Jack, Jack," includes a refrain that bears some resemblance to the legendary television theme song from *The Gong Show*.

As America's leading dance instructor, Murray sought out rich and famous pupils, including Eleanor Roosevelt, the Duke of Windsor, and John D. Rockefeller Jr. Throughout his career, Murray "promised social and even business success by developing confidence through dance skills."[32] Today, Arthur Murray Studios emphasize social poise as well as physical fitness: "Good dancing is a lifetime investment in fun, poise, confidence, improved personality and new friends. It is also a superb physical conditioner, providing fun without extreme effort."[33] Many midcentury Murray titles made it onto compact disc and remain dance instruction standards.

10 LET'S LEARN A LANGUAGE

Tourists? Spies? Soviet intelligence in disguise? A trio of hatted figures anchors the Cambridge Language Series RUSSIAN LP: a Humphrey Bogart character, looking befuddled in a fedora, shares a massive map with a startled cloche-and-fur-attired female whose round train case suggests light travel through France. The "local" (did the art director mean for that beard to look fake?) appears in a lamb-fur shepherd's hat, a striking red *cherkeska* decorated with *gazirnitsy*, small pockets made for packing gunpower (are those white drawing pencils, rather than bullets?). Introducing a Caucasus-based figure makes a postwar gesture toward conflicts in the USSR unification efforts and resonates with the US Cold War imagination.

Travel the globe, by boat, train, car, or plane, as the inner label's striking yellow and red drawing details—or by learning a language with lessons "designed in the same manner as the Army Language Courses during World War II and subsequent years." Ah, the Cold-War-suffused skullduggery and spy-filled subsequent years. Liner notes encourage beginning with what "interests you most," voicing the trend for learning "in the same manner as you did english as a child." Also offered are "a method of studying the manual" (to refer to "constantly as a reference and reminder and guide" when away from the record player) and "a method of studying the record." Active participation works best. However, "listening passively, while playing or working, within earshot of your record player will also aid in assimilating the language."

The Russian LP reference manual pages present six vertical columns in tiny six-point type. Guided by the Russian phrase (in Cyrillic, no sound transliteration) on the far right edge, "the ideas, not the words" are translated into, respectively, Italian, Spanish, English, French and German. It's a potentially overwhelming spectacle, but it does offer the opportunity to learn multiple languages simultaneously. The typical tourist scenarios are here (telling the time, at the hotel), but also more involved situations (rural visit, service of the state). "Before he bought a milking machine, the whole family helped milk the cows" and "Those who teach school are training the citizens of the future" are sure to spark heady conversation.

Janet, an enthusiastic language learner, put needle to groove and immediately got lost. The speaker begins with Russian pronunciation, so the words in the English column only represent a corresponding sound. Without knowing the Russian alphabet, it was difficult to discern which Russian word in the long list was being spoken. Eventually, the speaker began sounding out the alphabet, and it was possible to determine where he was on the page. (Here the manual's miniscule type size dropped down to something less than five-point. In Cyrillic typography.) As the next section started, the speaker articulated "Anna Karenina," and the Cyrillic looked similar enough to again locate the position on the page. Moving from phrase to phrase based on length of vocalization and scanning left past the German and French columns to find the English meanings pushed this language learning task into hopelessness before we even finished telling time. The male and female voices soldiered on about days of the week and double beds with normal language speed, leaving any possibility of a beginner accurately imitating or repeating these phrases well out of reach. Without knowing the meanings or Cyrillic representation of sounds, it was impossible to harmonize print and recording. Frustrating.

The second time through, Janet attended to every word or letter in conjunction with the sound and was able to follow the voice down the page while looking at the Cyrillic letters. "If you can devote enough time to the Cambridge Language Course to learn from ten to fifteen phrases a day, you will know your language in thirty to forty days," the notes promise. One's ear would become accustomed to the sounds. The alphabet would be familiar. But memorize ten to fifteen of these random phrases a day? What precisely would one know? "Remember, you are trying to communicate—not be taken as a native." Native? No risk of that. *Помогите!*

The Vatican with Saint Peter's Dome anchors the album cover's left edge—the Castel Sant'Angelo, the right—on LIVING ITALIAN: A COMPLETE LANGUAGE COURSE. In the detailed illustration, a smartly dressed couple rely on what looks to be the "Common Usage Dictionary" from this four record set, as they confidently engage a dark-hatted signore, who seems pleased with their efforts. Bold pronouncements such as "6 weeks from today speak this language fluently with a perfect native accent" adorn the cover. Two sizable booklets provide scripts that accompany the recordings and supplementary vocabulary. Ralph Weiman, "formerly Chief of Language Section U.S. War Department," receives credit for the instructional method.

The Conversation Manual presents thematically organized words and phrases, "based on U.S. Government methods to teach you quickly, easily, pleasantly." Three black disc icons mark the small percentage of sections that are actually read out on the four ten-inch records. The native speaker rolls his Rs and enunciates his vowels. But a beginner will find repeating the required phrases in the brief pause provided nearly impossible. Emphasizing "the commonest Italian words and their meanings," introducing "the most important 300" Italian sentences, and "learning Italian the way you learned English (hear it, say it, absorb it)" seems to make sense, yet working through the

FIGURE 10.1

Cambridge Language Series: Russian,
L 13, c. 1957.

eighty-eight-page manual, in conjunction with the recordings, represents an exercise in era-specific "curriculum and instruction."

As an experienced but impatient student of Italian, Janet almost skipped the introductory pronunciation practice, but then decided to follow the plan. Imitating the native speaker's vowel sounds made for excellent review and tiring mouth movement for an out-of-practice Italian speaker. Then, on to some basic phrases of introduction and greeting, a bit of work with the verbs *essere*, to be, and *avere*, to have, and the learning was underway! Rome already felt closer.

The Eiffel Tower, the Arc de Triomphe, café awnings, and a newspaper kiosk set the Parisian street scene for a man and woman in tailored suits, language manual in hand, addressing a uniformed gendarme. On **LIVING FRENCH**, a fleur-de-lis and bands of French flag red, white, and blue furl out below.

On **LIVING GERMAN**, somewhere in the vicinity of Neuschwanstein Castle and Cologne Cathedral (in fact separated by some 380 miles) the Grimm-Fairy-Tale Goose Girl and a man in a Bavarian *tracht*, holding close a Holstein cow, share the frame with a tweed-jacketed, pipe-smoking, less-mythical figure, perhaps a tourist trying out his phrases *auf Deutsche*. The listen-and-repeat method "grew out of the amazingly successful new speed-method devised by experts in World War II to teach foreign languages to overseas-bound soldiers."

A yellow casita wall topped by clay roof tiles opens a door on **LIVING SPANISH**, forty lessons on four LPs. The Toreador and the Flamenco dancer with black lace mantilla present a vision of travel to-dos, as a pith-helmeted customs official down on the docks inspects barrels of sherry and appears to question a local.

Two cheerful children sit on a red "magic carpet of learning" as it zooms across a pale blue globe. Armed with a portable turntable and, presumably, the vinyl record and instruction manual from **CHILDREN'S LANGUAGE COURSE: SPANISH**, they appear primed to excel at cross-border communication with "a proven method that combines sounds, words, and pictures." Beyond the pamphlet illustrations, no innovative method emerges. Listening is key, as is reading along with the manual. "Imagine the thrill of hearing your youngster speaking a foreign language!" crow the liner notes. Adult speakers pose as children (Pedro and Alicia): "Your child will eagerly follow their adventures together—and the language will come easily and naturally." Simple conversations present limited vocabulary for food, animals, colors, "rules of safety," and telling time.

Teaching language through song has the potential to offer words in context, demonstrate pronunciation, and introduce music of another culture, and it remains a popular pedagogical practice. This LP ends with four traditional folk songs, including "Cialito Lindo" (perhaps better known to some listeners as the "Frito Bandito" song) and "Cuatro Milpas," all sung by a wavery, mature female voice.

"It's fun! It's fabulous! It's fast!" **ROUND THE WORLD FRENCH** features bright orange, yellow, and blue and a small photo of a Pan American jet flying over a grid of tempting

FIGURE 10.2

Living Italian,
Living Language Records, 1956.

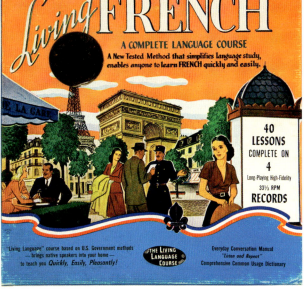

FIGURE 10.3

Living French,
Living Language Records, 1955.

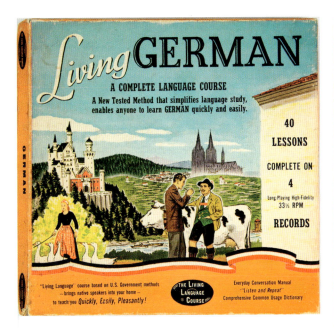

FIGURE 10.4

Living German,
Living Language Records, 1956.

FIGURE 10.5

Living Spanish,
Living Language Records, 1955.

FIGURE 10.6

Children's Language Course: Spanish,
Conversa-phone CX 135, 1973.

FIGURE 10.7

Round-the-World French,
Conversa-phone C 352;
cover illustration Boeing 707
courtesy Pan America World Airways, 1957.

illustrated travel scenarios: music in Munich, kimono in Kyoto, dancing in Paris. An ebullient young couple—she with smart handbag and wrist-length white gloves, he with rolled rim Hamburg—beam with anticipation. Hand in hand, they carry representative resources of readiness (formal hat, thick newspaper, purse) around the world. Access to the halls of power, awareness of current affairs, and organized personal finances set the stage for global influence. "Learn today . . . travel tomorrow." Learn "as a child learns his native tongue—the natural way, by listening." Native instructors with "perfect pronunciation" recite "interesting conversations." "Pennies a lesson," the album satisfied economic concerns, too. A midcentury scholarly review concluded that Conversa-phone recordings "will answer the need for recorded material that is linguistically sound and pedagogically useful."[1] An enclosed pamphlet features all phrases and their English translations.

Later releases in the Round-the-World series dispense with detailed cover art. Beyond random background colors, varying titles and font, and a meaninglessly multicolored Mercator projection that suggests Alaska is the size of West Africa, nothing differentiates a specific Conversa-phone Round-the-World Language record sleeve from any other.[2]

On Conversa-phone's Round-the-World SWEDISH LANGUAGE RECORD COURSE, a map with an inexplicable pastel color code and a characteristic misleading scale—Greenland looms larger than South America—suggests a fantasy world laid out for exploration. Broad capital letters mark a modern undertaking. Framed by chartreuse, our romantic young couple sets out for new horizons. This is a "Modern Method" for language learning, so spirits remain high.

"Which of 30 languages do you want to learn?" the liner notes ask, going on to extol the "proven Conversa-phone Method." Hungarian? Swahili? Malay? Dispensing with "dull verb conjugations" and presenting "no tiresome grammar," the LP churns through Swedish phrases read one after another, beginning with basic greetings, such as "God morgon" (Good morning). Worried friends won't find you later in the evening? Try telling the hotel concierge, "Om någon söker oss säg att vi äter middag på Berns" (If anyone looks for us we will be dining at Berns—a classic spot for dinner and music in central Stockholm). Menu items, telling time, and road signs close out the monologue.

Modeled more on a spoken-phrase book, this "quick easy way to learn a new language" likely leaves the deluded traveler with little hope of actually conversing with anyone. "See what you can learn by listening to records at home" speaks to the world of leisurely learning, with all the hard work of even simple language fluency unacknowledged. Still, a few key phrases are (usually) better than nothing. Other offerings, such as "Foreign Language for the Family" and a selection of children's records, include simple stories and song lyrics for sing-alongs. *Javisst!* (Of course!)

The cheerful couple—learning today, traveling tomorrow—turns their attention to Japanese on ROUND-THE-WORLD JAPANESE. The brush-stroke font suggests Asian calligraphy—the only cultural clue offered on the album. In familiar categories such as "Dining at your hotel" and "At the Japanese beauty salon," the instruction manual presents transliteration of Japanese characters meant to match phrases read by the recorded native speaker, along with the English translations. Generalized greetings and requests read in rapid succession allow little time for repetition. However, the native speaker's voice does offer an orienting set of sounds that become easier to follow as the lessons progress, and one can imagine after multiple listenings having a few words as entrée, even if any reply except the time of day will remain beyond our eager students' ken. Japanese characters are provided for common road signs. Interesting to note that *Round-the-World Japanese* was released just as Japanese cars were making impressive inroads to American markets.

Pale pink frames the **MODERN GREEK** language record course cover. The "Learn Today, Travel Tomorrow" instruction manual contained within features an uninspiring black-and-white photocopy-quality image of the Parthenon. Beginning with "special pronunciation points," the booklet's thirteen pages are divided into three vertical columns: English phrase, transliteration of the spoken Greek equivalent, and Greek translation of word or phrase, written in the Greek alphabet. Good morning! (ka-lee-ME-ra!) *Καλημέρα*! Thank you! (pa-ra-ka-LO!) *Παρακαλω*! No attempt is made to teach the Greek letters. However, hearing Greek words sounded out in relation to the transliteration in addition to the Greek word provides a useful foundation for future navigating: Hey! I can read that street sign!

On **ROUND-THE-WORLD ARABIC**, a calligraphic brush script gives the front cover an Orientalized flair. The back serves simply as advertising space for other Conversa-phone records, including *The Magic Key to Colorful Conversation* (1962) ("Make everything you say more meaningful, more exciting, more vivid and more impressive") and *Spelling Made Easy* (ca. 1962). The booklet inside informs the student that "the Arabic language employs its own characters." Nevertheless, Arabic letters and writing only appear in the last lesson. The introduction explains: "We use a transliteration, that is, we give the Arabic characters the equivalent English sounds." On the record, a native speaker reads out words and phrases in a careful meter to allow imitation and repetition. The final lesson, "How to Read Signs," presents the English for common street signs ("Danger," "Exit," "Hospital") as well as the transliteration and the equivalent Arabic words in pretty, legible cursive, allowing an experience of actually reading Arabic and hearing the sounds with the attendant meaning at hand. Arabic, read from right to left, does complicate the manual's layout, however, with Arabic writing filling both sides of the printed text's margins.

Jonathan vividly remembers a fellow student in his college French class performing Morris Albert's 1975 hit ballad "Feelings"—really, all he did was sing "*sentiments*" over and over—but he brought a guitar to class and really commanded the stage. This educational episode fluttered to consciousness when researching **LATIN-AMERICAN GAME SONGS**, "a teaching aid for language courses, voice pupils and home students." Our copy included the separately sold *Latin-American Game Songs* book (1959), with "simple piano arrangements" and both English and Spanish lyrics. The album offers

FIGURE 10.8

Round-the-World Swedish,
Conversa-phone CX 142, 1961.

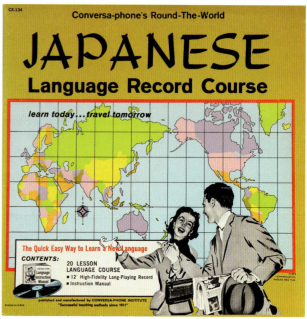

FIGURE 10.9

Round-the-World Japanese,
Conversa-phone CX 134, 1972.

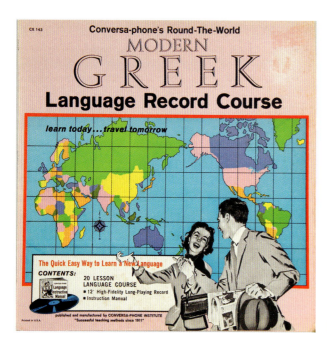

FIGURE 10.10

Round-the-World Modern Greek,
Conversa-phone CX 143, 1972.

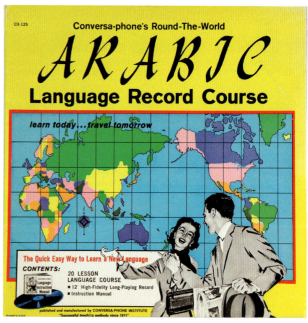

FIGURE 10.11

Round-the-World Arabic,
Conversa-phone CX 125, 1978.

FIGURE 10.12

Latin-American Game Songs,
Ruth De Cesare, Bowmar Records, M 4, 1959.

"16 folksongs with complete instructions for group activities." The cover, with the understated graphics of many instructional records, includes small drawings of several Latin American folk motifs, including straw hats, poncho-style striped blankets, and a palm tree. There are a few circles thrown in, perhaps to represent balloons for games.

One of a series of records from Mills Music that "beautifully integrate language study with music," *Latin-American Game Songs* features accomplished performers along with ethnomusicologically inspired background information for each selection. The liner notes declare: "Authentic performances assure complete accuracy as a study guide." Brief biographies are provided for the performers, which include singers Marni Nixon and Ken Remo and musicians María Arias Cruz, Antonio Alonzo, and José Barroso.

Nixon, an acclaimed soprano, provided the onscreen singing voice for several leading actresses, including Natalie Wood in *West Side Story* (1961) and Audrey Hepburn in *My Fair Lady* (1964), for which she was dubbed "American cinema's most unsung singer."[3] She recorded many albums and was featured on one of Leonard Bernstein's televised *Young People's Concerts*. Remo appeared on 1950s television programs such as *The Tennessee Ernie Ford Show* and *The Danny Kaye Show*, and in Broadway hits *Kismet* and *Oklahoma*. María Arias Cruz, marimba and piano player, "adds true flavor and charm to our album."

Latin-American Game Songs was released on Bowmar Records, which was founded by Stanley B. Bowmar. The label produced visual aids for classrooms, including a wonderful set of "Meet the Instrument" posters and filmstrips, along with the "Bowmar galaxy" of educational records, including *Science Concepts* (ca. 1962), *Songs for Children with Special Needs* (1965), and *North American Indian Songs* (1972). Bowmar also promoted a full range of physical fitness and dance records, including "action songs and games, couple dances and mixers, folk dances, health, modern dance, physical fitness, rhythms, and social and square dances."[4]

Music educator Ruth De Cesare produced *Latin-American Game Songs*. The cover indicates she taught at the Mills College of Education in New York City, which merged with the New School in the 1970s. Producer of numerous items for Bowmar Records, she published several instructional books, including *Myth, Music, and Dance of the American Indian: Teacher's Resource Book* (1988). In her liner notes, she writes, "the game songs of Latin America are both lively and charming, and serve as an ideal introduction to the appealing music of this area."

The songs, including "Rice and Milk (Arroz con Leche)," "Go Back to Your Cradle (Toma Tu Muñecu)," and "Breaking the Piñata (Al Quebrar La Piñata)," sound beautiful, each sung in c-l-e-a-r-l-y enunciated English, with some Spanish verses thrown in. As De Cesare spells out in her earnest, optimistic goals for integrating game songs into the curriculum: "Nothing, for instance, comes as a more pleasant surprise to youngsters than playing and singing the games of other countries, and finding them similar to their own. 'Little foreign children,' as they were known, become immediately fellow-humans in a common world."[5] A worthy ambition.

On the cover of **EVOLUTION OF THE BLUES SONG**, four-legged stools in pale pink, lilac, red, yellow, and dark blue harmonize with children dressed in their Sunday best as they gather around musician Jon Hendricks. This grouping echoes the 1960 Monterey Jazz Festival performance where Hendricks presented his original story "Evolution of the Blues Song" directly to a group of seated children. "The spirituals are the mother of the blues," he told them, "and the blues are the mother of jazz." This outstanding album blends spoken narration, poetry, and song, including versions of "Swing Low, Sweet Chariot," "Sufferin' Blues," and "See See Rider."

As Hendricks describes it: "I wrote about the music they sang all through their lives, the spirituals, which they gave freely to America and the world." As he writes in the liner notes, he wrote and sang about what he knew: "My people, about my great-grandmother who came from Guinea, Gold Coast, Africa. About my father, Alexander Brooks Hendricks who ran away from the master who sold his father, mother and sister separately." Clearly, this is not a typical "history of the blues" record.

Hendricks's presentation of "Evolution of the Blues Song" was by all accounts a highlight of that year's Monterey Jazz Festival. A hype sticker was affixed to the album cover with an excerpt from a glowing *DownBeat* review by jazz critic and Monterey Jazz Festival cofounder Ralph Gleason: "Members of the audience wept at Hendrick's narration of the development of the blues." The notes also reproduce jazz historian Frank Kofsky's judgment: "If in its three years, the Monterey Jazz Festival had done nothing other than present this program, it would have justified its existence."

Hendricks specialized in vocalizing, such as scat singing and vocalese. Lauded as an influential improvisational singer, he "created intricate narratives and tongue-in-cheek philosophical treatises that matched both the melody lines and the serpentine contours of the instrumental solos, note for note and inflection for inflection."[1] He performed with the group Lambert, Hendricks & Ross on several successful albums, including their heralded 1958 debut *Sing a Song of Basie*, which "expanded the horizons of jazz singing."[2]

For *Evolution of the Blues Song*, Hendricks called upon a host of exceptionally talented musicians, including the Ike Isaacs Trio led by bassist Ike Isaacs, who played with, among others, Count Basie, Ella Fitzgerald, and Carmen McRae; and saxophonist Ben Webster. Hailed as one of the "founding emperors of jazz tenor saxophone," Webster "developed an enormous lyrical sound and swinging directness."[3] Jimmy Witherspoon, called "one of the great postwar blues singers and a figure who naturally bridged the worlds of blues and jazz," provided vocals.[4] Gospel singer Hannah Dean—whose singing *Billboard* described as a "mixture of rhythm and blues and rock'n'roll sung with the feeling and unbuttoned phrasing of a gospel singer"—joined in as well.[5] Although Dean released a few records for Columbia in the early 1960s, she does not seem to have had much success.

Even the often curmudgeonly jazz writer Nat Hentoff praised *Evolution of the Blues Song*, which he described as "a simplified odyssey of Afro-American music, with illustrations and sociological asides."[6] Hentoff concluded: "It is especially encouraging to see a major record company carry through a project of such value."[7] Hendricks's obituary remarked that, "in his role as a teacher and a critic, Mr. Hendricks proved that he was adept at dealing with jazz in an analytical way. But he always maintained that words could go only so far in explaining the music's importance and endurance."[8]

Evolution of the Blues Song evolved into a theatrical production, *Evolution of the Blues*, with runs in the UK and the US during the 1970s and 1980s. Jazz writer and archivist Joe Maita recalls his experience at a San Francisco performance: "I will always remember him singing a spine-tingling, thrilling, and impeccable rendition of 'Everyday I Have the Blues.'"[9] For the way it weaves personal reflection, narrates history, and witnesses to the racial trauma that produced the blues—all with virtuoso musicianship—this record seems especially relevant today.

Tiny trumpets, drums, and directional arrows, among other symbols that create a computer-punch-card-like code for musical inputs and outputs adorn the cover of GUIDE TO JAZZ from Hugues Panassié. Artist Jason Kirby's striking grid design of irregular black, white, orange, and fuchsia rectangles against a turquoise background found a home on many LPs: the same modernist graphics appear on releases such as Duke Ellington and His Orchestra's *In a Mellowtone* (1956), Tito Puente's *Top Percussion* (1958), and the Mauna Loa Islanders' *Music of the Islands* (1959). Along with album covers for RCA and Columbia, Kirby designed book covers and textiles.

Guide to Jazz was "issued simultaneously with the publication of Hugues Panassié's book of the same title." Panassié, an eminent French jazz impresario and a critic, authored annotated liner notes for the sixteen musical selections. He provides interesting details about musicians and studio practices, creating a compelling tour through key moments in recorded jazz. "Some Sweet Day" with Louis Armstrong vocal starts off side 1. Count Basie's "One O'Clock Boogie," recorded in 1947, and John Estes's "Working Man Blues" from 1941, highlight connections to the genre's deep past and emphasize the blues' influence on jazz. "My Blue Heaven" from Coleman Hawkins, "Swingin'

FIGURE 11.1

Evolution of the Blues Song,
Jon Hendricks, Columbia CS 8383;
photo by Henry Parker, 1960.

Uptown" with Jimmy Lunceford, and Jimmy Yancy's 1939 recording of "The Mellow Blues," among others, offer appealing and memorable listening that admirably serves to introduce jazz to the uninitiated. Significant here is the all-Black roster of musicians. No Original Dixieland Jazz Band, no Benny Goodman, no Dave Brubeck—a noteworthy departure from most jazz history records of the era.

A CHILD'S INTRODUCTION TO JAZZ, narrated by Julian "Cannonball" Adderley, is part of the Wonderland series from Riverside Records. This wide-ranging set, produced by Riverside's cofounder Bill Grauer, included *A Child's Introduction to Gilbert and Sullivan* (1959) and *A Child's Introduction to Outer Space* (1959). Adderley, who played saxophone on Miles Davis's landmark 1959 album *Kind of Blue*, provides a "comprehensive and *authoritative* introduction to this important American music." His "highly articulate and well-informed" narration is useful for adults and well as children. As mentioned in his obituary, Adderley "believed in letting his audiences know, in an urbane and witty manner, what his music was about."[10]

The album offers a fascinating contrast to Leonard Bernstein's celebrated and cerebral *What Is Jazz* (1956), which seems serious and studious, if typically exuberant, in comparison to Adderley's warm and personal approach. As the liner notes point out, Adderley's commentary offers "an easy-going, conversational discussion of the highlights of the jazz story." The record features excerpts from early jazz legends Louis Armstrong, Duke Ellington, Scott Joplin, Jelly Roll Morton, and Ma Rainey, as well as Adderley's contemporaries John Coltrane, Thelonious Monk, and Wes Montgomery. As promised on the cover, the sound quality is excellent: "These records are conceived, planned and produced by an experienced, expert staff, and are recorded and processed at the finest modern high-fidelity sound studios."

The notes rave: "The story of jazz is the story of an exciting and truly American art form—a music bursting with the vitality of American life." To learn about jazz, Adderley asserts, "I can only recommend that you listen to records wherever you can and as much as you can." The fanciful cover art highlights a bowler-hatted man with a golden sax emitting colorful representations of unpredictable—even improvisational—sound. A young boy dressed in a boater and summer suit makes beginning efforts to play the drum. Given that the liner notes call no specific attention to the contribution of African Americans to jazz, nor to the blues and spirituals that preceded jazz (in contrast to Jon Hendricks's *Evolution of the Blues Song*), it's not surprising that Riverside failed to represent a Black musician on the album cover. Sonically, however, *A Child's Introduction to Jazz* is a marvelous record.

If the uninitiated are going to be lured into a relationship with jazz, clearly the conversion requires some seduction. After all, sexual tension and release permeate jazz.[11] Who better than a sexy teacher in pearls, a foamy cerulean shortie negligée, and coordinating kitten heels? On LET'S GET ACQUAINTED WITH JAZZ . . . FOR PEOPLE WHO HATE JAZZ! a befuddled, overage schoolboy in scarlet polo shirt, matching socks, and

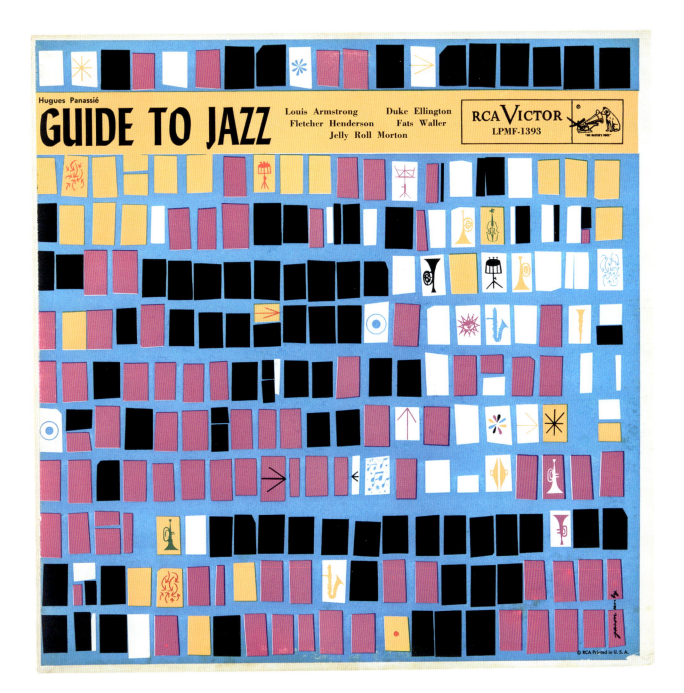

FIGURE 11.2

Guide to Jazz,
Hugues Panassié, RCA Victor LPMF 1393;
cover design: Jason Kirby, 1956.

FIGURE 11.3

A Child's Introduction to Jazz,
narrated by Julian "Cannonball" Adderley,
Wonderland Records RLP 1435, 1961.

rolled-up trousers bites his tongue as he shies away from her gaze. Holding a cone—somewhere between a dunce cap and a megaphone—Junior's fascination with a woman's legs may delay his education in the Swing, Cool, and Progressive schools, but, as the notes proclaim, "I'm sure words are wasted. It's the music we're after and the sounds." Beginning with basic bars of bachelor-pad easy-listening piano, "Lullaby of Birdland" calms the beginner's nerves and gently leads the listener into syncopation and traded solos.

Tampa Records, founded in Los Angeles in 1955, emphasized West Coast jazz. With "Supersonic Sound" and "realism in recording this all newly recorded album offers a wonderful spatial dimensional quality which completely envelopes the listener." (Envelopment. Also a midcentury military strategy.) Side 1 ends with more energetic beats on "El Tigre" and gives way—with an ear to winning over the haters—to side 2's boppier bass and horns on "Cheeta's for Two" and a vibes and improv feel on "The Cobra" and "Perdido." Players include Jimmy Rowles on piano, Barney Kessel on guitar, and Larry Bunker on vibes.[12] *Billboard* gave the LP three stars ("good potential—will sell"), termed the jazz style "languorous," and found the stereo separation effect "on the exaggerated side."[13] Our copy is mono. Only the sexual stereotypes are exaggerated.

A book and a slightly bruised apple pale in comparison with teacher's crimson hair-ribbon, short skirt, and lipstick. No boring homework here. Whoever left the iconic gift on her desk may be hoping to learn something more than 4 LESSONS IN JAZZ. A piece of white chalk and a globe complete the midcentury educational setting. The buxom expert, eyeglasses off and ruler in hand, points to the chalkboard, highlighting the album's musicians. Art Blakey Jazz Messengers, Charlie Mingus, Australian Jazz Quintet, and Johnny Richards each provide a lesson: Mingus as "a bold experimentalist" and "a searcher," Richards as an arranger, the Detroit-based Quintet for "thought-out jazz interpretations," and the Jazz Messengers, the prolific and long-running group that featured many legendary players, expounding on the school of hard bop.

JAZZ GOES TO JUNIOR COLLEGE documents the Dave Brubeck Quartet's campus tour that garnered national attention and landed Brubeck on the cover of *Time* magazine in 1954, with the headline "The Joints Are Really Flipping." Not quite as celebrated as the quartet's first collegiate release, the best-selling *Jazz Goes to College* (1954), the junior version featured Paul Desmond on alto sax, Norman Bates on bass, and Joe Morello on drums. As the liner notes explain: "The five outstanding Brubeck Quartet interpretations in this set came from two concerts at junior colleges—Fullerton and Long Beach." Brubeck's emphasis on seeking out audiences beyond nightclubs required getting people "acquainted with jazz." His mission included helping "the students learn about the jazz heritage which is theirs to enjoy" and defy the "past generations of educators" who had the sense that jazz was "something to be ignored or considered undignified or downright bad."

The album includes a fantastic version of "One Moment Worth Years," along with "Bru's Blues" and extended interpretation of standards "These Foolish Things," "The

FIGURE 11.4

Let's Get Acquainted with Jazz . . . for People Who Hate Jazz!,
the Jimmy Rowles Sextet, Tampa Records TP 8,
produced by Robert Sherman;
cover design by Bud Costello, 1957.

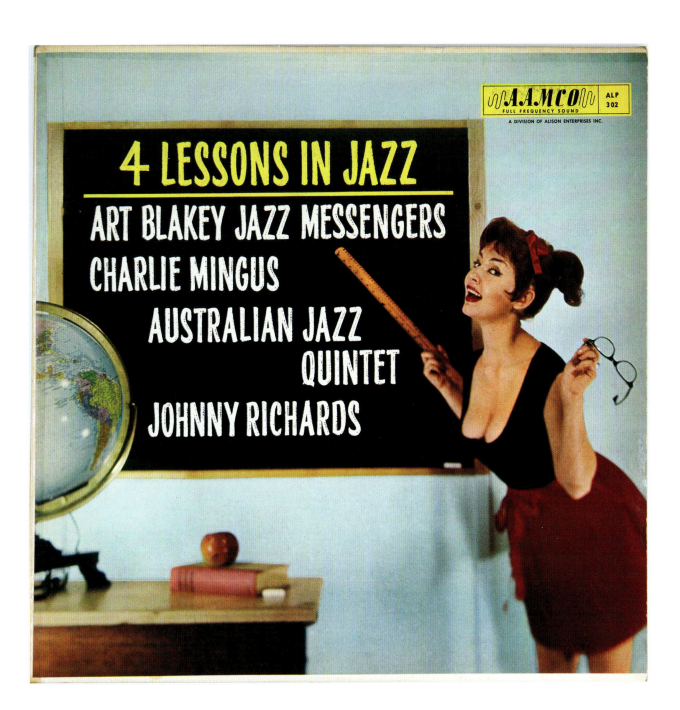

FIGURE 11.5

4 Lessons in Jazz,
AAMCO ALP 302, 1958.

Masquerade Is Over," and "St. Louis Blues," all enthusiastically received by the collegiate audiences, as evidenced by the approving applause on the record. The erudite, enlightening notes were penned by legendary producer George Avakian, who, as noted upon his death at ninety-eight in 2017, "was involved in virtually every facet of the music industry. He helped popularize the long-playing record; organized the first jazz reissue series, preserving the recorded legacies of Louis Armstrong and other pioneers."[14] Avakian helped transform Brubeck and other jazz luminaries, such as Miles Davis, "from artists with a loyal but limited audience to international celebrities."[15] Avakian's notes provide context for Brubeck's college tours: "Campus concerts prior to the early fifties consisted of classical music series sponsored by the schools; beginning in 1952, student organizations, or small groups of students acting with the faculty permission but independently of an official university group, began to engage jazz artists to appear on individual concerts."

On the cover, striking white space sets off a convertible with three passengers, two of them clearly of the younger set. Red, yellow, and blue painted lettering spell out "Dave Brubeck Quartet." The cover photo was shot by Garry Winogrand, "widely considered one of the greatest photographers of the twentieth century."[16] (His name is misspelled as "Gary" on the front cover.) Winogrand shot hundreds of thousands of photographs in his lifetime, but only a few ended up on album covers. Aptly, one can be found on Leonard Bernstein and the New York Philharmonic's recording of *Pictures at an Exhibition* (1959). Another showed up on the cover of the rock band Interpol's *Marauder* in 2018. The back cover of *Jazz Goes to Junior College* includes a promotion for Columbia's line of record players and hi-fi consoles, with a photo of model 530. They promise "guaranteed high fidelity and hemispheric sound."

LEONARD BERNSTEIN CONDUCTS FOR YOUNG PEOPLE was a spinoff of Bernstein's cherished Young People's Concerts with the New York Philharmonic. Running from 1958 to 1972, the concerts, according to Bernstein's legacy website, "stand among his greatest achievements. These televised programs introduced an entire generation to the joys of classical music."[17]

The notes emphasize the "story" aspect of classical music, but insist that "one of the qualities that all great orchestral compositions have in common is that they can be enjoyed purely as musical sound." The album was produced by John McClure, who worked with Bernstein on almost two hundred albums. McClure, who won several Grammy Awards for classical albums, "helped shape some of the most celebrated classical recordings of the 20th century."[18] His production work ranged beyond Bernstein and Beethoven—he helped produce Dave Brubeck and Peter, Paul, and Mary, and he also contributed to engineering Pink Floyd's *The Wall* (1979).

Cover photography is by Don Hunstein, a staff photographer for Columbia Records, who produced hundreds of album covers from the 1950s through to the 1980s. Perhaps best known for the cover of *The Freewheelin' Bob Dylan* (1963), he also shot several covers for the eccentric and exceedingly talented pianist Glenn Gould, who often refused to have his picture taken.

FIGURE 11.6

Jazz Goes to Junior College,
Dave Brubeck Quartet, Columbia CL 1034;
photo by Garry Winogrand, 1957.

Leonard Bernstein Conducts for Young People provides a voluminous amount of recording data: recorded in Columbia's "360 Sound," "the ultimate in listening enjoyment," with "sixteen-channel consoles and custom-calibrated tape machines," using microphones "chosen for their individual sound properties depending upon the orchestration," and edited on equipment "hand-tooled by Columbia's engineering staff." The cover art mixes colorful illustrated brass instruments and black-and-white photos, but the liner notes specifically call attention to the lettering for album and song titles. The handwriting was done by "Tako Suzuki, age 9." The son of two commercial artists, Suzuki grew up to be an artist in his own right and now teaches at the School of the Arts in New York City. When contacted in 2022, Suzuki reported that he recognized his handwriting, but had little memory of contributing to the cover design. He was delighted to hear from us, and we were delighted to connect with the precocious album cover artist.

CLASSICAL MUSIC FOR PEOPLE WHO DON'T KNOW ANYTHING ABOUT CLASSICAL MUSIC turns out to be less of an instructional album and more of an orchestral music sampler. Most of the selections are firmly in the canon of classical music—that is, they are widely played in concerts and have been recorded over and over again. Many are considered exemplars of the "romantic" period, which exerted a profound influence on twentieth-century film music.

So, even if listeners are unfamiliar with the music, the pieces may sound familiar from movies. And, of course, Merrie Melodies cartoons regularly ransacked the classics. Who can forget Bugs Bunny and Elmer Fudd in *What's Opera, Doc?* (1957), singing selections, in their own special way, from Richard Wagner's bombastic and impossibly romantic operatic works? For Fudd fans, *Classical Music for People Who Don't Know Anything About Classical Music* includes an excerpt from Wagner's *Tannhäuser Overture*. Other highlights include the *Peer Gynt Suite*, by Norwegian composer Edvard Grieg, written for his countryman Henrik Ibsen's surrealist play *Peer Gynt* (1876) and memorably whistled by the actor Peter Lorre in Fritz Lang's haunting film *M* (1931); Beethoven's Symphony No. 5, with its famous first four notes; and Tchaikovsky's Symphony No. 6, known as Sonata Pathétique, which had often been used in films and popular songs.

These "warhorses" certainly provide a thoughtful introduction to classical music, but it remains unclear if they will be enjoyed by "people who don't know anything about classical music." The RCA Victor Orchestra is conducted by Robert Russell Bennett, known for his Tony Award–winning work for Broadway and Hollywood; he orchestrated for Irving Berlin, George Gershwin, Cole Porter, and Richard Rogers, among others. The cover photo, which resembles a fashion magazine layout, shows a model coyly cocking her head, caressing her ear with its large, sparkly earring, perhaps to better hear the music. Blurred in the background sits her listening companion, apparently enthralled with . . . the music. One of our favorite midcentury album cover artists, Wendy (Wendlyn) Hilty, shot the photo in his characteristic stagey, glamorous style.[19] It may be his wife, Violette, in the picture—he included her on several album covers,

FIGURE 11.7

Leonard Bernstein Conducts for Young People,
New York Philharmonic, Columbia MS 6441;
photos by Robert F. Seraping–Birnback Publishing Service/Don Hunstein,
lettering by Taro Suzuki, age 9, 1963.

FIGURE 11.8

*Classical Music for People Who Don't Know Anything
About Classical Music*,
RCA Victor Symphony conducted by Robert Russell Bennett,
RCA Victor LM 2140;
photo by Wendy Hilty, 1957.

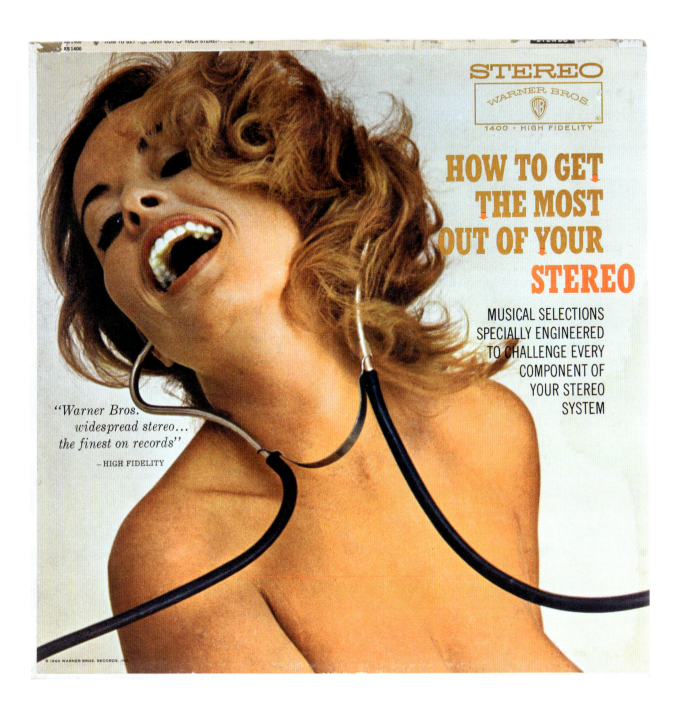

FIGURE 11.9

How to Get the Most Out of Your Stereo,
Warner Bros. WB XS 1400, 1960.

including RCA's *A Night in Acapulco* (1956) and, apparently, *Music for a Backyard Barbecue* (1959), although she was not credited.[20]

An elated honey-blonde throws back her head in dual channel ecstasy on **HOW TO GET THE MOST OUT OF YOUR STEREO**. Fueled by stethoscope signals from two separate "hearts," each ear receives distinct stimulations. The record includes "musical selections specially engineered to challenge every component of your stereo system" and apparently is best enjoyed in the nude.

Technological innovations pronounce improvement, and the stereo LP was no different. Dozens of records introduced listeners to stereo when it was launched in 1958. Stereo demonstration records showed off the innovative qualities of the new stereo sound, with tracks for "balancing signals" or doing "speaker-response checks." Curious listeners could hear trains chugging from left to right, wow at the roar of passing warplanes, and catch children's energetic voices as they dashed across playgrounds.[21]

But how to visually communicate stereo? Catchy graphics, of course, such as Columbia's 360 Sound "arrows," RCA Living Stereo's flowing diagram, and Stereo Fidelity Records' full-color sound spectrum. Midcentury RCA Victor records came with an inner sleeve full of helpful stereophonic schematics: "For the first time, your ears will be able to distinguish where each instrument and voice comes from—left, right or center."

And Warner Bros.? How about sex appeal? *How to Get the Most Out of Your Stereo*, from 1960, with its cheesecake cover, is just what the doctor ordered. The liner notes provide titillating details about recording technique—left, center, and right—for "spaciousness and depth." The director of engineering at Warner Bros. Records describes "the illusion of a Center or Third Track."

The back cover includes ten critical review snippets that sing the praises of Warner Bros.' stereo sound. *High Fidelity Magazine* notes: "From the stereo there issues forth a widespread cascade of sparkling notes from a golden background of sumptuous orchestral sound." Each track demonstrates some aspect of stereo sound reproduction. There's "excellent separation" in "Theme from Mickey Mouse Club"; right and left stereo tracks for "the two 'chambers' of the orchestra" on "Singin' in the Rain"; and "spectacular ping-pong effects, extreme movement, and other deliberate distortions of the 'aural third dimension'" on "Two Heads Are Better than One." Hear, hear.

IV

ON VINYL AND CULTURAL HISTORY

The vast range of midcentury records provides a unique portal into the hopes and dreams of the United States. Whereas the cultural, political, and social facets of midcentury film, literature, television, and art are well established, less attention had been paid to vinyl record albums and the roles they played at midcentury. We set out to change that. Record albums, as multimedia objects, offer numerous dimensions to consider, including cover design, liner notes, the recording itself, the physicality of the object, and how records are consumed, listened to, marketed, collected, and integrated into daily lives and social practice.

At midcentury, phonographs and records functioned as something of an equalizing force: they disseminated knowledge, news, and entertainment and sometimes offered a platform for those who would not have had their voices widely heard. Mainstream broadcasting didn't host all voices; many kinds of music didn't get played on the airwaves either. But if you could make a record and find a path for distribution, the previously unheard voice might cultivate an audience. In addition, the usually unaddressed audience gained integrity, community, and otherwise-unavailable know-how for appropriate vocal tone, Latin dance steps, or swimming strokes.

The history of the recording industry often focuses on greatness—great inventors, great musical artists, greatest hits. But another facet of the story concerns the early promise of records as instructional tools, and the ways in which such records tapped into America's deepest longings.

12

A HISTORY OF
INSTRUCTIONAL
RECORDINGS

Midcentury records designed for success and promoting self-improvement, whether preserving the hunting advice of a famous bowman or offering *Bazaar* magazine–approved exercise regimens, fell within the phonograph's original verbal purview. Whereas spoken-word vinyl records might initially seem like outliers, familiar as we are with music recordings for dancing and romancing, the phonograph in fact emerged with goals and intentions for capturing and reproducing the human voice—though not always a singing voice.

Recorded music dominates the perception of the recording industry and its histories, yet instructional records have been produced since the earliest days of recorded sound. Instructional records amplify a parallel history to music-centered narratives of the recording industry.[1] The call to listen and learn was not limited to scales, sonatas, and symphonies. Recording technology provided the means to capture the world of sound, including, of course, the human domains of music and speech. The sounds of nature, too, wound up on record—birdsong, ocean waves, even injured rabbit cries.

Instructional records can be considered a form of educational technology. Long before computers entered the classroom, phonographs played their part in pedagogical practice.[2] By 1906, International Correspondence Schools introduced a set of Language System records, "approved by the highest educational authorities in the land, and by the French, German, and Spanish embassies."[3] By the 1910s, schools were urged to adopt phonographs for instructional purposes, along with motion picture machines, lantern slides, and player pianos.[4] By the 1960s, almost every US classroom had at least one record player.

THE PHONOGRAPH: LAYING THE GROOVES FOR INSTRUCTION

The educational use of recordings tells a compelling story: "As an instructional technology, the phonograph marked a new era and challenged traditional conceptions of when, where, and how learning could take place."[5] Further, "with the introduction of the telephone, the phonograph, and then radio, there was a revolution in our aural environment that prompted a major perceptual and cognitive shift in the country, with a new emphasis on hearing."[6] As media theorist John Durham Peters has proposed, "In many ways the phonograph is a more shocking emblem of modernity than the photograph."[7] Preserving images had numerous historical precedents, such as drawing and painting, preserving sound had none.

Soon after inventing the phonograph, Thomas Edison sketched out what he thought were its most promising uses, including recording dictated letters for business, documents for family chronicles, and materials for education, as well as literature and music.[8] "Of all the writer's inventions," he wrote, "none has commanded such profound and earnest attention throughout the civilized world as has the phonograph. This fact he attributes largely to that peculiarity of the invention which brings its possibilities within range of the speculative imaginations of all thinking people, as well as to the almost universal applicability of the foundation principle, namely, the gathering up and retaining of sounds hitherto fugitive, and their reproduction at will."[9] The phonograph, which media historian Lisa Gitelman calls "mechanically inscribed sound," excited Edison's imagination for "automatic" reproduction of the human voice. "As Edison conceived it," Gitelman writes, "the phonograph would be a business machine for the conversion of aural experience into *records*—permanent, portable, reproducible inscriptions. The aural experience he had foremost in mind was clearly speech, not music."[10]

Edison focused on the way recording transformed sound into a repeatable phenomenon; the phonograph provided "for an indefinite repetition of the same thing."[11] He identified education as a primary function of the phonograph, particularly for music: "As a musical teacher it will be used to enable one to master a new air, the child to form its first songs, or to sing him to sleep."[12] In the 1890s, although educational recordings continued to be produced, the industry shifted its focus to selling recordings of music, as the talking machine transformed into a kind of musical instrument itself.[13]

Early uses of the phonograph also included recording sales pitches and product instructions, in a protoadvertising format, sometimes amplified with megaphones to reach more potential customers.[14] However, business uses of recordings were soon surpassed by entertainment.[15] Pioneering firms in the recording business, such as Columbia, originally attracted by the corporate applications of recording technology, such as dictation, soon realized that they were in the music business.[16]

Most media historians think Edison got it wrong. Indeed, as musical recordings came to dominate the phonograph industry, the use of recorded dictation largely faded away. However, instructional records played significant roles in each phase of the recording industry's growth, and their educational purposes offered potent propaganda for the industry's positive social role. In particular, music appreciation and spoken word records were touted as a way to lift the cultural literacy of the United States.

Recordings of complete books were introduced in the 1930s, spurred on by the Library of Congress's Books for the Adult Blind Project, which included over one thousand titles by 1945. The long-playing format album, introduced in 1948, sparked a boom in recording, including instructional and spoken-word albums; its longer length allowed for extended readings of literature, plays, and poetry, as well as more detailed instructional records.

Spoken-word records helped pave the way for today's audiobooks, which now make up a considerable share of publisher profits.[17] Caedmon Records, founded in 1952 by Barbara Holdridge and Marianne Mantell, specialized in spoken word and produced such well-received recordings as the complete works of Shakespeare and Arthur Miller's *Death of a Salesman*.[18] Caedmon offered "a third dimension for the printed page" with their efforts "to translate traditional forms of high culture into media formats associated with modern popular culture."[19] In this way, "spoken word genres played an important role in establishing a popular market for the LP and demonstrated that the long-playing record could be defined in a variety of ways. When the economic and cultural ascendancy of rock music coincided with the emergence of new media platforms that usurped some of the LP's functions in the home, spoken word genres were pushed to the peripheries of the industry."[20]

Along with recorded books and poetry, spoken-word titles range beyond the instructional. In the industry's initial phases, these records encompassed field recordings by anthropologists, family conversations, oral histories, recordings for the blind, comedy acts, theatrical productions, and political speeches. As media historian Jacob Smith observed: "Between the 1890s and 1920s, record companies released a wide range of material in a surprising array of genres, including historical reenactments, descriptive sketches, and comedy routines from the vaudeville and minstrel stage: a stunning diversity of cultural artifacts whose utility for historians is only beginning to be appreciated. Music became the dominant recorded genre only in the 1910s and 1920s, in part as a means to secure middle class consumers, for whom highbrow music was an important form of social distinction."[21]

From the earliest days of the phonograph, customers were encouraged to think of their purchases as acts of discernment aimed at "improving" their musicality, showing off their taste, and signaling their modernity and sophistication. The Victor Talking Machine Company "succeeded brilliantly in making the phonograph into something that many middle-class Americans wanted to listen to in their homes, and they claimed that they improved the musical tastes of the nation."[22] In 1927, on the fiftieth anniversary of Thomas Edison's introduction of the "talking machine," the phonograph was celebrated as "a medium of entertainment and education."[23]

According to Gitelman, in early incarnations of the phonograph Edison, along with influential cultural critic Matthew Arnold, looked to esteemed cultural and individual human accomplishment as potential "preserved" content. Such recordings included literature read by the author, philosophical thought, and presidential speeches.[24] In what she deems an "enactment of cultural hierarchy," opportunities for designating distinctions in mechanical amusement—for example, between edifying and uncouth, with the latter often attracting attention and dollars—immediately emerged.

The reproducibility and repetition of sound, including the human voice, along with sonic scenarios, made possible not only the hoped-for "capture" of the great and good but also something quite different: "The public capaciousness of the phonograph seemed to ask for the low, the other, the infantile—the pro- or protosemiotic—all performed cathartically within the respectability of the middle-class lecture space and its rational, technocratic weal."[25] Elements of "low" culture may have met industry expectations for the entertainment value of sound recordings—jokes, stereotypical accents, humorous scenarios.

Whereas classical music albums signaled high culture, many recordings offered fun and frolic and fantasy, including music for dancing, romancing, and dreaming. However, midcentury records promising *Music for Courage and Confidence*, training for *Effective Listening*, and the basic principles to *Think and Grow Rich* present enlightened reflections and a reach for public betterment in the original spirit of Edison's invention.

MUSIC APPRECIATION BY PHONOGRAPH: IMPROVING THE MASSES AND MARKETING PLOY

Music appreciation was recruited to burnish the phonograph's reputation. The burgeoning recording industry promoted the notion that having a phonograph in the home brought "refinement and taste" through listening to classical music. A 1906 article in the industry journal *Talking Machine World* emphasized the phonograph's role in "spreading civilization."[26] Aside from spoken-word instruction, recordings were considered a crucial way to introduce "refined" music to the masses. As fittingly named music educator Francis Horn remarked: "The tremendous upsurge in popularity of the phonograph, especially of high fidelity instruments, and the lowered cost of long-playing records, bring the world's finest music within reach of increasing numbers of individuals."[27]

During the early twentieth century, the popularity of jazz, "race" records, and other, less "cultured" genres had prompted widespread—and often racist—criticism of the recording industry's cultural influence. Under attack for promoting "the moral dangers associated with popular music," recording companies and gramophone manufacturers emphasized the educational and uplifting potential of listening to and learning about classical music in the comfort of home.[28] For example, in the 1920s, Victor stressed the enriching, instructional aspects of their records—"to create the impression, mainly through advertising, that the phonograph could be an educational instrument without peer that would be an asset in any home or classroom."[29]

In his history of the classical recording industry, educational theorist Colin Symes discusses the cultural discourses that supported the recording industry's growth and suggests that people could "be persuaded that it might be in their social interest to do so [buy records], on the grounds that owning discs offers manifold moral and aesthetic dividends."[30] One such discourse, the music appreciation movement, responded to the growing market for popular (and for some, less desirable) music, by emphasizing the classical tradition. As one music educator explains: "There is actually no reason why music—traditionally known as the common language—cannot lead the school community and develop, through the sharing of vital and meaningful educational materials, wiser and better-prepared world citizens."[31]

As the music appreciation movement endorsed classical recordings, record players were developed into articles of furniture and promoted as part of any sophisticated home.[32] Manufacturers marketed the phonograph "by distancing it from its own technological past and role as an arcade novelty" and emphasizing "its role as edifying musical furniture, an unobtrusive presence in the idealized environment of family life."[33] Thus, the phonograph "was part of a larger context of consumption, during a period when domestic space was modernized and commercialized."[34]

Part of the phonograph's appeal—at least as described in early twentieth-century advertising and promotion—was its potential to educate and uplift. Phonographs were touted as tools to turn the home into "more than an escape from job, market, and public strife; it could become a haven of family togetherness."[35] By 1914, phonographs outsold pianos, and, by the early 1920s, there were over 150 phonograph manufacturers in the United States alone.[36]

An early instructional "hit" was well-known baritone Oscar Saenger's vocal-training records—a complete course of study for the tenor voice released on Victor records in 1916. A Victor gramophone ad from 1918 "emphasized the educational potential of its product in helping to teach roller-skating, calisthenics, kindergarten games, penmanship, maypole dancing, typewriting, something called 'girls' classes in rhythmic expression,' wireless telegraphy to the Army and Navy, and French to the doughboys, all of this in addition to the history of music."[37] Instructional records were not limited to academic subjects—in 1922, Victor introduced Records for Health Exercises, paving the way for midcentury albums like Bonnie Prudden's *Keep Fit / Be Happy*, Debbie Drake's *Feel Good! Look Great!*, and Indra Devi's *Yoga for Americans*.

The recording industry enthusiastically embraced the notion that listening to and learning from records helped to establish and maintain the "right" musical taste: "The advocates of music appreciation determined that recording would have an assured place in the classroom and play its role in combating the damaging effects of inferior music. In this respect, music teachers enlisted the services of the gramophone to broaden the musical tastes of the population and establish the foundations of more discriminating musical taste."[38]

From 1928 to 1942, the NBC radio network broadcast *The Music Appreciation Hour*, which presented live performances of orchestral music, analysis, and commentary during school hours "to supplement rather than supplant local instruction in the appreciation of music, by presenting through the medium of broadcasting a type of program not otherwise available in the average school."[39] Lists of phonograph recordings were provided to schools, teachers were urged to play recordings from the broadcast, and students were encouraged to buy their own records for home study. The music appreciation movement mirrored efforts to make literature and "great books" readily available through reading groups, the Book-of-the-Month Club, university extension courses, radio programs, as well as spoken-word and instructional records.[40]

THE TALKING MACHINE AS TEACHING MACHINE: PHONOGRAPHS AS EDUCATIONAL TECHNOLOGY

The phonograph's impact on teaching and pedagogy offers a counterpoint to its influence on recorded music. Early critics of the phonograph worried that listening to and learning from records might interfere with literacy development. Responding to such concerns, the Victor Talking Machine Company "took the high road in defense of its national cultural influence."[41] In 1911, Victor created an educational division, headed by Frances E. Clark, who defined her mission as "serving the children of America and building business for Victor dealers through work in the schools teaching millions of children to think of the Victor."[42] The company also introduced a "School House" phonograph, designed for educational use.

Victor called the phonograph a "universal pedagogic machine," with an enlightened mission: "The coming of the Victrola into the schools and into the homes of the millions has been a godsend to the race. It has brought music, greatest of all arts, to the many, to every child, and to every human heart."[43] Their extensive *Educational Catalog and Graded List of Victor Records for Home, School, and College*, distributed during the 1920s and 1930s, included "records selected because of cultural and educational value or, especially made for some definite educational purpose."[44] The list encompassed children's records, broken down by grade and subject; instrumental and vocal recordings; music history; language (including ancient Hebrew and Latin); music instruction, whereby "children first hear the melodies on records, then they go to the piano"; as well as "correlation of music with other subjects," such as American history, geography, and physical education, which included ballet, folk dances, and rhythmic activity and mimetic play.

The phonograph's distinctive qualities included affordability, portability, and repeatability.[45] Composer Aaron Copland recognized a key quality of recorded music: "The phonograph has the inestimable advantage of giving the listener what he wants when he wants it."[46] Particularly when compared to radio and television, the repetitive possibilities of records offered listeners unique opportunities for repeat playing and rote learning.

In contrast to broadcast programs, instructional records did not include advertising. Records could be listened to on your own schedule, repeatedly, and were an owned or loaned object. As a 1934 Decca Records advertisement proclaimed about their recordings: "Hear them when you want—as *often* as you want."[47] For instructors, "recordings are 'two-way' communication. You can stop a recording to discuss passages, to answer questions, and to clarify certain points. Recordings are controlled by *you*."[48] One principal extolled the benefits of not just using audiovisual equipment in the classroom, but "the value that accrues to the boys who are taught to operate and maintain this equipment."[49] (It seems only boys were offered a chance to "crew.")

During World War II, the US Army developed Specialized Training Programs, which deployed an array of audiovisual aids, including phonographs and magnetic tape recorders to teach foreign languages, Morse code, air traffic signals, and communications protocol.[50] Recordings were "effectively employed to simulate sounds of equipment, actual combat noises, and other sounds of military life."[51] Training records produced for the British military during World War II taught listeners to distinguish between the sounds of German and of British submarines and led to significant advances in high-fidelity recording that eventually found their way to the mass market.[52] Phonographs were also noted for their use in teaching displaced persons English in the wake of World War II.[53] Several records included here, such as *Learn the International Morse Code* and the Living Language series, evolved from military use.

Classroom use of instructional records expanded after the war, too. In an influential manual on audiovisual instruction from 1954, educational theorist Edgar Dale pointed out: "The delight that a record player can stimulate in children is obvious here. And the wide variety of excellent recordings readily available makes it easy for the teacher to use the machine as a regular teaching tool. These children are not sitting quietly at their desk. But are they listening intently?"[54] In considering records for teaching literature, he suggested that recordings can be used to "teach listening," to "provide background for the study of literature and language," to "help students experience the dramatic in the classroom," to "enliven the reading of poetry," and to "celebrate holidays."[55] A focus on "critical listening" informs these insights into the phonograph's educational potential. For Dale, the "the critical listener . . . makes it a point to listen attentively to materials that are important to his life."[56]

In response to Cold War concerns over the state of American education, the National Defense Education Act of 1958 "made funds available for the utilization of new media of communication in the educational program offered by the public schools. The purpose of this provision was to bring about improved educational opportunities for youth and thus strengthen the security of the nation."[57] Along with extensive funding from the Rockefeller Foundation, the Ford Foundation, and the Payne Fund, the act financed a boom in audiovisual equipment in classrooms throughout the country, including phonographs and instructional recordings, and promoted their use by schools.[58]

Thus, by midcentury, record players were an essential tool for most schools in the United States. A 1962 guide to audiovisual instruction stipulates one record player per classroom for primary grades, one per two classrooms for intermediate grades.[59] Another period primer notes: "Phono equipment is manufactured largely for the 'home market.' Many of the models, styles and brands from which the educator must choose have modern lines, but not ruggedness; compactness, but not fidelity; excellent reproduction, but not durability."[60] In setting up a language lab, one writer offered this detailed advice: "It should be mentioned that when buying such phonograph records, stipulation must be made that individual recordings be replaced as needed or desired, for obviously the introductory platters are worn out far more rapidly than the more advanced."[61]

Of course, instructional technology is big business, and successful selling to school districts could mean big profits. Writing in 1961, a financial analyst predicted profitability for "programmed teaching" that included phonographs and other instructional technology: "The tools of programmed teaching are thus already being translated into commercial services and products, around which an entire industry is just coming into being and significant sales and profits should not be too long in coming."[62]

As a 1963 *New York Times* review stated: "The latest releases in children's records give assurance . . . that no phase of the child's development—physical, cultural, intellectual—is being neglected."[63] Folkways Records released extensive educational record catalogs, which included titles like *Children's Jamaican Songs and Games* (1957) and *Teaching Reading in the Elementary School* (1965).[64] Although classroom use of phonographs waned by the 1980s, up until then, record players, used for solo listening through headphones and for communal instruction, formed a significant component of educational technology. Today, of course, podcasts, YouTube videos, Zoom sessions, educational subscriptions like Masterclass with their slogan "gain new skills in 10 minutes," and television shows have taken over the instructional realm, as virtual reality and artificial intelligence loom as the next paradigm shifting instructional technologies.

INSTRUCTIONAL FILM VERSUS INSTRUCTIONAL RECORDS

Like instructional records, classroom, educational, and training films tackled an incredibly broad range of topics, including etiquette, interpersonal skills, personal hygiene, career training, industrial skills, languages, anthropology, and history.[65] Instructional film comprises an extensive array of documentaries, newsreels, and public service messages. (Jonathan has fond memories of watching the 1968 National Geographic documentary *The Lonely Dorymen* in elementary school—lights dimmed, projector whirring, popcorn brought in under special dispensation.)

Both instructional films and instructional records strain against the category of "entertainment." Analogous to the way music dominates research on the recording industry, considering film as primarily entertainment obscures the large and tremendously varied realm of "useful cinema."[66] Both instructional records and instructional films have fallen under the radar.[67] Both are important—if unheralded—contributors to the imaginative world of self-improvement, uplift, and pedagogical histories.

However, several significant distinctions mark differences between instructional records and instructional films. First, of course, instructional films emphasize looking as well as listening. Second, instructional films were usually shown in communal settings, such as workplaces, schools, churches, public libraries, private clubs, and community organizations.[68] Instructional records were also played in such settings, especially schools, but most were marketed to the home listener. Third, films were usually owned or rented by organizations, whereas records were generally meant for private consumption, with the exception of language records, which often belonged to school or university language labs. Record players and record collections formed a ubiquitous part of the modern home. Records were portable, and could be played by anyone with access to a record player, including one of the many portable record players that were produced. During midcentury, relatively few households had access to personal projectors; the market for consumer film equipment, which took off in the 1960s, was driven by shooting your own home movies, not viewing commercially produced titles. Fourth, records were meant to be listened to repeatedly—an aspect stressed on many instructional albums. Instructional and industrial films generally were meant to be viewed once, limiting their intended effect and freezing their viewing experience in time.

The ownability, portability, and repeatability of instructional records mark a major experiential difference from instructional film. Further, instructional film hews toward public, civic, and corporate uses. Instructional records, while embodying a public dimension, were generally experienced in private, in the home, heard on the domestic hi-fi set, or through language lab headphones. In this way, instructional records blurred lines between private and public, between home and work, and between occupation and leisure.

THE TRANSFORMATIONAL PHONOGRAPH

The utopian author Edward Bellamy foresaw the phonograph's potential for the self-improvement and designed for success genre. In his 1889 *Harper's* story "With the Eyes Shut," the narrator notes how people change after listening to "new-fashioned phonographed books and magazines"; they appear "emotionally" altered. The phonographic texts "also bodily liberate them: posture is better and eyesight improved."[69] Quite a transformation.

CONCLUSION
MIDCENTURY RECORDS AND
THE CREATION OF MODERN AMERICA

We had a hunch.

Midcentury vinyl record albums were neglected. Especially the ones we loved and collected.

These record albums, we mused, are unexpectedly spectacular elements of midcentury media. They reveal fascinating aspects of the era's cultural history. No one else has taken these records seriously, we thought. We should write a book!

As we conclude the third volume of our *Designed For* trilogy, we recognize that our insight proved more profound than we initially anticipated.

Yes: as a vital component of US material culture, midcentury records did serve as an information distribution format for shaping modern visions. They also played an essential role in building participatory democracy in postwar America, aligning the populace with strategic postwar projects. Yet, beyond this, midcentury records mobilized the most basic individual human processes and practices for molding mind and body and transforming self and country.

By explicating and laying out for examination midcentury vinyl records and their covers, we witness their influence on domestic spaces, social relationships, aspirational self-development, educational technology, and career training. Record albums embraced not only practices of consumption but also pedagogical ideologies—teaching a citizenry the basics of learning how to learn. Consuming ideas, consuming identities, consuming knowledge: these all are crucial in a participatory democracy. The willingness and ability to take in, process, and mobilize information—indeed, the willingness to be instructed—form the most basic aspects of a consumer culture populace. In this sense, education is a consumption practice, the consumption of information, most obviously, and also, perhaps, knowledge. There is no postwar consumer culture (or enlightenment, for that matter) without developing and evolving philosophies and techniques of education, instruction, and training. There is no marketing, branding, or advertising for the future of postwar modern America without this.

Teaching and learning for the sake of building a participatory democracy in a consumer culture requires philosophies, strategies, lessons, and even visual schematics

—dance steps, exercise routines, atomic particles—that, it turns out, fit, folded and flat, inside midcentury record albums.

Designed-for-success LPs encouraged better living—at work, home, and leisure. They provided recorded advice on topics as varied as raising a family, playing bongos, cooking Italian, and expanding mind power. Instructional records recruited private domestic space for training and skill development.[1] They also depended on personal motivation for self-improvement. For example, the US Army's *How to Succeed* record, with its charmingly earnest set of radio spots, promises that "with Army, a future you can choose." These often prosaic instructional records promoted progress and reinforced the United States' deeply rooted do-it-yourself aesthetic. In this way, they offer an unexpected yet enlightening lens for understanding midcentury contributions to the American prospect.

The predilection for self-improvement, whether honing innate abilities, deepening comprehension, or keeping one's body toned and strong, is surely not a uniquely US phenomenon, yet instructional and self-improvement records from the United States do offer a distinctly national narrative. For example, albums from Amway Corporation specifically name and honor the "American Way"—a biblical claim to capitalist free enterprise, entrepreneurial invention, and deep anti-communist instincts. Many other records build upon ostensibly long-term American values and traditions involving individual ingenuity and initiative in the face of vast territory, opportunity, and choice in ways that echo notions of manifest destiny.[2]

Motivational inducements to claim more and to reach farther suggest possibilities of endless growth, progress, and wealth for individuals bold enough to continue moving forward, onward, and up. Midcentury instructional records promised gratifying achievements, fulfilled fantasies, and satisfied desires and offered inroads to previously unknown destinies. Certainly, the implications of such visions—for the realities of competition, cooperation, and negotiation—reverberate more broadly on the global stage.

At midcentury, the Cold War suffused contemporary living in the United States. Indeed, the home formed an important site for embodying visions of a good life during a period dominated by dueling superpowers and American concerns to "contain" Soviet Communism. The capitalist realism that infuses so much designed-for-success album art reconfigured national goals and domestic soft power communications. On these covers, monochrome images free of fantasy capture ordinary midcentury Americans experiencing progress, equality of opportunity, and new challenges in everyday settings.

In his analysis of the intricate history of how modernism—which started as a "cause" and became a "style"—engaged with ideological propaganda, cultural historian Greg Barnhisel identifies what he deems "Cold War modernism." The argument is complex: what began as a modernist rejection of tradition came, in time, to stand in for fundamental "American" values, including freedom of expression, cultural achievement, and individual (and consumer) sovereignty. Even as modernism "retained its associations with innovation and the drive for the new, modernism also came to be presented as a pro-Western, pro-'freedom,' and pro-bourgeois movement, evidence of the superiority of the Western way of life."[3] In this way, "tradition"—often lauded on the home front—took a backseat internationally to modernist ideals that were adapted for propaganda purposes.[4] We see that capitalist realism helped to conjure traditional "let's get down to business" values while at the same time pushing agendas for a more modern, market-driven America.

The United States recruited "cultural weapons" of modern design, abstract art, and jazz in its claims for modern consumer sovereignty and freedom of expression. Abstract art, with its emphasis on creativity and subjectivity, was held up as an example of American freedom; jazz, with its integral mode of individual improvisation, was extolled as a key contribution to world culture. For example, at the American National Exhibition held in Moscow in 1959, the US Information Agency exhibited American art, including Jackson Pollock's abstract canvasses. The free expression seen in modern abstract art served as a riposte against state-sanctioned Soviet realism as commandeered for political propaganda. Billed as a trade fair, the Moscow exhibition became a battleground for a riveting cultural clash in the era's Cold War skirmishes. US manufacturers were invited to ship over their best and brightest products, in a concerted effort to show the Soviets—and the world—the superiority of the American free enterprise system. Soviet visitors marveled at gleaming kitchen appliances (the backdrop for the famous "kitchen debate" between Soviet premier Nikita Khrushchev and US vice president Richard Nixon), streamlined automobiles, the latest American fashion, and shelves of books.

Also on display in Moscow? A selection of midcentury vinyl records, favoring classical and jazz, their $12'' \times 12''$ covers celebrating a world beyond the Iron Curtain.

Thus, basic components of US consumer culture, such as appliances, art, books, fashion, furniture, and vinyl records contributed to Cold War cultural diplomacy and pinpoint how the rise of postwar consumer culture intersected with global politics and ideology.

Midcentury records promoting international travel and language learning resonate with the potential of an affable, global citizen: meet new friends; gain an appreciation of other cultures; bring home memories, souvenirs, expanded vocabularies, and novel ideas. This genre opens understandings to previously unknown peoples and suggests positive forms of attachment and admiration. For example, studying Italian or Arabic or Japanese may serve as the overture to an unforgettable romantic encounter (often hinted at on language instruction records) that alters feelings of homegrown supremacy and fundamentally changes the way one sees the world. Learning to cook Brazilian dishes and dance the Rhumba might lead to increased enjoyment of exotic flavors and steps, as well as suitably matched musical accompaniment. Becoming more cosmopolitan through awareness of worlds beyond one's own can be relatively benign, if not wholly beneficial.

However, learning a country's language or dances or traditional foodways is often a first step toward mining its potentials, whether for conducting academic research, influencing international policy, or extracting natural resources. (Some midcentury language records mention the US military and Department of Defense, drawing on government teaching techniques and earning commendation from them.) Further, the quest for engagement with other cultures can take the form of acquisition, or collection. International travel opens up opportunities to buy and own (legally or otherwise) other peoples' material culture, whether souvenir scarves and traditional musical instruments or chunks of historical structures and once-buried treasures. Such artifacts may simply be displayed and shared as mementos; they also offer raw materials for creating profitable music, design, or "new" cuisine that passes no recognition or advantage back to the originators. Foreign appropriation of cultural resources may disrupt the ability of native peoples to value their history, tell their own stories, and benefit from their own innovations and cultural developments.

Most of the LPs presented here involve instruction and improvement for the US environments of work, home, and leisure. In these contexts, individuals focus on and alter themselves. In so doing, listeners potentially improve their social as well as economic community, within what has been called the "therapeutic discourse."[5] However, by suggesting that the viewpoints, priorities, advice, and admonitions heard on midcentury records addressed and suited everyone—including unknown others in different circumstances and from varied cultural backgrounds, whether within the United States or abroad—the albums paint a homogenizing, if imperialist, picture. We love our records, but they are not without their limitations.

Our first volume in the trilogy, *Designed for Hi-Fi Living: The Vinyl LP in Midcentury America*, provided a broad framework for thinking about midcentury vinyl albums. We showed how album covers could be productively considered media objects with communicative functions beyond identifying performers, recording genres, or album content. Indeed, midcentury album covers taught lessons about modern values.[6] We argued that covers from the 1950s and 1960s offered postwar America modernist visions and alluring lessons for achieving cosmopolitan and contemporary lifestyles fueled by a consumer culture of options, choice, and consumer sovereignty in contrast to Soviet models. The ideal home, the ideal living room, the ideal romance, the ideal honeymoon, and the ideal family—not to mention national Cold War victories in the kitchen and in outer space—all were visible, tangible, achievable, in the fantastical frame of the LP cover.

Our second record-related volume, *Designed for Dancing: How Midcentury Records Taught America to Dance*, revealed that fun, colorful, and sometimes provocative cha-cha-cha, tango, limbo, and twist records reflected similar concerns. Dances, from the waltz to Watusi, square dance to the swim, polka to hula, filled with vibrant, sensual, and seductive poses and personas, demonstrated broader cultural themes, often in surprising ways. A host of dreams and desires come to life with a dance record and taking a turn around the floor. Soundtracks for dancing as well as soundtracks for dreaming, midcentury dance records became an aspirational instrument for the fulfillment of national fantasy. Dance records tell tales of American identity.

In conjunction with *Designed for Hi-Fi Living* and *Designed for Dancing*, *Designed for Success* has explored the contribution of consumer artifacts to the imagination and construction of modern US identity and global citizenship at midcentury. We examined the ways in which instructional records—whether for salesmanship, speed reading, or sport—express core values of US culture, including self-reliance, opportunity, and upward mobility; embody the self-help movement's focus on self-improvement; and illuminate that fundamental American notion of self-motivated success.

In this *Designed For* trilogy, we unveiled vinyl records designed, implicitly and explicitly, to teach and guide midcentury Americans. By paying attention to neglected genres, such as instructional, lifestyle, travel, and dance records, we have tried to add an engaging and enlightening chapter to the cultural history of vinyl. Inspired by our interest in midcentury design, music, visual culture, and recording industry history—as well as an inexhaustible enthusiasm for our captivating record collection—we revealed the integral role played by midcentury record albums in the modernist project.

ACKNOWLEDGMENTS

Thank you to everyone at music companies, both large and small, who helped out with permissions, including Alisa Coleman, Jade Rose, and Lauren Wintermute at ABKCO Music & Records, Inc.; Shari Mostad and Lindsay Fox at Hal Leonard; Melanie Clarkson at GNP Crescendo Records Co.; Jamey Aebersold, Matt Eve, and Jason Lindsey at Jazzbooks; Alex Livadas and Toby Silver at Sony Music; Todd Waxler, Janelle Fuchigami, Anne Leopard, Scott Ravine, Susan Hilderly, and Brooklynn Gigliotti at Universal Music; Jim Kimble at Kimbo Educational; Will Griffin, Sahara Naini, and Sayem Sharif at Smithsonian Folkways Recordings; Erin Casey at Documentary Recordings; and Gene Lee at Rhino Entertainment Company, a Warner Music Group Company.

Researching reproduction rights for this book sent us to many companies to seek permissions, some not in the music or record business. We deeply appreciate the assistance with our requests. Thank you to Linda M. Byrne and Lisa Joyce, the Toro Company; Heather Anderson, Copyright and Trademark Licensing, the Boeing Company; Jocelyn Damgaard-Ensinger and Tiziana Kauth-Otto at Boeing Global Services; Tammy Sodia at Boeing Digital Solutions, Inc. d/b/a Jeppesen; Didona Tudorachi, Georgina Van Der Heijden, Claire Villeneuve, and Fatma Rahal at Technicolor SA; Hall O'Donnell at Talisman Brands, Inc.; Meghan Winston at McCormick & Company; Steve Hardy, Rosemarie McGowan, Lynn Richardson, and the Licensing Team at Boy Scouts of America; Christopher Aguirre at Penguin Random House permissions; Maddie, Rachel Fudge, and Shellie LaCombe at David C. Cook Ministries; Justin Capella, Heidi Martinez, and Lauren Silveri at Xerox Corporation; Richard Hersh at Celebrity Consultants; Elaine LaLanne and Befit Enterprises Inc.; and Ludo Wurfbain and James Reed at *Sports Afield*.

We also thank Joyce Faust at Art Resource; Jacklyn Burns at the J. Paul Getty Museum; David Howe at the George Eastman Museum; Kay Peterson at the National Museum of American History; Kurt H. Taylor at Wilson Marshall & Taylor LLP, Mimi Muray Levitt, and the Nickolas Muray Photo Archives; Thomas V. Keppler; and Susan Hawkins at the G. Ray Hawkins Gallery for assistance with permissions to reproduce midcentury photographs by Paul Outerbridge Jr., Victor Keppler, Nickolas Muray, and Ralph Bartholomew Jr.

We deeply appreciate being able to tap into the rich reservoirs of archival materials, both online and in person, including the Hagley Center for the History of Business, Technology, and Society; the Bentley Historical Library, University of Michigan; the National Museum of African American History & Culture; the Wallace Center at Rochester Institute of Technology; HaithiTrust Digital Library; Online Archive of California; Smithsonian Archives of American Art; Smithsonian Folkways Recordings online resources; Peter Losin's Miles Ahead: A Miles Davis website; Both Sides Now Publications online discographies; Joe Maita's Jerry Jazz Musician site; Michael Pieper's Glamour Photographers site; Craig Swank's Popboprocktiludrop site; Discogs; Mike Goldstein's Album Cover Hall of Fame site; the *Public Domain Review*; US Modernist Radio, the British Library Sounds collection; the National Park Service early sound recording collection; Texas Tech University's Southwest Music Archive; the Western Reserve Historical Society; and the fabulous Fonts in Use website.

Special thanks to the team at Discographical Research, including Mike Callahan, Publisher and Editor, David Edwards, Patrice Eyries, Tim Neely, and Randy Watts; Lucas Clawson at the Hagley Center; Meg McKenzie and Madeleine Bradford at the Bentley Historical Library, University of Michigan; Shevon Desai, Director, Social Sciences and Clark Library, University of Michigan; Cami Goldowitz, Morna Hildebrand, and Joan Naturale at the RIT library; and to RIT's Interlibrary Loan and the IDS Express request system (who never failed to find our disparate and at times obscure requests).

Thank you to friends and colleagues Victoria Cherry, Bill Cherry, Jane Burchfield, Penny Milliken, Michael Brown, Rebecca DeRoo, Denise A. Gray, Alex Reed, Mike and Libby Robold, Jann Nyffler, Tom Kohn, Joe Maita, Rebekah Modrak, Nick Tobier, Dana Polan, Martha Meek, Andrew Mansour, Milina Berry, Vanessa Schwartz, Claudia Pretelin, Ben Tucker, Dean Yeotis, Susie Baity, Hope Schroeder, John Kropf, Darrell Brogdon, Aaron Stander, Craig Manning, Daniel M. Warner, George Smart, Ron Hicklin, Mark Kingsley, Tom Perchard, Carol Summerfield, Tako Suzuki, Jeff Gold, and colleagues at the October 2022 RIT College of Liberal Arts writing workshop. Thanks also to the Popular Music Books in Process Series from the International Association for the Study of Popular Music, organized and hosted by Kimberly Mack, Francesca Royster, Gus Stadler, Eric Weisbard, and Carl Wilson. Special thanks to Scott Earl, Maureen Earl, and Michelle Schmaltz.

Deep thanks to the team at the MIT Press, including Noah Springer, Alyssa Napier, Lillian Dunaj, Pamela Quick, Jessica Pellien, Zoë Kopp-Weber, Deborah Cantor-Adams, Charles Hale, Emily Gutheinz, Nicholas DiSabatino, Helen Weldon, and Debora Kuan, as well as the insightful anonymous reviewers. Tip of the pen, er, keyboard, to freelance editor Emily Shelton.

This project was made possible with the assistance of the William A. Kern endowment at the Rochester Institute of Technology and the RIT College of Liberal Arts. Thank you to Elizabeth Lamark at RIT photo services for photographing the records, and to Cassandra Shellman, Kelly Norris Martin, Israel Brown, and Tracy Worrell for administrative support.

NOTES

INTRODUCTION

1. For an insightful examination of how musical compositions, as well as records, are canonized and valued, see "Who Constructs a Canon?," in *Twentieth-Century Music in the West: An Introduction*, Tom Perchard, Stephen Graham, Tim Rutherford-Johnson, and Holly Rogers (Cambridge: Cambridge University Press, 2022), 113–115.

2. Daniel J. Boorstin, *The Americans: The Democratic Experience* (New York: Vintage, 1973), 370.

3. Union Trading Co. advertisement, "Hear How Records," *Black Belt*, February 1963, 68.

4. Max Brzezinski, *Vinyl Age: A Guide to Record Collecting Now* (New York: Black Dog & Leventhal, 2020). Few instructional records appear in Eilon Paz's landmark compendium, *Dust & Grooves: Adventures in Record Collecting* (Brooklyn, NY: Dust & Grooves, 2014).

5. Brett Milano, *Vinyl Junkies: Adventures in Record Collecting* (New York: St. Martin's, 2003), 99.

6. Jon Moshier, "Learn the Secrets of Self-improvement with Vintage Instructional Records," WDET 101.9 FM, January 31, 2022, https://wdet.org/2022/01/31/learn-the-secrets-of-self -improvement-with-vintage-instructional-records.

7. Alan Dein, "The Bizarre World of Instructional LPs," BBC News, July 18, 2015, https://www .bbc.com/news/uk-33464722.

8. Steven A. Benko, ed. *Better Living through TV: Contemporary TV and Moral Identity Formation* (Lanham, MD: Lexington, 2022), back cover.

9. See Lynn Spigel, *Make Room for TV: Television and the Family Ideal in Postwar America* (Chicago: University of Chicago Press, 1992), 5–6.

10. For an insightful exploration of midcentury cultural erasure, see Kate A. Baldwin, *The Racial Imaginary of the Cold War Kitchen: From Sokol'niki Park to Chicago's South Side* (Lebanon, NH: Dartmouth College Press, 2016).

11. On the role of experts in midcentury America, see Michael J. Brown, *Hope and Scorn: Eggheads, Experts, and Elites in American Politics* (Chicago: University of Chicago Press, 2020).

12. Billboard, "Album Reviews—*You Be a Disc Jockey*," *Billboard*, December 28, 1963, 10.

13. Richard M. Huber, *The American Idea of Success* (New York: McGraw-Hill, 1971), 8.

14. Erving Goffman, *The Presentation of Self in Everyday Life* (New York: Doubleday Anchor, 1959).

15. Richard Weiss, *The American Myth of Success: From Horatio Alger to Norman Vincent Peale* (Urbana: University of Illinois Press, 1969), 3.

16. Weiss, *American Myth of Success*, 15.

17. Huber, *American Idea of Success*, 456.

18. Ralph Waldo Emerson, *Success* (Boston: Houghton Mifflin, 1912), 22.

19. Emerson, *Success*, 19.

20. Emerson, 16–17.

21. Emerson, 54.

22. Janet Borgerson and Jonathan Schroeder, *Designed for Hi-Fi Living: The Vinyl LP in Midcentury America* (Cambridge, MA: MIT Press, 2017); Janet Borgerson and Jonathan Schroeder, *Designed for Dancing: How Midcentury Records Taught America to Dance* (Cambridge, MA: MIT Press, 2021).

23. Michael Schudson, *Advertising, the Uneasy Persuasion: Its Dubious Impact on American Society* (New York: Basic Books, 1984), 215.

24. Erika L. Paulson and Thomas C. O'Guinn, "Marketing Social Class and Ideology in Post-World-War-Two American Print Advertising," *Journal of Macromarketing* 38 no. 1 (March 2018): 24.

25. Michael Schudson, "Advertising as Capitalist Realism," *Advertising & Society Review* 1, no. 1 (2000): 10.

26. Spigel, *Make Room for TV*.

27. Schudson, "Advertising as Capitalist Realism," 8.

28. On the relationships between advertising and photographic style, see Jonathan E. Schroeder, "Snapshot Aesthetics and the Strategic Imagination," *InVisible Culture* 18 (Spring 2013), http://ivc.lib.rochester.edu/snapshot-aesthetics-and-the-strategic-imagination.

29. Elspeth H. Brown, *The Corporate Eye: Photography and the Rationalization of American Commercial Culture* (Baltimore, MD: Johns Hopkins University Press, 2005), 22.

30. Brown, *Corporate Eye*, 219.

31. Jean Baudrillard, *The Consumer Society: Myths and Structures*, trans. Chris Turner (London: Sage, 1998), 166.

32. Erika L. Paulson and Thomas C. O'Guinn, "Working-Class Cast: Images of the Working Class in Advertising, 1950–2010," *Annals of the American Academy of Political and Social Science* 64, no. 1 (November 2012): 50–69. See also Jonathan E. Schroeder, *Visual Consumption* (New York: Routledge, 2002).

33. William Leiss, Stephen Kline, Sut Jhally, Jacqueline Botterill, and Kyle Asquith, *Social Communication in Advertising: Consumption in the Mediated Marketplace*, 4th ed. (New York: Routledge, 2018), 9.

34. Elspeth H. Brown, "Rationalizing Consumption: Lejaran à Hiller and the Origins of American Advertising Photography, 1913–1924," *Enterprise & Society* 1, no. 4 (December 2000): 736.

35. Tim B. Wride, *Retail Fictions: The Commercial Photography of Ralph Bartholomew Jr.* (Los Angeles: Los Angeles County Museum of Art, 1998), 11.

36. Robert A. Sobieszek, *The Art of Persuasion* (New York: Harry N. Abrams, 1988), 100.

37. Brown, *Corporate Eye*, 148.

38. Wride, *Retail Fictions*, 17.

39. Wride, 19.

40. Wride, 23.

41. Sobieszek, *Art of Persuasion*, 13.

42. Wride, *Retail Fictions*, 28.

43. Wride, 27.

44. Jennifer Weaver, "Ralph Bartholomew Jr.'s Postwar America," *Photo District News* 18, no. 4 (April 1998): 198.

45. John Szarkowski, *Looking at Photographs: 100 Pictures from the Collection of the Museum of Modern Art* (New York: Harry N. Abrams, 1973).

46. Ken Johnson, "Always Something Unnerving in Paul Outerbridge Photographs," *New York Times*, September 9, 2016, C20.

47. Marvin Heiferman, "Paul Outerbridge," *Art in America*, October 23, 2009, https://www.artnews.com/art-in-america/features/paul-outerbridge-62816.

48. Andy Grundberg, "Photography View: Commercial Work was Best," *New York Times*, February 14, 1982, A33.

49. Robert A. Sobieszek, *The Art of Persuasion* (New York: Harry N. Abrams, 1988), 71.

50. Sobieszek, *Art of Persuasion*, 70.

51. Tim J. Anderson, "Listening to the Promise of a Better You: Considering the Instructional Record," *Leonardo Music Journal* 26 (December 2016): 30. Anderson published two of the few scholarly articles on instructional records: one focusing on music instruction records, the other on stereo demonstration discs that introduced stereo to (mostly male) listeners. He suggests that instructional records "have connections with other audio-enabled practices such as karaoke, exercise and gaming." Anderson, "Listening to the Promise," 28. On gender and hi-fi culture, see Kelli Smith-Biwer, "'The Silent Partner': Tonearms and Modular Masculinities in U.S. Midcentury Hi-Fi Culture," *Journal of the Society for American Music* 16, no. 3 (August 2022): 319–342.

52. Michel Foucault, *Résumé des Cours* (Paris: Gallimard, 1989), 133–134.

53. Michel Foucault, "Technologies of the Self," in *Technologies of the Self: A Seminar with Michel Foucault*, ed. Luther H. Martin, Huck Gutman, and Patrick H. Hutton (Amherst: University of Massachusetts Press, 1988), 18.

54. Jan Goldstein, "Foucault's Technologies of the Self and the Cultural History of Identity," *Arcadia* 33, no. 1 (January 1998), 62.

55. Anderson, "Listening to the Promise," 30.

56. Hal Leonard, "Music Minus One," 2022, https://www.halleonard.com/series/MMONE?keywords=chicago&subsiteid=1&&dt=item#products.

57. Music Minus One catalog, New York, Music Minus One, n.d.

58. Harold C. Schonberg, "Records: Play Along," *New York Times*, September 13, 1953, X9.

59. Ben Ratliff, "Mal Waldron, 77, Composer of the Jazz Ballad 'Soul Eyes,'" *New York Times*, December 6, 2002, A33.

60. David Gahr photographs, 2023, https://www.davidgahr.com.

61. Alan Dein, "The Bizarre World of Instructional LPs," BBC News, July 18, 2015, https://www.bbc.com/news/uk-33464722. For a useful compendium of original sources about the phonograph's introduction, see Timothy D. Taylor, Mark Katz, and Tony Grajeda, eds., *Music, Sound, and Technology in America: A Documentary History of Early Phonograph, Cinema, and Radio* (Durham, NC: Duke University Press, 2012).

62. Victor Talking Machine, advertisement, *Saturday Evening Post*, December 7, 1901, 22.

63. Jacob Smith, *Spoken Word: Postwar American Phonograph Cultures* (Berkeley: University of California Press, 2011), 2. In his singular book on spoken word records, Smith argues, "For a time, that new media format was mobilized for children's entertainment, home education, cutting-edge comedy, risqué material, and poetic recitation. It was only when the economic ascendancy of rock music—spurred by the baby-boom demographic and a shift from singles to albums as rock's central medium—coincided with the emergence of new home media outlets that usurped some of the LP's social functions that a range of spoken word genres faded from the cultural stage" (4). See also David Suisman, *Selling Sounds: The Commercial Revolution in American Music* (Cambridge, MA: Harvard University Press, 2009).

64. For an insightful and amusing look at self-improvement, see Carl Cederström and André Spicer, *Desperately Seeking Self-Improvement: A Year Inside the Optimization Movement* (New York: OR, 2017).

65. William H. Whyte Jr., *The Organization Man* (Garden City, NY: Doubleday, 1957).

66. Henry Clews quoted in Whyte, *Organization Man*, 16–17.

67. Micki McGee, *Self-Help, Inc.: Makeover Culture in American Life* (New York: Oxford University Press, 2005), 36.

68. Weiss, *American Myth of Success*, 11.

69. Weiss, 14.

70. McGee, *Self-Help, Inc.*, 37.

71. Given the midcentury gender playbook, perhaps it's not surprising that US history lessons often emphasize alignment with ancient Greek civilization's notions of democracy. The Greek democratic citizen, always male, that sets out into the world, bearing privilege to seek knowledge and enlightenment, depends upon women and slaves to make such a life possible—at the most basic level of food acquisition and preparation, for example. The particular choice to trace US history back to the Greeks was always masked as a deep connection to "democracy," not the necessity of second-class citizens. And slavery.

72. Paul Goodman, *Growing Up Absurd: Problems of Youth in the Organized Society* (New York: Vintage, 1960), 13.

73. Goodman, *Growing Up Absurd*, 13.

74. Helen Gurley Brown, *Sex and the Single Girl* (New York: Pocket Books, 1962), 29.

75. Veit Elrmann, "The Invention of the Listener: An(other) History," in *Sound as Popular Culture: A Research Companion*, ed. Jens Gerrit Papenburg and Holger Schulze (Cambridge, MA: MIT Press, 2016), 166.

76. Elrmann, "Invention of the Listener," 164–165.

77. Jennifer Lynn Stoever, *The Sonic Color Line: Race and the Cultural Politics of Listening* (New York: New York University Press, 2016).

78. Sayan Dey, "Pedagogy of Performative Silence," *Philosophy and Global Affairs* 2, no. 1 (2022), 24 [footnote 20].

79. Deaf culture depends on learning without listening. See Lois Bragg, ed., *Deaf World: A Historical Reader and Primary Sourcebook* (New York: New York University Press, 2001).

80. Pierre Bourdieu and Jean-Claude Passeron, *Reproduction in Education, Society and Culture*, (London: Sage, 1977). See also Paul Willis, *Learning to Labor: How Working Class Kids Get Working Class Jobs* (New York: Columbia University Press, 1977).

81. Scholars have interrogated the weakness of Bourdieu's strict analytical binaries. However, his distinctions do map certain tendencies in teaching and learning philosophies and shine light on ways of understanding how certain children typically fail in traditional school

settings. Educational philosopher Michael Apple writes that, despite scholarly disagreements, "none would deny the importance of examining the relationship between schooling and the maintenance of these unequal relations." Michael Apple, *Education and Power*, 2nd ed. (New York: Routledge, 1995), 9.

82. The 1960s ushered in greater awareness of alternative philosophies of teaching and learning. For example, experimental schools such as Summerhill in the UK, and similarly guided experiments throughout the United States, focused on freedom, play, and social development over academic development, memorization, and rule following. The authors attended such a school in Flint, Michigan, that embraced a hands-on, create-your-own-goals, develop-your-own-projects approach, which generally involved very little listening to teachers. See A. S. Neill, *Summerhill: A Radical Approach to Child Rearing* (New York: Hart, 1960).

83. Anderson, "Listening to the Promise," 30. On pedagogical powers of vinyl, see Tim J. Anderson, "Training the Listener: Stereo Demonstration Discs in an Emerging Consumer Market," in *Living Stereo: Histories and Cultures of Multichannel Sound*, ed. Paul Théberge, Kyle Devine, and Tom Everett (London: Bloomsbury, 2015), 107–124; and Jon Austin, ed., *Spinning Popular Culture as Public Pedagogy: Critical Reflections and Transformative Possibilities* (Boston: BrillSense, 2017).

84. Jonathan Sterne, *The Audible Past: Cultural Origins of Sound Reproduction* (Durham, NC: Duke University Press, 2003), 2.

85. Sterne, *Audible Past*, 24–25.

86. Kate Lacey, *Listening Publics: The Politics and Experience of Listening in the Media Age* (London: Polity, 2013), 78.

87. Greg Goodale, *Sonic Persuasion: Reading Sound in the Recorded Age* (Champaign: University of Illinois Press, 2011).

88. Mladen Dolar, *A Voice and Nothing More* (Cambridge, MA: MIT Press, 2006). For an insightful discussion of hearing and listening into the digital era, see Damon Krukowski, *Ways of Hearing* (Cambridge, MA: MIT Press, 2019).

89. Smith, *Spoken Word*, 4.

90. Marshall McLuhan, *The Mechanical Bride: Folklore of Industrial Man* (New York: Vanguard, 1951).

91. Ellen Lupton, *Thinking with Type: A Critical Guide for Designers, Writers, Editors & Students* (New York: Princeton Architectural Press, 2004), 8.

PART I

1. Michael Schein, "The Real Reason Napoleon Hill Grew Rich (Hint: It's Not What You Think)," *Inc.*, February 14, 2017, https://www.inc.com/michael-schein/brthe-real-reason-napoleon-hill-grew-rich-hint-its-not-what-you-think.html.

2. Our favorite Amway story belongs to the dynamic, energetic, and successful Lillian Gill. Born in Mississippi, Gill moved as a young woman to Grand Rapids, Michigan, in 1936. She was the first Black woman to "sell products for a local company called Nutrilite Food Supplements," now a subsidiary of Amway. She was a "Top Ten" distributor in 1958. Hers is one of the few Black faces in the 1959 Nutrilite Products Convention photo: dressed in fashionable black hat and dark coat, she sits in the center front row with her son, Dr. Robert Gill (the talented cartoonist of *Sugar*, a strip that followed the antics of a seven-year-old Black girl). When Nutrilite offered a correspondence "Success Course" called Think and Grow Rich by Napoleon Hill, Gill completed it. She took their Dale Carnegie course, too. As we can see from the bounty of her archived

ephemera, Gill heard Amway founder Richard DeVos speak several times, so she may have been in the audience for the recording of *Selling America.* All information is derived from the Lillian Gill collection at the Bentley Library, University of Michigan.

3. Amway Corporation, *Amagram* 17, no. 10 (October 1976): 3.

4. Amway, *Amagram,* 7.

5. Ellen Lupton, *Mechanical Brides: Women and Machines from Home to Office* (New York: Cooper Hewitt National Museum of Design / Princeton Architectural Press, 1993), 44. Writing in 1993, well before the smartphone, Lupton noted: "Many jobs pegged as 'women's work' in the twentieth century center on the phone, including secretary, receptionist, customer service agent, and telephone operator" (29). For a nuanced history of how typewriters functioned, similar to record players, as "fluid historical objects defined by their social contexts," see Rachel Plotnick, "Tethered Women, Mobile Men: Gendered Mobilities of Typewriting," *Mobile Media & Communication* 8, no. 2 (May 2020): 188.

CHAPTER 1

1. Thanks to Mark Kingsley for graphic insight into the *Learn the International Morse Code* album cover.

2. HQ Staff, "Learn Morse Code the Boy Scout Way," Radio Relay International, April 15, 2017, https://radio-relay.org/learn-morse-code-the-boy-scout-way.

3. Lisa Gitelman, *Scripts, Grooves, and Writing Machines: Representing Technology in the Edison Era* (Stanford, CA: Stanford University Press, 1999).

4. Gitelman, *Scripts, Grooves, and Writing Machines,* 41.

5. Boorstin, *The Americans: The Democratic Experience* (New York: Vintage, 1973), 463.

6. Lee H. Salisbury, "Audio-Visual Aids: Speak Well Off the Record," *Speech Teacher* 12, no. 4 (November 1963): 356. In his scholarly review, Mr. Salisbury was clearly not impressed with the *Speak Well* album: "Speech correction like brain surgery cannot be taught on a do-it-yourself basis."

7. Billboard, "Reviews and Ratings of New Albums—*Speak Well,*" *Billboard,* October 5, 1959, 30.

8. Thanks to Peggy Joyner Johnson and Chris Johnson for insights into the military albums included here.

CHAPTER 2

1. Steven Heller, "Advertising Layout Handbook of Don May," The Daily Heller, October 14, 2018, https://www.printmag.com/daily-heller/rough-rough-rough.

2. For a concise, illuminating exploration of typography, see Bradbury Thompson, *The Art of Graphic Design* (New Haven, CT: Yale University Press, 1988).

3. Arthur Miller, *Death of a Salesman* (New York: Viking, 1949), 11.

4. Thanks to Mark Kingsley for insights into the *Birth of a Salesman* cover.

5. Josh Hinds, "Dottie Walters, Motivational Speakers Hall of Fame," Get Motivation, n.d., https://www.getmotivation.com/dottie-walters-hof.htm.

6. Wilson Learning, "Wilson Learning Announces the Passing of Larry Wilson: Founder, Speaker, and Author," Wilson Learning Worldwide, February 11, 2013, https://global.wilsonlearning.com/resources/20130411passingoflarrywilson.

7. Wilson Learning, "About," 2023, https://global.wilsonlearning.com/about.

CHAPTER 3

1. Discogs, "Elba Corp.," 2023, https://www.discogs.com/label/160643-Elba-Corp.

2. *Nation's Business* magazine, which was published from 1912 to 1999 by the US Chamber of Commerce, is available online. Hagley Library, *"Nation's Business* Magazine Online," Hagley Library News, April 11, 2012, https://www.hagley.org/librarynews/digital-collections-nations -business-online.

3. Bill Miller, "Amway Merits Support," *Grand Rapids Press*, December 15, 1982, 14A.

4. Alex Taylor, "Amway: Up from the Basement," *Detroit Free Press*, November 19, 1978, 1B.

5. Taylor, "Amway."

PART II

1. Mary and Russel Wright, *Guide to Easier Living* (Salt Lake City: Gibbs Smith, [1950] 2003), 5.

2. Wright and Wright, *Guide to Easier Living*. 6.

3. Smith writes: "Just as radio and television production and consumption were profoundly influenced by their introduction into the domestic sphere, so LPs were shaped by the rhythms of female domestic labor and suburban social life, and women were encouraged to make 'educational' records part of their domestic routine." Jacob Smith, *Spoken Word; Postwar American Phonograph Cultures* (Berkeley: University of California Press, 2011), 7.

4. Leslie Paris, "The Sexual Clock: Middle-Aged American Women and Sexual Vitality in the 1960s and 1970s," *Journal of Social History* 53, no. 4 (Fall 2020): 926.

5. Stephanie Coontz, *A Strange Stirring: The Feminine Mystique and American Women at the Dawn of the 1960s* (New York: Basic Books, 2011), xv.

6. Betty Friedan, *The Feminine Mystique* (New York: Norton, 1963), 2.

7. Friedan, *Feminine Mystique*, 1.

8. Suman Mishra, "From Self-Control to Self-Improvement: Evolving Messages and Persuasion Techniques in Weight Loss Advertising (1930–1990)," *Visual Communication* 16, no. 4 (November 2017): 467.

9. Shelly McKenzie, "Weak Hearts and Wedding Day Figures: Exercise and Health Promotion in the 1960s," in *Women, Wellness, and the Media*, edited by Margaret C. Wiley (Newcastle upon Tyne: Cambridge Scholars, 2008), 213.

10. McKenzie, "Weak Hearts and Wedding Day Figures," 215.

11. Burçak Ertimur and Gokcen Coskuner-Balli, "Navigating the Institutional Logics of Markets: Implications for Strategic Brand Management," *Journal of Marketing* 79, no. 2 (February 2015): 46.

12. McKenzie, "Weak Hearts and Wedding Day Figures," 207.

13. Leslie Paris, "The Sexual Clock: Middle-Aged American Women and Sexual Vitality in the 1960s and 1970s," *Journal of Social History* 53, no. 4 (Fall 2020): 926.

14. Paris, "Sexual Clock," 922.

15. Julie Sturgeon and Janice Meer, "The President's Council on Physical Fitness and Sports Revisits Its Roots and Charts Its Future," in *President's Council on Fitness and Sports: The First Fifty Years, 1956–2006* (St. Petersburg, FL: Faircount, 2006), 40.

16. Douglas Martin, "Bonnie Prudden, 97, Dies; Promoted Fitness for TV Generation," *New York Times*, December 20, 2011, B10.

17. Jeffrey Montez de Oca, "'As Our Muscles Get Softer, Our Missile Race Becomes Harder': Cultural Citizenship and the 'Muscle Gap,'" *Journal of Historical Sociology* 18, no. 3 (September

2005): 145–172. Bonnie Prudden helped inspire the President's Council on Youth Fitness, which influenced more than just flabby arms and stomachs: "The achievement of the Council on Youth Fitness was as much political as educational. The program produced a measurable improvement in fitness nationwide as well as a shift in public attitudes and wider participation. The work of the council also helped identify President Kennedy with fitness, vigor, and preparedness." "The Federal Government Takes on Physical Fitness," John F. Kennedy Presidential Library and Museum, National Archives, n.d., https://www.jfklibrary.org/learn/about-jfk/jfk-in-history /physical-fitness.

18. In the 1960s and 1970s, the women's movement, along with books like *Our Bodies, Ourselves* (1970), worked to redefine women's relationships to their bodies, recast aging as a natural process, and reexamine sexual satisfaction. But beliefs about women's bodies, sexuality, and aging have been slow to change.

19. "In the 60s, Men and Women Both Tuned in to Debbie Drake," OrangeBean Indiana, January 20, 2021, https://orangebeanindiana.com/2021/01/20/in-the-60s-men-and-women-both-tuned-in-to -debbie-drake.

20. A selection of vintage fitness recordings can be heard on WFMU Radio, "Fantastic Family Fitness Fun, Session 1," Beware of the Blog, September 29, 2007, https://blog.wfmu.org /freeform/2007/week39.

21. McKenzie, "Weak Hearts and Wedding Day Figures," 199.

22. Sarah Archer, *The Midcentury Kitchen: America's Favorite Room from Workspace to Dreamscape, 1940s–1970s* (New York: Countryman, 2019), 144–145.

23. Greg Castillo, *Cold War on the Home Front: The Soft Power of Midcentury Design* (Minneapolis: University of Minnesota Press, 2009); and Andrew James Wulf, *U.S. International Exhibitions during the Cold War: Winning Hearts and Minds through Cultural Diplomacy* (Lanham, MD: Rowman & Littlefield, 2015).

24. Smith, *Spoken Word*, 12.

25. Billboard, "Coast Department Stores in All-Out Kidisk Xmas Drives; Supply Plentiful," *Billboard*, November 23, 1946, 18.

26. Smith, *Spoken Word*, 31.

27. Beatrice Landeck, "New Records for Children," *New York Times*, November 20, 1955, XX9.

28. Herbert Mitgans, "A Christmas Guide to Children's Records," *HiFi/Stereo Review*, December 1963, 43–46.

29. Casey Cep, "Diary of a Made-Up Kid," *New Yorker*, "August 1, 2022, 62. Beatrice Sparks, the "anonymous" author of the best-selling druggy diary *Go Ask Alice* (1971), wrote the text for many Family Achievement Institute records.

30. Hank Fox, "Educational Emphasis Aids Sale of Children's Records." *Billboard*, October 15, 1965, 38.

31. Fox, "Educational Emphasis," 38.

32. Fox, 38.

33. Huber, *The American Idea of Success* (New York: McGraw-Hill, 1971), 454.

CHAPTER 4

1. Richard Goldstein, "Jack LaLanne, Founder of Modern Fitness Movement, Dies at 96," *New York Times*, January 23, 2011, A25. Thank you to Elaine LaLanne for her generous assistance in providing details about Jack LaLanne.

2. Goldstein, "Jack LaLanne."

3. Goldstein, "Jack LaLanne."

4. Trisha Lucey, "Catching Up with . . . Bonnie Prudden, Fitness Pioneer," *Sports Illustrated*, June 6, 1999, 12.

5. Douglas Martin, "Bonnie Prudden, 97, Dies; Promoted Fitness for TV Generation," *New York Times*, December 20, 2011, B10.

6. "About Bonnie Prudden," Bonnie Prudden Myotherapy, n.d., https://bonnieprudden.com /about-bonnie-prudden.

7. "About Bonnie Prudden."

8. Bonnie Prudden, *How to Keep Slender and Fit after Thirty* (New York: Pocket, 1961).

9. Daniel J. King, "Chuck Stewart's Legendary Photographs (1927–2017)," Ohio News: Chuck Stewart," Alumni, June 30, 2017, https://www.ohio.edu/fine-arts/news/chuck-stewarts -legendary-photographs-1927-2017.

10. Marcus Crowder, "Soul and Essence: The Jazz Photography of Chuck Stewart," SF Jazz, June 18, 2021, https://www.sfjazz.org/onthecorner/photography-of-chuck-stewart.

11. "Bonnie to the Rescue," *Sports Illustrated*, November 25, 1957, 52–54.

12. Masterwork, advertisement, "4 New Models for Spring Sales from Your Newest Profit Line," *Billboard*, January 26, 1963, 49.

13. McKenzie, "Weak Hearts and Wedding Day Figures: Exercise and Health Prmotion in the 1960s," in *Women, Wellness, and the Media*, ed. Margaret C. Wiley (Newcastle upon Tyne: Cambridge Scholars, 2008), 208.

14. Douglas Martin, "Noel Regney, Songwriter Known for 'Do You Hear What I Hear?' Is Dead at 80," *New York Times*, December 1, 2002, Section 1, 58.

15. Larry Wolters, "Channel 9 Figures to get Flying Start," *Chicago Tribune*, September 14, 1964, 46.

16. Carl Fisher, who photographed the cover for *Modern Screen's Hollywood Method*, shot some of the famous *Esquire* covers in the 1960s. As design historian Steven Heller has reflected, the *Esquire* covers—including Muhammad Ali pierced as Saint Sebastian, smiling Lieutenant William Calley with four Asian children before his court-martial and conviction for his role in the My Lai massacre during the Vietnam War, and Andy Warhol sucked down into a Campbell's tomato soup can—"are considered the most powerful propaganda imagery in any medium and certainly the most memorable magazine covers ever." Fischer also taught photography at Rochester Institute of Technology. See Carl Fischer Photography, n.d., https://carlfischerphotography.com/brief -reviews.html.

17. Billboard, "Periodicals Turn New Leaf in Ties with LP Producers," *Billboard Music Week*, August 7, 1961, 1.

18. "Nicholas Kounovsky, Fitness Expert, 80," *New York Times*, December 8, 1993, B8.

19. Lynn Peril, *Pink Think: Becoming a Woman in Many Uneasy Lessons* (New York: W. W. Norton, 2002), 183.

20. Peril, *Pink Think*, 183.

21. "Programming: One & Kick & Two, and Stick Out Your Tongue," *Time*, February 16, 1968, https://content.time.com/time/subscriber/article/0,33009,837873-1,00.html.

22. "Programming: One & Kick & Two."

CHAPTER 5

1. Jancis Robinson, "Peter M. F. Sichel—from CIA to Blue Nun," February 27, 2016, https://www.jancisrobinson.com/articles/peter-m-f-sichel-from-cia-to-blue-nun.

2. Online Archive of California, "Inventory of the Bern C. Ramey Papers, 1858–1998," Department of Special Collections, University of California, Davis, n.d., https://oac.cdlib.org/findaid/ark:/13030/kt5q2nc5wk/entire_text.

3. Lawry's, "Adolph's® Unseasoned Meat Tenderizer," McCormick & Company, 2023, https://www.mccormick.com/lawrys/flavors/adolphs/adolphs-original-meat-tenderizer.

CHAPTER 6

1. Michael Pieper, "Photographers—Peter James Samerjan," Glamour Photographers of the 1950s and 60s, 2020, http://glamourphotographers.yolasite.com/more-photographers.php.

2. Margalit Fox, "Helen Gurley Brown, Who Gave 'Single Girl' a Life in Full (Sex, Sex, Sex), Dies at 90," *New York Times*, August 13, 2012, A1.

3. Jennifer Scanlon, *Bad Girls Go Everywhere: The Life of Helen Gurley Brown* (New York: Oxford University Press, 2009), xiii.

4. Fox, "Helen Gurley Brown."

5. Vern L. Bullough, "Alfred Kinsey and the Kinsey Report: Historical Overview and Lasting Contributions," *Journal of Sex Research* 35, no. 2 (May 1998): 131.

6. Kinsey Institute, "Learn More about Our Research," Indiana University, 2020, https://kinseyinstitute.org/research/research-topics.php.

7. Shalyn Isaacs, "Profile of Joyce Brothers," Psychology's Feminist Voices Digital Archive, ed. A. Rutherford, 2016, https://feministvoices.com/profiles/joyce-brothers.

8. Valerie J. Nelson, "Dr. Joyce Brothers dies at 85; Popular TV Psychologist," *Los Angeles Times*, May 13, 2013, https://www.latimes.com/local/obituaries/la-me-joyce-brothers-20130514-story.html.

9. Sydney Stahl Weinberg, "Joyce Brothers," Shalvi/Hyman Encyclopedia of Jewish Women, December 31, 1999, https://jwa.org/encyclopedia/article/brothers-joyce.

10. Weinberg, "Joyce Brothers."

11. Alice Thompson Beaton, according to the liner notes of *The Family All Together*, was founder and editor of *Glamour* magazine and publisher of *Seventeen*.

12. Kathryn A. Ostrofsky, "Learning from *Sesame Street* Soundtrack Albums," in *The Soundtrack Album: Listening to Media*, ed. Paul N. Reinsch and Laurel Westrup (New York: Routledge, 2020), 91–106.

13. Golden Records, advertisement, *Billboard*, October 16, 1965, 36.

14. Craig Swank, "Music Storytelling for the Young! The Imaginative World of Arthur Shimkin & Golden Records," Poprockboptiludrop, August 26, 2021, https://kimsloans.wordpress.com/tag/arthur-shimkin-and-golden-records.

15. Billboard, "Point-of-Purchase Display Sells Children's Records for Golden," *Billboard*, March 6, 1965, 35.

16. The Popmythology website features an entire set of the "Teaching Your" Sunday School records. Marianne Spellman, "What We Can Learn from these Vintage School Instructional Albums," Popthomology, August 22, 2012, https://www.popthomology.com/2012/08/what-we-can-learn-from-these-vintage.html.

17. Douglas Martin, "Tom Glazer, Folk Singer, Is Dead at 88," *New York Times*, February 26, 2003, A23.

18. Craig Swank, "Tom Glazer: ("On Top of Spaghetti")," Popboprocktiludrop, n.d., https://kimsloans.wordpress.com/spotlight-tom-glazer.

19. Argosy Music Corp., "Ballads for the Age of Science," Argosy Music Corp., 2019, https://www.argosymusiccorp.com/Science/Science.html.

20. David Bonner, *Revolutionizing Children's Records: The Young People's Records and Children's Record Guild Series, 1946–1977* (Lanham, MD: Scarecrow, 2007).

21. "Reviews and Ratings of New Popular Albums—*Now We Know (Songs to Learn By)* Album 2," *The Billboard*, May 28, 1955, 56.

22. The move to admit women to Ivy League universities may have had less to do with addressing inequality—and expanding female access to elite resources and prestigious degrees—and more to do with male students desiring female presence on campus. See for example, Carlos Lozada, "How Harvard, Princeton, and Yale Discovered Women," *Washington Post*, October 14, 2016, https://www.washingtonpost.com/news/book-party/wp/2016/10/14/how-harvard-princeton-and-yale-discovered-women.

23. Peter Wyden, *The Overweight Society* (New York: Pocket Books, 1965), 97–98.

24. Wyden, *Overweight Society*, 99.

25. Staff, "'Chaplain of Bourbon Street' Dies at 89," *Baptist Press*, July 5, 2017, https://www.baptistpress.com/resource-library/news/chaplain-of-bourbon-street-dies-at-89.

26. Staff, "'Chaplain of Bourbon Street.'"

CHAPTER 7

1. Richard Severo, "Steve Allen, Comedian Who Pioneered Late-Night TV Talk Shows, Is Dead at 78," *New York Times*, November 1, 2000, B13.

2. James Alvino, "On Educating Gifted Children," *New York Times*, November 13, 1983, 11NJ, 36.

3. Arthur Crabtree, dir., "1959 *Horrors of the Black Museum* trailer," Producers Library Service, 2023, https://producerslibrary.com/preview/VT-0050_012.

4. For more information about Living Strings recordings, see "String Groups," Space Age Pop, 2019, http://www.spaceagepop.com/strings.htm.

5. Jill Lepore, "How Longfellow Woke the Dead," *American Scholar*, March 2, 2011, https://theamericanscholar.org/how-longfellow-woke-the-dead.

6. Florian Hardwig, "*Affect Your Emotions through Music* Album Art," Fonts in Use, July 4, 2021, https://fontsinuse.com/uses/38055/affect-your-emotions-through-music-album-art.

7. David Flint, "Are You Ready for the Burgess Method?," The Reprobate, March 24, 2022, https://reprobatepress.com/2022/03/24/are-you-ready-for-the-burgess-method.

8. Nicole Palina, "Hypnotic Performance Given by Russ Burgess," *The Heights* (student weekly of Boston College) 72, no. 20 October 21, 1991, 1, 15.

9. Steven Starker, *Oracle at the Supermarket: The American Preoccupation with Self-Help Books* (New Brunswick, NJ: Transaction, 1989), 115.

PART III

1. David Scott, "A Narrative Analysis of a Declining Social World: The Case of Contract Bridge," *Play & Culture* 4, no. 1 (February 1991): 22.

2. Henry Dreyfuss, *Designing for People* (New York: Allworth, [1955] 2013), 238; citation refers to the Allworth edition.

3. Billboard, "Disk Course LP's to Sell for $9.95," *Billboard*, December 24, 1955, 14.

4. Ren Gravett, "Album Education Kick Grows; Indie Companies Lead Way," *Billboard*, November 21, 1960, 24.

5. "Disk Course LPs to Sell for $9.95," *Billboard*, December 24, 1955, 14

6. Gravett, "Album Education Kick Grows," 24.

7. Gravett, "Album Education Kick Grows," 24. In 1967, a Canadian retailer reported "a continuing upswing in sales of French courses to English-speaking Canadians and English courses to French-Canadians as national unity remains an issue and a surprise surge in sales of Japanese courses, now selling more per month than per year in the past. This reflects interest in Expo 70 in Tokyo." Billboard, "From the Music Capitols of the World," *Billboard*, December 9, 1967, 90.

8. Sheet Music Plus, "Music Minus One," Sheet Music Plus, 2023, https://www.sheetmusicplus.com.

9. Rudolf A. Bruil, "What is it about Remington Records?," The Remington Site, n.d., http://www.soundfountain.org.

10. Billboard, "Take a Chorus: MMO Debs Two More LP Vols.," *Billboard*, November 24, 1956, 30.

11. Charles Sinclair, "Top Jazz Names Climb NBC-TV Bandwagon," *Billboard*, April 7, 1958, 10.

12. Leonard Bernstein Office, "Omnibus," https://leonardbernstein.com/about/educator/omnibus, 2023.

13. Our book *Designed for Dancing* devoted a chapter to dance instruction records.

14. Esquire editors, *Esquire Etiquette*: *A Guide to Business Sports and Social Conduct* (Philadelphia: Lippincott, 1953), 115.

15. Billboard, "Carlton Distrib Meeting Brings Big Sales Hike," *Billboard Music Week*, January 16, 1961, 8.

16. Billboard, "Carlton Distrib Meeting," 58.

17. Rudolf Müllner, "Self-Improvement In and Through Sports: Cultural-Historical Perspectives," *The International Journal of the History of Sport* 33, no. 14 (2006), 1593.

CHAPTER 8

1. Dave Anderson, "Arnold Palmer, the Magnetic Face of Golf in the '60s, Dies at 87," *New York Times*, September 25, 2016, A1.

2. Anderson, "Arnold Palmer."

3. Robin Finn, "Arthur Ashe, Tennis Star, Is Dead at 49," *New York Times*, February 8, 1993, B9.

4. Arthur Ashe, International Tennis Hall of Fame, https://www.tennisfame.com/hall-of-famers/inductees/arthur-ashe.

5. "Leslie Allen on Arthur Ashe's 'Learn Tennis,' record," Tennis, February 10, 2022, https://www.tennis.com/news/videos/allen-ashe-album-2-short.

6. Jerry Cooke, photographs, "Skeeter Tunes Up," *Sports Illustrated*, November 21, 1955, 50–53.

7. A vintage film of Skeeter Werner demonstrating her downhill teaching technique can be viewed on YouTube: "1960s Film Footage of Ski Instruction on Mt. Werner," Colorado Snowsports Museum and Hall of Fame, 10:07, April 6, 2021, https://www.youtube.com/watch?v=yg1zdas6wag.

8. In 2021, at his local Sons in Retirement branch, *Hear How to Improve Your Fishing*'s expert John Dieckman gave a slide presentation on three recent fishing trips to Alaska. Old fisherman never die . . . and Dieckman clearly maintained his passion for the sport.

9. Sam Roberts, "Ralph Morse, Life Photographer of Big Events, Is Dead at 97," *New York Times*, January 23, 2015.

10. Roberts, "Ralph Morse."

11. Sharon Osburg, "Bring Bridge Back to the Table," *New York Times*, November 27, 2005, 4, 10.

12. On the postwar decline of bridge, see David Scott, "A Narrative Analysis of a Declining Social World: The Case of Contract Bridge," *Play & Culture* 4, vol. 1 (February 1991): 11–23.

13. Thomas Vinciguerra, "The Gamester Who Went All In," *Columbia College Today*, Winter 2020–21, https://www.college.columbia.edu/cct/issue/winter-2020%E2%80%9321/article/gamester -who-went-all.

14. A nod to Jeff Missinne's post about canary training records in Facebook's Exotica . . . and other Cool, Unusual Music group, July 25, 2022.

CHAPTER 9

1. George A. Woods, "Easing the Pain of Education," *New York Times*, March 15, 1964, X17.

2. Smithsonian Folkways, "Chicago Celebrates Ella Jenkins at the DuSable Museum," Smithsonian Institution, April 10, 2019, https://ellajenkins.com/news-press.html.

3. Smithsonian Folkways, "Ella Jenkins: The First Lady of Children's Music," Smithsonian Institution, 2023, https://folkways.si.edu/ella-jenkins-first-lady-childrens/african-american -folk/music/article/smithsonian.

4. For more about Elektra records, see Mick Houston, *Becoming Elektra: The True Story of Jac Holzman's Visionary Record Label* (New York: Jawbone, 2016).

5. "Reviews and Ratings of New Popular Albums—*Folk Song Kit*," *Billboard*, May 18, 1959, 37.

6. Mikiko Tachi, "Commercialism, Counterculture, and the Folk Music Revival: A Study of *Sing Out!* Magazine, 1950–1967," *Japanese Journal of American Studies*, 15 (2004): 187–211.

7. Tachi, "Commercialism, Counterculture, and the Folk Music Revival."

8. Jim Tranquada and John King, *The Ukulele Book: A History* (Honolulu: University of Hawai'i Press), 2012, 115. Tranquada and King provide a concise introduction to the ukulele:

> As an instantly recognizable symbol of Hawaii, the 'ukulele has been many things over the past 130 years: a promise of an island paradise; a tool of political protest; an instrument central to a rich and celebrated musical culture; a musical joke; a symbol of youthful rebellion; a highly sought-after collectible; a cheap airport souvenir; a lucrative industry; an early adapter to new technologies; and the product of a remarkable synthesis of Western and Pacific cultures. (2)

9. Tranquada and King, *Ukulele Book*, 118.

10. Emily I. Dolan, "'. . . This Little Ukulele Tells the Truth': Indie Pop and Kitsch Authenticity," *Popular Music* 29 no. 3 (October 2010): 457–469.

11. Fender, "How to Play Ukulele," Fender, 2023, https://www.fender.com/articles/how-to/how-to -play-ukulele.

12. Budd Rude, "Some Gene Lies Memories," Gene Leis, n.d., http://www.hermosarecords.com /geneBuddRude.html.

13. Wilbur M. Savidge, "The Official History of Guitar Phonics," Guitar Phonics, 2021, https://guitarphonics-playguitar.com.

14. "Volume 8—Sonny Rollins—Autographed," Jazzbooks, n.d., https://www.jazzbooks.com/mm5/merchant.mvc?Screen=PROD&Store_Code=JAJAZZ&Product_Code=V08LP.

15. Tom Ervin and Jodi Goalstone, "Plays Well with Others: Jamey Aebersold and the Jazz Play-A-Longs," Plays Well with Others, n.d., https://www.jazz-play-a-longs.com.

16. Ervin and Goalstone, "Plays Well with Others." [Jamey Aebersold's original quote is from a 2019 interview with Matt Oestreicher on the *Mindful Musician* program.]

17. Tom Ervin and Jodi Goalstone, "How Play-A-Longs Came Along," Plays Well with Others, n.d., https://www.jazz-play-a-longs.com.

18. Tom Ervin and Jodi Goalstone, "Randy Brecker, Trumpeter," Plays Well with Others, n.d., https://www.jazz-play-a-longs.com. Rufus Reid, who played drums on numerous Play-A-Long records, was hired by legendary trombonist J. J. Johnson after he heard Reid playing on a Play-A-Long recording. Tom Ervin and Jodi Goalstone, "Rufus Reid, Bassist," Plays Well with Others, n.d., https://www.jazz-play-a-longs.com.

19. Bongos represented many things over the years—a touch of exotica, Latin, and beatnik: "At the tail end of the 1950s, the bongos also grew popular with the beat generation. Easy to carry, the instrument accompanied coffee-house poetry readings and exemplified subculture moodiness, discontent and rebellion against conformity and the status quo." Marc Myers, "Jack Costanzo (1919–2018)," Jazzwax, August 27, 2018, https://www.jazzwax.com/2018/08/jack-costanzo-1919-2018.html?utm_source=dlvr.it&utm_medium=twitter.

20. Neil Genzlinger, "Jack Costanzo, Who Helped Popularize the Bongos and Latin Jazz, Is Dead at 98," *New York Times*, August 26, 2018, A25.

21. George Varga, "Obituary: Jack 'Mr. Bongo' Costanzo, Dead at 98, Collaborated with Judy Garland, Nat 'King' Cole, Marlon Brando," *San Diego Union*, August 19, 2018, https://www.sandiegouniontribune.com/entertainment/music/sd-me-music-jack-costanzo-obit-20180819-story.html.

22. Michael H. Little, "Graded on a Curve: Mr. Bongo, *Learn, Play Bongos with "Mr. Bongo,"* *Vinyl District*, July 22, 2020, https://www.thevinyldistrict.com/storefront/2020/07/graded-on-a-curve-mr-bongo-learn-play-bongos-with-mr-bongo.

23. Louise Sandhaus, *Earthquakes, Mudslides, Fires & Riots: California & Graphic Design 1936–1986*, New York: Metropolis, 2014.

24. Art Chantry, "Judge by the Cover," Madame Pickwick Art Blog, January 22, 2012, http://www.madamepickwickartblog.com/2012/01/judge-by-the-cover/?replytocom=12636.

25. For an extended discussion of dancing other's steps, see Borgerson and Schroeder, *Designed for Dancing*, 12–13.

26. Leona Hipp, "Kids: Children's Dance Theatre," *Routes: A Guide to African-American Culture*, February 1978, https://routes-mag.com/issue-1978-2-3.

27. Hipp, "Kids."

28. DJ Asma, "Forgotten Treasure: *Har-You Percussion Group: Sounds of the Ghetto Youth* (1967), Music is my Sanctuary, blog, July 12, 2016, https://www.musicismysanctuary.com/forgotten-treasure-har-you-percussion-group-sounds-of-the-ghetto-youth-1967.

29. Arthur Murray contributed to the visual language of social dance:

> The silhouetted dancing couple that adorns Arthur Murray Dance Studios advertisements and storefronts has become a recognizable sign of reputable dance instruction and romantic connotations associated with forms of ballroom dance. The

> hallmark footprint patterns in Murray's dance instructions that date back to the 1920s have also become a pervasive visual symbol of ballroom dance.

Libby Smigel, "Arthur Murray (1895–1991) and Arthur Murray Dance Studios," Dance Heritage Coalition, 2012, http://www.danceheritage.org.

30. Capitol Records, advertisement, *Billboard*, February 1, 1960, 31.

31. Dance Guild, *Rumba Made Easy* (New York: Book Guild of America, 1956), 9.

32. Cynthia R. Millman, "Arthur Murray," in *The International Encyclopedia of Dance*, online ed., ed. Selma Jeanne Cohen and Dance Perspectives Foundation (New York: Oxford University Press, 2005), http://www.oxfordreference.com.

33. Arthur Murray International, "What's the Benefit of Taking Dance Lessons?," Arthur Murray International, 2019, https://arthurmurray.com.

CHAPTER 10

1. Richard D. Abraham, "The 'Conversaphone Courses' in Foreign Languages," *Hispania* 30, no. 3 (August 1947): 360.

2. The back cover of Conversa-phone records advertised four LP box sets that travel beyond the familiar French, German, and Italian to Portuguese, Russian, and Swedish. More specialized courses in Ukrainian, Persian, Afrikaans, Tagalog, and Cantonese were released in single record packages. Conversa-phone's expanded list of "Steno booster" LPs for medical and legal dictation, children's spelling, Makers of History (e.g., Katherine the Great and Oliver Cromwell), and Betty White dance discs offer a sense of what was worth learning.

3. Margalit Fox, "Marni Nixon, the Singing Voice behind the Screen, Dies at 86," *New York Times*, July 25, 2016, B8.

4. Stanley Bowmar Co., advertisement, "Records for the Classroom," *Journal of Health, Physical Education, and Recreation* 38, no. 6 (June 1967): 68.

5. Ruth De Cesare, "Music to the Fore," *Music Educators Journal* 47, no. 4 (February–March 1961): 90.

CHAPTER 11

1. Peter Keepnews, "Jon Hendricks, 96, Who Brought a New Dimension to Jazz Singing, Dies," *New York Times*, November 22, 2017, B13.

2. Ralph J. Gleason, *Conversations in Jazz: The Ralph J. Gleason Interviews* (New Haven, CT: Yale University Press, 2016), 264.

3. Whitney Balliet, "Big Ben: Once Upon a Time, Ben Webster Was the King of Tenor Saxophonists," *New Yorker*, August 20, 2001, 158.

4. Ben Ratliff, "Jimmy Witherspoon, Singer of Blues and Jazz, Dies at 74," *New York Times*, September 22, 1997, D16.

5. "Discourse from the *Billboard* Sales Department—Hannah Dean," *Billboard*, September 5, 1960, 20.

6. Nat Hentoff, "Blues Odyssey by a Hip Homer," *Stereo Review*, July 1961, 61.

7. Hentoff, "Blues Odyssey." 62.

8. Keepnews, "Jon Hendricks," B13.

9. Joe Maita, "Remembering Jon Hendricks, 1921–2017," JerryJazzMusican, https://jerryjazzmusician.com/remembering-jon-hendricks-1921-2017.

10. John S. Wilson, "Cannonball Adderley, Jazzman, Dead," *New York Times*, August 9, 1975, 15.

11. Herina Ayot, "Tension and Release: A History of Jazz and Sex," *Ebony*, February 27, 2013, https://www.ebony.com/a-history-of-jazz-and-sex-405.

12. Larry Bunker, percussionist on *Let's Get Acquainted with Jazz*, had quite a varied career. He was in the US Army Band in the late 1940s; he played in Gerry Mulligan's group, which included Art Pepper and Chet Baker; he was a member of the Bill Evans Trio; and he played timpani for the Los Angeles Philharmonic. He also helped create memorable scores for films such as *Breakfast at Tiffany's* (1961), *THX 1138* (1971), and *The Matrix Revolutions* (2003).

13. "Reviews—*Let's Get Acquainted with Jazz*," *Billboard*, November 3, 1958, 42.

14. Peter Keepnews, "George Avakian, Record Producer and Talent Scout, Dies at 98," *New York Times*, November 22, 2017, A24.

15. Keepnews, "George Avakian."

16. "Garry Winogrand: Exhibition Overview," Metropolitan Museum of Art, 2014, https://www.metmuseum.org/exhibitions/listings/2014/garry-winogrand.

17. "Leonard Bernstein's Young People's Concerts with the New York Philharmonic," Leonard Bernstein Office, 2023, https://www.leonardbernstein.com/about/educator/young-peoples-concerts.

18. William Yardley, "John McClure Dies at 84; Produced Classic Records," *New York Times*, June 25, 2014, A15.

19. Wendy Hilty shot many classic midcentury album covers. For a brief selection, see Janet Borgerson and Jonathan Schroeder, "Recovering and Discovering Album Cover Artists and Photographers," MIT Press, November 1, 2017, https://mitpress.mit.edu/blog/recovering-and-discovering-album-cover-artists-and-photographers.

20. Susan Ellis, "The Legacy of Violette Hilty," The Source: US Virgin Islands, September 17, 2020, https://stthomassource.com/content/2020/09/17/the-legacy-of-violette-hilty.

21. Jonathan Schroeder and Janet Borgerson, "How Stereo Was First Sold to a Skeptical Public," The Conversation, December 12, 2018, https://theconversation.com/how-stereo-was-first-sold-to-a-skeptical-public-103668.

CHAPTER 12

1. Histories of recorded sound focus almost exclusively on music. For example, Andre Millard's comprehensive history of the US recording industry doesn't mention spoken-word, comedy, or instructional records at all. Andre Millard, *America on Record: A History of Recorded Sound*, 2nd ed. (Cambridge: Cambridge University Press, 2005).

2. Rodney S. Earle, "The Integration of Instructional Technology into Public Education: Promises and Challenges," *Educational Technology* 42, no. 1 (January–February 2002): 5–13.

3. International Correspondence Systems, advertisement, "Sell Them I.C.S. Records and Textbooks," *Talking Machine World* 24, no. 7 (July 15, 1906): 5.

4. Mark Katz, "Making America More Musical through the Phonograph, 1900–1930," *American Music* 16, no. 4 (Winter 1998): 448–475.

5. Jordan Mroziak, "Exiles on Main Street: A Pedagogy of Popular Music through Technology and Aesthetic Education," PhD diss., School of Education, Duquesne University, 2017, 48.

6. Susan J. Douglas, *Listening In: Radio and the American Imagination* (New York: Times Books, 1999), 7. As both radio and records rose up to dominate the listening sphere, "radio was above all seen as a communicative medium and sound recordings were seen as an entertainment

medium." Kyle Barnett, *Record Cultures: The Transformation of the U.S. Recording Industry* (Ann Arbor: University of Michigan Press, 2020), 7.

7. John Durham Peters, *Speaking into the Air: A History of the Idea of Communication* (Chicago: University of Chicago Press, 1999), 160.

8. Thomas A. Edison, "The Phonograph and Its Future," *North American Review* 126, no. 262 (May–June 1878), 533–534.

9. Edison, "Phonograph and Its Future," 527.

10. Gitelman, *Scripts, Grooves, and Writing Machines*, 63.

11. Edison, "Phonograph and Its Future," 531.

12. Edison, 533.

13. Marsha Siefert, "Aesthetics, Technology, and the Capitalization of Culture: How the Talking Machine Became a Musical Instrument," *Science in Context* 8, no. 2 (Summer 1995): 417–449.

14. Patrick Feaster, "'The Following Record': Making Sense of Phonographic Performance, 1877–1908," PhD diss., Indiana University, 2007.

15. David Morton, *Off the Record: The Technology and Culture of Sound Recording in America* (New Brunswick, NJ: Rutgers University Press, 2000).

16. Gary Marmorstein, *The Label: The Story of Columbia Records* (New York: Thunder's Mouth, 2007).

17. Matthew Rubery, *The Untold Story of the Talking Book* (Cambridge, MA: Harvard University Press, 2016).

18. Mike Evans, *Vinyl: The Art of Making Records* (New York: Sterling, 2015), 78–81.

19. Rubery, *The Untold Story*, 189.

20. Smith, *Spoken Word*, 204–205.

21. Smith, *Spoken Word*, 3. Remarkable historic recordings are available online, including recordings of Thomas Edison and early "advertisements" for the phonograph. See, for example, "Early Spoken Word Recordings," British Library: Sounds, n.d., https://sounds.bl.uk/Oral-history /Early-spoken-word-recordings; "Listen to Edison Sound Recordings," National Park Service, US Department of the Interior, 2015, https://www.nps.gov/edis/learn/photosmultimedia/the -recording-archives.htm; and "I Am the Edison Phonograph (1906)," *Public Domain Review*, 2016, https://publicdomainreview.org/collection/i-am-the-edison-phonograph-1906.

22. William Howland Kenney, *Recorded Music in American Life: The Phonograph and Popular Memory, 1890–1945* (New York: Oxford University Press 1999), 55. See also Gideon Schwartz, *Revolution: The History of Turntable Design* (New York: Phaidon, 2022).

23. Talking Machine World, "Fiftieth Anniversary of the Phonograph," *Talking Machine World* 23, no. 8 (August 1927): 34b.

24. Lisa Gitelman, *Always Already New: Media, History, and the Data of Culture* (Cambridge, MA: MIT Press, 2006), 35.

25. Gitelman, *Always Already New*, 35.

26. "Spreads Civilization," *Talking Machine World* 2, no. 7 (July 15, 1906): 5.

27. Francis H. Horn, "Music for Everyone," *Music Educators Journal* 42, no. 4 (February-March 1956): 27.

28. Colin Symes, "A Sound Education: The Gramophone and the Classroom in the United Kingdom and the United States, 1920–1940," *British Journal of Music Education* 21, no. 2 (July 2004): 163.

29. Symes, "Sound Education," 165.

30. Colin Symes, *Setting the Record Straight: A Material History of Classical Music Recording* (Middletown, CT: Wesleyan University Press, 2004), 8.

31. Ruth De Cesare, "Music to the Fore," *Music Educators Journal*, 47, no. 4 (February–March 1961): 91.

32. Kyle S. Barnett, "Furniture Music: The Phonograph as Furniture: 1900–1930," *Journal of Popular Music Studies* 18 no. 3 (December 2006): 301–324.

33. Barnett, "Furniture Music," 301.

34. Barnett, 302.

35. Gary S. Cross and Robert N. Proctor, *Packaged Pleasures: How Technology & Marketing Revolutionized Desire* (Chicago: University of Chicago Press, 2014), 160.

36. Barnett, "Furniture Music," 301–324.

37. Kenney, *Recorded Music in American Life*, 58. See also *The Oscar Saenger Course in Vocal Training* (1916), The Victor Talking Machine Company, HathiTrust, 2023, https://babel.hathitrust .org/cgi/pt?id=inu.39000018564976&seq=1.

38. Symes, "Sound Education," 175.

39. Quote from Sondra Wieland Howe, "The NBC Music Appreciation Hour: Radio Broadcasts of Walter Damrosch, 1928–1942," *Journal of Research in Music Education* 51, no. 1 (Spring 2003): 67. See also the posthumously published critique, Theodor W. Adorno, "Analytical Study of the NBC 'Music Appreciation Hour,'" *The Musical Quarterly* 78, no. 2 (Summer 1994): 325–377.

40. Joan Shelley Rubin, *Making of Middlebrow Culture* (Chapel Hill: University of North Carolina Press, 1992), 1. In a wide-ranging discussion of efforts to expose midcentury Americans to "high" culture, Rubin mentions books, book clubs, magazines, night courses, public lecture series, and university extension programs—but not instructional records. See also Keir Keightley, "Music for Middlebrows: Defining the Easy Listening Era, 1946–1966," *American Music* 26, no. 3 (Fall 2008): 309–335.

41. Kenney, *Recorded Music in American Life*, 58.

42. Frances E. Clark, quoted in Kenney, 58.

43. Frances E. Clark, "Introduction," in *Educational Catalog and Graded List of Victor Records for Home School and College*, by RCA Victor Education Department (Camden, NJ: RCA Victor, 1930), 5.

44. *Educational Catalog and Graded List of Victor Records for Home School and College* (Camden, NJ: RCA Victor, 1930), 1.

45. Katz, "Making America More Musical," 450.

46. Aaron Copland, "The World of the Phonograph," *American Scholar* 6, no. 1 (Winter 1937): 30.

47. Decca Records advertisement quoted in Daniel J. Boorstin, *The Americans: The Democratic Experience* (New York: Vintage, 1973), 370.

48. Edgar Dale, *Audio-Visual Methods in Teaching*, rev. ed. (New York: Dryden, 1954), 297.

49. Lyle E. Siverson, "Audio-Visual Equipment Is Material for Instruction," *National Elementary Principal* 36, no.1 (September 1956): 202.

50. Daniel P. Girard, "Unit in Use of Audio-Visual Aids," *Modern Language Journal* 30, no. 2 (February 1946): 62–68.

51. Paul Saettler, *The Evolution of American Educational Technology* (Englewood, CO: Libraries Unlimited, 1990), 187.

52. Boorstin, *Americans*.

53. "English for DPs: Audio-Visual Methods Are Used To Teach Them Quickly," *New York Times*, June 13, 1948, E9.

54. Dale, *Audio-Visual Methods in Teaching*, 297.

55. Dale, 464–465. See also Effie G. Bathurst, "Phonograph Records as Aids to Learning," *Journal of Educational Psychology* 34, no. 7 (October 1943): 385–406.

56. Dale, *Audio-Visual Methods in Teaching*, 295.

57. Max Rafferty, "Foreword," in William A. Allen, ed., *Improving Instruction through Audio-Visual Media: Techniques in Teaching Science, Mathematics, and Modern Foreign Languages*, Report No-NDEA-3B (Washington, DC: US Department of Health, Education, and Welfare, Office of Education, 1963), ii.

58. William A. Allen, ed., *Improving Instruction through Audio-Visual Media: Techniques in Teaching Science, Mathematics, and Modern Foreign Languages*, Report No-NDEA-3B (Washington, DC: US Department of Health, Education, and Welfare, Office of Education, 1963).

59. *The School Instructional Materials Center and the Curriculum: The Library Audio-visual Center, Pennsylvania Curriculum Development Program* (Harrisburg, PA: Commonwealth of Pennsylvania, Department of Public Instruction, 1962).

60. Hubert Wheeler, *Audio-Visual Instruction: An Administrative Handbook* (Jefferson City: Missouri State Board of Education, 1961), 31.

61. Fritjof A. Raven, "Spoken Spanish Instruction at the Massachusetts Institute of Technology," *Hispania* 31, no. 2 (May 1948), 177.

62. Tadeusz Kozlowski, "Programmed Teaching," *Financial Analysts Journal* 17, no. 6 (November-December 1961), 47.

63. George A. Woods, "Easing the Pain of Education," *New York Times*, March 15, 1964, X17.

64. Excerpts from *Teaching Reading in the Elementary School* (1965) can be heard on the Smithsonian Folkways website: "Teaching Reading in the Elementary School, Morris Schreiber," Smithsonian Institution, 2023, https://folkways.si.edu/morris-schreiber/teaching-reading-in -the-elementary-school/language-instruction/album/smithsonian.

65. Books about instructional film include Kelly Ritter, *Reframing the Subject: Postwar Instructional Film and Class-Conscious Literacies* (Pittsburgh: University of Pittsburgh Press, 2015); Vinzenz Hediger and Patrick Vonderau, ed., *Films that Work: Industrial Film and the Productivity of Media* (Amsterdam: Amsterdam University Press, 2009); Haidee Wasson, *Everyday Movies: Portability and the Transformation of American Culture* (Berkeley: University of California Press, 2019); Geoff Alexander, *Academic Films for the Classroom* (Jefferson, NC: McFarland, 2010); and Devon Orgeron, Marsha Orgeron, and Dan Streibel, eds., *Learning with the Lights Off: Educational Film in the United States* (New York: Oxford University Press, 2012).

66. Charles R. Acland and Haidee Wasson, ed., *Useful Cinema* (Durham, NC: Duke University Press, 2011).

67. Steve Young and Sport Murphy's wonderful book *Everything's Coming Up Profits: The Golden Age of Industrial Musicals* (New York: Blast, 2013) celebrates industrial musicals—often elaborate, big-budget Broadway-inspired productions staged for sales conventions and industry conferences. Many were recorded and released on records that focused more on entertainment than instruction.

68. Conferences and conventions also represent a relatively underappreciated mode of midcentury communication and pedagogy. Several albums included here were recorded at such events. See Justus Nieland, *Happiness by Design: Modernism and Media in the Eames Era* (Minneapolis: University of Minnesota Press, 2020).

69. Edward Bellamy's story "With the Eyes Shut," referenced in Gitelman, *Scripts, Grooves, and Writing Machines*, 65.

CHAPTER 13

1. For insights into the spatial dimensions of postwar culture, see Beatriz Colomina, AnnMarie Brennan, and Jeanine Kim, eds., *Cold War Hothouses: Inventing Postwar Culture, from Cockpit to Playboy* (Princeton, NJ: Princeton Architectural Press, 2004).

2. See, for example, Fred Turner, *The Democratic Surround: Multimedia and American Liberalism from World War II to the Psychedelic Sixties* (Chicago: University of Chicago Press, 2013), 218–220.

3. Greg Barnhisel, *Cold War Modernists: Art, Literature, and American Cultural Diplomacy* (New York: Columbia University Press, 2015).

4. Barnhisel, *Cold War Modernists*, 2.

5. Eva Illouz, *Saving the Modern Soul: Therapy, Emotions, and the Culture of Self-Help* (Berkeley: University of California Press, 2008).

6. Borgerson and Schroeder, *Designed for Hi-Fi Living*.

BIBLIOGRAPHY

Abraham, Richard D. "The 'Conversaphone Courses' in Foreign Languages." *Hispania* 30, no. 3 (August 1947): 358–360.

Acland, Charles R., and Haidee Wasson, ed. *Useful Cinema*. Durham, NC: Duke University Press, 2011.

Adorno, Theodor W. "Analytical Study of the NBC 'Music Appreciation Hour.'" *Musical Quarterly* 78, no. 2 (Summer 1994): 325–377.

Alexander, Geoff. *Academic Films for the Classroom*. Jefferson, NC: McFarland, 2010.

Allen, William A., ed. *Improving Instruction through Audio-Visual Media: Techniques in Teaching Science, Mathematics, and Modern Foreign Languages*, Report No-NDEA-3B. Washington, DC: US Department of Health, Education, and Welfare, Office of Education, 1963.

Alvino, James. "On Educating Gifted Children." *New York Times*, November 13, 1983, 11NJ, 36.

Amway Corporation. *Amagram* 17, no. 10 (October 1976): 3.

Anderson, Dave. "Arnold Palmer, the Magnetic Face of Golf in the '60s, Dies at 87." *New York Times*, September 25, 2016, A1.

Anderson, Tim J. "Listening to the Promise of a Better You: Considering the Instructional Record." *Leonardo Music Journal* 26 (December 2016): 28–31.

Anderson, Tim. J. *Making Easy Listening: Material Culture and American Recording*. Minneapolis: University of Minnesota Press, 2006.

Anderson, Tim J. "Training the Listener: Stereo Demonstration Discs in an Emerging Consumer Market." In *Living Stereo: Histories and Cultures of Multichannel Sound*, edited by Paul Théberge, Kyle Devine, and Tom Everett, 107–124. London: Bloomsbury, 2015.

Apple, Michael. *Education and Power*. 2nd ed. New York: Routledge, 1995.

Archer, Sarah. *The Midcentury Kitchen: America's Favorite Room from Workspace to Dreamscape, 1940s–1970s*. New York: Countryman, 2019.

Argosy Music Corp. "Ballads for the Age of Science." 2019. https://www.argosymusiccorp.com/Science/Science.html.

Arthur Murray International. "What's the Benefit of Taking Dance Lessons?" 2019. https://arthurmurray.com.

Austin, Jon, ed. *Spinning Popular Culture as Public Pedagogy: Critical Reflections and Transformative Possibilities*. Boston: BrillSense, 2017.

Ayot, Herina. "Tension and Release: A History of Jazz and Sex." *Ebony*, February 27, 2013. https://www.ebony.com/a-history-of-jazz-and-sex-405.

Baldwin, Kate A. *The Racial Imaginary of the Cold War Kitchen: From Sokol'niki Park to Chicago's South Side*. Lebanon, NH: Dartmouth College Press, 2016.

Balliet, Whitney. "Big Ben: Once Upon a Time, Ben Webster Was the King of Tenor Saxophonists." *New Yorker*, August 20, 2001, 158.

Barnett, Kyle S. "Furniture Music: The Phonograph as Furniture: 1900–1930." *Journal of Popular Music Studies* 18, no. 3 (December 2006): 301–324.

Barnett, Kyle. *Record Cultures: The Transformation of the U.S. Recording Industry*. Ann Arbor: University of Michigan Press, 2020.

Barnhisel, Greg. *Cold War Modernists: Art, Literature, and American Cultural Diplomacy*. New York: Columbia University Press, 2015.

Bathurst, Effie G. "Phonograph Records as Aids to Learning." *Journal of Educational Psychology* 34 no.7 (October 1943): 385–406.

Baudrillard, Jean. *The Consumer Society: Myths and Structures*. Translated by Chris Turner. London: Sage, 1998.

Benko, Steven A. ed. *Better Living through TV: Contemporary TV and Moral Identity Formation*. Lanham, MD: Lexington, 2022.

Billboard. "Album Reviews—*You Be a Disc Jockey*." *Billboard*, December 28, 1963, 10.

Billboard. "Carlton Distrib Meeting Brings Big Sales Hike." *Billboard Music Week*, January 16, 1961, 8, 58.

Billboard. "Coast Department Stores in All-Out Kidisk Xmas Drives; Supply Plentiful." *Billboard*, November 23, 1946, 18.

Billboard. "Discourse from the Billboard Sales Department—Hannah Dean." *Billboard*, September 5, 1960, 20.

Billboard. "Disk Course LPs to Sell for $9.95." *Billboard*, December 24, 1955, 14.

Billboard. "From the Music Capitols of the World." *Billboard*, December 9, 1967, 17, 79, 83, 84, 86, 90.

Billboard. "Periodicals Turn New Leaf in Ties with LP Producers." *Billboard Music Week*, August 7, 1961, 1.

Billboard. "Point-of-Purchase Display Sells Children's Records for Golden." *Billboard*, March 6, 1965, 35.

Billboard. "Reviews—*Let's Get Acquainted with Jazz*." *Billboard*, November 3, 1958, 42.

Billboard. "Reviews and Ratings of New Popular Albums—*Folk Song Kit*." *Billboard*, May 18, 1959, 37.

Billboard. "Reviews and Ratings of New Popular Albums—*Now We Know (Songs to Learn By)* Album 2." *Billboard*, May 28, 1955, 56.

Billboard. "Reviews and Ratings of New Albums—*Speak Well*." *Billboard*, October 5, 1959, 30.

Billboard. "Take a Chorus: MMO Debs Two More LP Vols." *Billboard*, November 24, 1956, 30.

Bonner, David. *Revolutionizing Children's Records: The Young People's Records and Children's Record Guild Series, 1946–1977*. Lanham, MD: Scarecrow, 2007.

"Bonnie to the Rescue." *Sports Illustrated*, November 25, 1957, 52–54.

Boorstin, Daniel J. *The Americans: The Democratic Experience*. New York: Vintage, 1973.

Borgerson, Janet, and Jonathan Schroeder. *Designed for Dancing: How Midcentury Records Taught America to Dance*. Cambridge, MA: MIT Press, 2021.

Borgerson, Janet, and Jonathan Schroeder. *Designed for Hi-Fi Living: The Vinyl LP in Midcentury America*. Cambridge, MA: MIT Press, 2017.

Borgerson, Janet, and Jonathan Schroeder. "Recovering and Discovering Album Cover Artists and Photographers." MIT Press, November 1, 2017. https://mitpress.mit.edu/blog/recovering -and-discovering-album-cover-artists-and-photographers.

Bourdieu, Pierre, and Jean-Claude Passeron. *Reproduction in Education, Society, and Culture*. London: Sage, 1977.

Bragg, Lois, ed. *Deaf World: A Historical Reader and Primary Sourcebook*. New York: New York University Press, 2001.

Brown, Elspeth H. *The Corporate Eye: Photography and the Rationalization of American Commercial Culture*. Baltimore, MD: Johns Hopkins University Press, 2005.

Brown, Elspeth H. "Rationalizing Consumption: Lejaran à Hiller and the Origins of American Advertising Photography, 1913–1924." *Enterprise & Society* 1, no. 4 (December 2000): 715–738.

Brown, Helen Gurley. *Sex and the Single Girl*. New York: Pocket, 1962.

Brown, Michael J. *Hope and Scorn: Eggheads, Experts, and Elites in American Politics*. Chicago: University of Chicago Press, 2020.

Bruil, Rudolf A. "What Is It about Remington Records?" The Remington Site, n.d. http://www .soundfountain.org.

Brzezinski, Max. *Vinyl Age: A Guide to Record Collecting Now*. New York: Black Dog & Leventhal, 2020.

Bullough, Vern L. "Alfred Kinsey and the Kinsey Report: Historical Overview and Lasting Contributions." *Journal of Sex Research* 35, no. 2 (May 1998): 127–131.

Capitol Records. Advertisement. *Billboard*, February 1, 1960, 31.

Castillo, Greg. *Cold War on the Home Front: The Soft Power of Midcentury Design*. Minneapolis: University of Minnesota Press, 2009.

Cederström, Carl, and André Spicer. *Desperately Seeking Self-Improvement: A Year inside the Optimization Movement*. New York: OR, 2017.

Cep, Casey. "Diary of a Made-up Kid." *New Yorker*, August 1, 2022, 60–64.

Chantry, Art. "Judge by the Cover." Madame Pickwick Art Blog, January 22, 2012. http://www .madamepickwickartblog.com/2012/01/judge-by-the-cover/?replytocom=12636.

"'Chaplain of Bourbon Street' dies at 89." *Baptist Press*, July 5, 2017. https://www.baptistpress .com/resource-library/news/chaplain-of-bourbon-street-dies-at-89.

Friedan, Betty. *The Feminine Mystique*. New York: Norton, 1963.

Friedman, Danielle. *Let's Get Physical: How Women Discovered Exercise and Reshaped the World*. New York: Putman, 2022.

Gahr, David. Photographs. 2023. https://www.davidgahr.com.

Genzlinger, Neil. "Jack Costanzo, Who Helped Popularize the Bongos and Latin Jazz, Is Dead at 98." *New York Times*, August 26, 2018, A25.

Girard, Daniel P. "Unit in Use of Audio-Visual Aids." *Modern Language Journal* 30, no. 2 (February 1946): 62–68.

Gitelman, Lisa. *Always Already New: Media, History, and the Data of Culture*. Cambridge, MA: MIT Press, 2006.

Gitelman, Lisa. *Scripts, Grooves, and Writing Machines: Representing Technology in the Edison Era*. Stanford, CA: Stanford University Press, 1999.

Gleason, Ralph J. *Conversations in Jazz: The Ralph J. Gleason Interviews*. New Haven, CT: Yale University Press, 2016.

Goffman, Erving. *The Presentation of Self in Everyday Life*. New York: Doubleday Anchor, 1959.

Golden Records. Advertisement. *Billboard*, October 16, 1965, 36.

Goldstein, Jan. "Foucault's Technologies of the Self and the Cultural History of Identity." *Arcadia* 33, no. 1 (January 1998): 46–63.

Goldstein, Richard. "Jack LaLanne, Founder of Modern Fitness Movement, Dies at 96." *New York Times*, January 23, 2011, A25.

Goodale, Greg. *Sonic Persuasion: Reading Sound in the Recorded Age*. Champaign: University of Illinois Press, 2011.

Goodman, Paul. *Growing Up Absurd: Problems of Youth in the Organized Society*. New York: Vintage, 1960.

Grevatt, Ren. "Album Education Kick Grows; Indie Companies Lead Way: LP's Teach Language, Dancing, Golf, Flying, Do-It-Yourself Music." *Billboard*, November 21, 1960, 4, 24.

Grundberg, Andy. "Photography View: Commercial Work Was Best." *New York Times*, February 14, 1982, A33.

Hardwig, Florian. "*Affect Your Emotions Through Music* Album Art." Fonts in Use, July 4, 2021. https://fontsinuse.com/uses/38055/affect-your-emotions-through-music-album-art.

Hediger, Vinzenz, and Patrick Vonderau, ed. *Films That Work: Industrial Film and the Productivity of Media*. Amsterdam: Amsterdam University Press, 2009.

Heiferman, Marvin. "Paul Outerbridge," *Art in America*, October 23, 2009. https://www.artnews .com/art-in-america/features/paul-outerbridge-62816.

Heller, Steven. "Advertising Layout Handbook of Don May." The Daily Heller, October 14, 2018. https://www.printmag.com/daily-heller/rough-rough-rough.

Hentoff, Nat. "Blues Odyssey by a Hip Homer." *Stereo Review*, July 1961, 61–62.

Hinds, Josh. "Dottie Walters, Motivational Speakers Hall of Fame." Get Motivation, n.d. https:// www.getmotivation.com/dottie-walters-hof.htm.

Hipp, Leona. "Kids: Children's Dance Theatre." *Routes: A Guide to African-American Culture*, February 1978. https://routes-mag.com/issue-1978-2-3.

Horn, Francis H. "Music for Everyone." *Music Educators Journal* 42, no. 4 (February–March 1956): 27–29.

Houston, Mick. *Becoming Elektra: The True Story of Jac Holzman's Visionary Record Label*. New York: Jawbone, 2016.

Howe, Sondra Wieland. "The NBC Music Appreciation Hour: Radio Broadcasts of Walter Damrosch, 1928–1942." *Journal of Research in Music Education* 51, no. 1 (Spring 2003): 64–77.

HQ Staff. "Learn Morse Code the Boy Scout Way." Radio Relay International, April 15, 2017. https://radio-relay.org/learn-morse-code-the-boy-scout-way.

Huber, Richard M. *The American Idea of Success*. New York: McGraw-Hill, 1971.

Illouz, Eva. *Saving the Modern Soul: Therapy, Emotions, and the Culture of Self-Help*. Berkeley: University of California Press, 2008.

International Correspondence Systems. Advertisement. "Sell Them I.C.S. Records and Textbooks." *Talking Machine World* 24, no. 7 (July 15, 1906): 5.

International Tennis Hall of Fame. "Arthur Ashe." 2022. https://www.tennisfame.com/hall-of -famers/inductees/arthur-ashe.

Isaacs, Shalyn. "Profile of Joyce Brothers." In Psychology's Feminist Voices Digital Archive, edited by A. Rutherford, 2016. https://feministvoices.com/profiles/joyce-brothers.

Jazzbooks. "Volume 8—Sonny Rollins—Autographed." n.d. https://www.jazzbooks.com/mm5 /merchant.mvc?Screen=PROD&Store_Code=JAJAZZ&Product_Code=V08LP.

Johnson, Ken. "Always Something Unnerving in Paul Outerbridge Photographs." *New York Times*, September 9, 2016, C20.

Katz, Mark. "Making America More Musical through the Phonograph, 1900–1930." *American Music* 16, no. 4 (Winter 1998): 448–475.

Keightley, Keir. "Music for Middlebrows: Defining the Easy Listening Era, 1946–1966." *American Music* 26, no. 3 (Fall, 2008): 309–335.

Keepnews, Peter. "George Avakian, Record Producer and Talent Scout, Dies at 98." *New York Times*, November 22, 2017, A24.

Keepnews, Peter. "Jon Hendricks, 96, Who Brought a New Dimension to Jazz Singing, Dies." *New York Times*, November 22, 2017, B13.

Kenney, William Howland. *Recorded Music in American Life: The Phonograph and Popular Memory, 1890–1945*. New York: Oxford University Press, 1999.

King, Daniel J. "Chuck Stewart's Legendary Photographs (1927–2017)." Ohio University College of Fine Arts News, June 30, 2017. https://www.ohio.edu/fine-arts/news/chuck-stewarts -legendary-photographs-1927-2017.

Kinsey Institute. "Learn More about Our Research." 2020. https://kinseyinstitute.org/research /research-topics.php.

Kozlowski, Tadeusz. "Programmed Teaching." *Financial Analysts Journal* 17, no. 6 (November– December 1961): 47, 50–52, 54.

Krukowski, Damon. *Ways of Hearing*. Cambridge, MA: MIT Press, 2019.

Lacey, Kate. *Listening Publics: The Politics and Experience of Listening in the Media Age.* London: Polity, 2013.

Landeck, Beatrice. "New Records for Children." *New York Times*, November 20, 1955, XX9.

Lawry's. "Adolph's® Unseasoned Meat Tenderizer." McCormick & Company, Inc, 2023. https://www.mccormick.com/lawrys/flavors/adolphs/adolphs-original-meat-tenderizer.

Leiss, William, Stephen Kline, Sut Jhally, Jacqueline Botterill, and Kyle Asquith. *Social Communication in Advertising: Consumption in the Mediated Marketplace.* 4th ed. New York: Routledge, 2018.

Leonard Bernstein Office. "Leonard Bernstein's Young People's Concerts with the New York Philharmonic." 2023. https://www.leonardbernstein.com/about/educator/young-peoples-concerts.

Lepore, Jill. "How Longfellow Woke the Dead." *The American Scholar*, March 2, 2011. https://theamericanscholar.org/how-longfellow-woke-the-dead.

"Leslie Allen on Arthur Ashe's 'Learn Tennis,' Record." Tennis, February 10, 2022. https://www.tennis.com/news/videos/allen-ashe-album-2-short.

Little, Michael H. "Graded on a Curve: Mr. Bongo, *Learn, Play Bongos with "Mr. Bongo."* Vinyl District, July 22, 2020. https://www.thevinyldistrict.com/storefront/2020/07/graded-on-a-curve-mr-bongo-learn-play-bongos-with-mr-bongo.

Lucey, Trisha. "Catching Up with . . . Bonnie Prudden, Fitness Pioneer." *Sports Illustrated*, June 6, 1999, 12.

Lupton, Ellen. *Mechanical Brides: Women and Machines from Home to Office.* New York: Cooper Hewitt National Museum of Design / Princeton Architectural Press, 1993.

Lupton, Ellen. *Thinking with Type: A Critical Guide for Designers, Writers, Editors, and Students.* New York: Princeton Architectural Press, 2004.

Maita, Joe. "Remembering Jon Hendricks 1921–2017." JerryJazzMusician, November 22, 2017. https://jerryjazzmusician.com/remembering-jon-hendricks-1921-2017.

Marmorstein, Gary. *The Label: The Story of Columbia Records.* New York: Thunder's Mouth, 2007.

Martin, Douglas. "Bonnie Prudden, 97, Dies; Promoted Fitness for TV Generation." *New York Times*, December 20, 2011, B10.

Martin, Douglas. "Noel Regney, Songwriter Known for 'Do You Hear What I Hear?' Is Dead at 80." *New York Times*, December 1, 2002, Section 1, 58.

Martin, Douglas. "Tom Glazer, Folk Singer, Is Dead at 88." *New York Times*, February 26, 2003, A23.

Masterwork. Advertisement. "4 New Models for Spring Sales from Your Newest Profit Line." *Billboard*, January 26, 1963, 49.

McGee, Micki. *Self-Help, Inc.: Makeover Culture in American Life.* New York: Oxford University Press, 2005.

McKenzie, Shelly. "Weak Hearts and Wedding Day Figures: Exercise and Health Promotion in the 1960s." In *Women, Wellness, and the Media*, edited by Margaret C. Wiley, 199–229. Newcastle upon Tyne: Cambridge Scholars, 2008.

McLuhan, Marshall. *The Mechanical Bride: Folklore of Industrial Man*. New York: Vanguard, 1951.

Metropolitan Museum of Art. "Garry Winogrand: Exhibition Overview." 2014. https://www.metmuseum.org/exhibitions/listings/2014/garry-winogrand.

Middleton, Richard. *Studying Popular Music*. Milton Keynes: Open University Press, 1990.

Milano, Brett. *Vinyl Junkies: Adventures in Record Collecting*. New York: St. Martin's, 2003.

Millard, Andre. *America on Record: A History of Recorded Sound*. 2nd ed. Cambridge: Cambridge University Press, 2005.

Miller, Arthur. *Death of a Salesman*. New York: Viking, 1949.

Miller, Bill. "Amway Merits Support." *Grand Rapids Press*, December 15, 1982, 14A.

Millman, Cynthia R. "Arthur Murray." In *The International Encyclopedia of Dance*, edited by Selma Jeanne Cohen and Dance Perspectives Foundation. New York: Oxford University Press, 2005. http://www.oxfordreference.com.

Mishra, Suman. "From Self-Control to Self-Improvement: Evolving Messages and Persuasion Techniques in Weight Loss Advertising (1930–1990)." *Visual Communication* 16, no. 4 (November 2017): 467–494.

Mitgans, Herbert. "A Christmas Guide to Children's Records." *HiFi/Stereo Review*, December 1963, 43–46.

Montez de Oca, Jeffrey. "'As Our Muscles Get Softer, Our Missile Race Becomes Harder':" Cultural Citizenship and the 'Muscle Gap." *Journal of Historical Sociology* 18, no. 3 (September 2005): 145–172.

Morton, David. *Off the Record: The Technology and Culture of Sound Recording in America*. New Brunswick, NJ: Rutgers University Press, 2000.

Moshier, Jon. "Learn the Secrets of Self-improvement with Vintage Instructional Records." WDET 101.9 FM, January 31, 2022. https://wdet.org/2022/01/31/learn-the-secrets-of-self-improvement-with-vintage-instructional-records.

Mroziak, Jordan. "Exiles on Main Street: A Pedagogy of Popular Music through Technology and Aesthetic Education." PhD diss., School of Education, Duquesne University, 2017.

Müllner, Rudolf. "Self-Improvement in and through Sports: Cultural-Historical Perspectives." *International Journal of the History of Sport* 33, no. 14 (2006): 1592–1605.

Music Minus One catalog. New York: Music Minus One, n.d.

Myers, Marc. "Jack Costanzo (1919–2018)." Jazzwax, August 27, 2018. https://www.jazzwax.com/2018/08/jack-costanzo-1919-2018.html?utm_source=dlvr.it&utm_medium=twitter.

National Archives. "The Federal Government Takes on Physical Fitness." John F. Kennedy Presidential Library and Museum, n.d. https://www.jfklibrary.org/learn/about-jfk/jfk-in-history/physical-fitness.

Neill, A. S. *Summerhill: A Radical Approach to Child Rearing*. New York: Hart, 1960.

Nelson, Valerie J. "Dr. Joyce Brothers Dies at 85; Popular TV Psychologist." *Los Angeles Times*, May 13, 2013. https://www.latimes.com/local/obituaries/la-me-joyce-brothers-20130514-story.html.

"Nicholas Kounovsky, Fitness Expert, 80." *New York Times*, December 8, 1993, B8.

Nieland, Justus. *Happiness by Design: Modernism and Media in the Eames Era*. Minneapolis: University of Minnesota Press, 2020.

Orgeron, Devon, Marsha Orgeron, and Dan Streibel. ed. *Learning with the Lights Off: Educational Film in the United States*. New York: Oxford University Press, 2012.

Online Archive of California. "Inventory of the Bern C. Ramey Papers, 1858–1998." Department of Special Collections, University of California, Davis, n.d. https://oac.cdlib.org/findaid/ark:/13030 /kt5q2nc5wk/entire_text.

Orange Bean, Indiana. "In the 60s, Men and Women Both Tuned in to Debbie Drake." January 20, 2021. https://orangebeanindiana.com/2021/01/20/in-the-60s-men-and-women-both-tuned-in-to -debbie-drake.

Osburg, Sharon. "Bring Bridge Back to the Table." *New York Times*, November 27, 2005, 4, 10.

Ostrofsky, Kathryn A. "Learning from *Sesame Street* Soundtrack Albums." In *The Soundtrack Album: Listening to Media*, edited by Paul N. Reinsch and Laurel Westrup, 91–106. New York: Routledge, 2020.

Ouelette, Laurie, and James Hay. *Better Living through Reality TV: Television and Post-Welfare Citizenship*. Malden, MA: Blackwell, 2008.

Palina, Nicole. "Hypnotic Performance Given by Russ Burgess." *The Heights* (student weekly of Boston College), October 21, 1991, 1, 15.

Paris, Leslie. "The Sexual Clock: Middle-Aged American Women and Sexual Vitality in the 1960s and 1970s." *Journal of Social History* 53, no. 4 (Fall 2020): 922–938.

Paulson, Erika L., and Thomas C. O'Guinn. "Marketing Social Class and Ideology in Post-World-War-Two American Print Advertising." *Journal of Macromarketing* 38, no. 1 (March 2018): 7–28.

Paulson, Erika L., and Thomas C. O'Guinn. "Working-Class Cast: Images of the Working Class in Advertising, 1950–2010." *Annals of the American Academy of Political and Social Science* 64, no. 1 (November 2012): 50–69.

Paz, Eilon. *Dust and Grooves: Adventures in Record Collecting*. Brooklyn: Dust & Grooves, 2014.

Perchard, Tom, Stephen Graham, Tim Rutherford-Johnson, and Holly Rogers. *Twentieth-Century Music in the West: An Introduction*. Cambridge: Cambridge University Press, 2022.

Pieper, Michael. "Photographers—Peter James Samerjan." Glamour Photographers of the 1950s and 60s, 2020. http://glamourphotographers.yolasite.com/more-photographers.php.

Peril, Lynn. *Pink Think: Becoming a Woman in Many Uneasy Lessons*. New York: W. W. Norton, 2002.

Peters, John Durham. *Speaking into the Air: A History of the Idea of Communication*. Chicago: University of Chicago Press, 1999.

Plotnick, Rachel. "Tethered Women, Mobile Men: Gendered Mobilities of Typewriting." *Mobile Media & Communication* 8, no. 2 (May 2020): 188–208.

"Programming: One & Kick & Two, and Stick Out Your Tongue." *Time*, February 16, 1968. https:// content.time.com/time/subscriber/article/0,33009,837873-1,00.html.

Prudden, Bonnie. "About Bonnie Prudden." Bonnie Prudden Myotherapy, n.d. https:// bonnieprudden.com/about-bonnie-prudden.

Prudden, Bonnie. *How to Keep Slender and Fit after Thirty.* New York: Pocket Books, 1961.

Rafferty, Max. "Foreword." In *Improving Instruction through Audio-Visual Media: Techniques in Teaching Science, Mathematics, and Modern Foreign Languages,* edited by William A. Allen, ii. Report No-NDEA-3B. Washington, DC: US Department of Health, Education, and Welfare, Office of Education, 1963.

Ratliff, Ben. "Jimmy Witherspoon, Singer of Blues and Jazz, Dies at 74." *New York Times,* September 22, 1997, D16.

Ratliff, Ben. "Mal Waldron, 77, Composer of the Jazz Ballad 'Soul Eyes.'" *New York Times,* December 6, 2002, A33.

Raven, Fritjof A. "Spoken Spanish Instruction at the Massachusetts Institute of Technology." *Hispania* 31, no. 2 (May 1948): 175–180.

RCA Victor Education Department. *Educational Catalog and Graded List of Victor Records for Home School and College.* Camden, NJ: RCA Victor, 1930.

Ritter, Kelly. *Reframing the Subject: Postwar Instructional Film and Class-Conscious Literacies.* Pittsburgh: University of Pittsburgh Press, 2015.

Roberts, Sam. "Ralph Morse, Life Photographer of Big Events, Is Dead at 97." *New York Times,* January 23, 2015.

Robinson, Jancis. "Peter M. F. Sichel—from CIA to Blue Nun." February 27, 2016. https://www.jancisrobinson.com/articles/peter-m-f-sichel-from-cia-to-blue-nun.

Rubery, Matthew. *The Untold Story of the Talking Book.* Cambridge, MA: Harvard University Press, 2016.

Rubin, Joan Shelley. *The Making of Middlebrow Culture.* Chapel Hill: University of North Carolina Press, 1992.

Rude, Budd. "Some Gene Lies Memories." Hermosa Records, n.d. http://www.hermosarecords.com/geneBuddRude.html.

Saettler, Paul. *The Evolution of American Educational Technology.* Englewood, CO: Libraries Unlimited, 1990.

Salisbury, Lee H. "Audio-Visual Aids: Speak Well Off the Record." *Speech Teacher* 12, no. 4 (November 1963): 356.

Sandhaus, Louise. *Earthquakes, Mudslides, Fires, and Riots: California and Graphic Design 1936–1986.* New York: Metropolis, 2014.

Savidge, Wilbur M. "The Official History of Guitar Phonics." Guitar Phonics, 2021. https://guitarphonics-playguitar.com/Home_Page.html.

Scanlon, Jennifer. *Bad Girls Go Everywhere: The Life of Helen Gurley Brown.* New York: Oxford University Press, 2009.

Schein, Michael. "The Real Reason Napoleon Hill Grew Rich (Hint: It's Not What You Think)." *Inc.,* February 14, 2017. https://www.inc.com/michael-schein/brthe-real-reason-napoleon-hill-grew-rich-hint-its-not-what-you-think.html.

Schonberg, Harold C. "Records: Play Along." *New York Times,* September 13, 1953, X9.

Schroeder, Jonathan E. "Snapshot Aesthetics and the Strategic Imagination." *InVisible Culture* 18 (Spring 2013). http://ivc.lib.rochester.edu/snapshot-aesthetics-and-the-strategic-imagination.

Schroeder, Jonathan E. *Visual Consumption*. New York: Routledge, 2002.

Schroeder, Jonathan, and Janet Borgerson. "How Stereo Was First Sold to a Skeptical Public." The Conversation, December 12, 2018. https://theconversation.com/how-stereo-was-first-sold -to-a-skeptical-public-103668.

Schudson, Michael. "Advertising as Capitalist Realism." *Advertising & Society Review* 1, no. 1 (2000): 1–23.

Schudson, Michael. *Advertising, the Uneasy Persuasion: Its Dubious Impact on American Society*. New York: Basic Books, 1984.

Schwartz, Gideon. *Revolution: The History of Turntable Design*. New York: Phaidon, 2022.

Scott, David. "A Narrative Analysis of a Declining Social World: The Case of Contract Bridge." *Play & Culture* 4, no. 1 (February 1991): 11–23.

Severo, Richard. "Steve Allen, Comedian Who Pioneered Late-Night TV Talk Shows, Is Dead at 78." *New York Times*, November 1, 2000, B13.

Siefert, Marsha. "Aesthetics, Technology, and the Capitalization of Culture: How the Talking Machine Became a Musical Instrument." *Science in Context* 8, no. 2 (Summer 1995): 417–449.

Sinclair, Charles. "Top Jazz Names Climb NBC-TV Bandwagon." *Billboard*, April 7, 1958, 10.

Siverson, Lyle E. "Audio-Visual Equipment Is Material for Instruction." *National Elementary Principal* 36 no.1 (September 1956): 202–203.

Smigel, Libby. "Arthur Murray (1895–1991) and Arthur Murray Dance Studios." Dance Heritage Coalition, 2012. http://www.danceheritage.org.

Smith, Jacob. *Spoken Word: Postwar American Phonograph Cultures*. Berkeley: University of California Press, 2011.

Smith-Biwer, Kelli. "'The Silent Partner': Tonearms and Modular Masculinities in U.S. Midcentury Hi-Fi Culture." *Journal of the Society for American Music* 16, no. 3 (August 2022): 319–342.

Smithsonian Folkways. "Chicago Celebrates Ella Jenkins at the DuSable Museum." Smithsonian Institution, April 10, 2019. https://ellajenkins.com/news-press.html.

Sobieszek, Robert A. *The Art of Persuasion*. New York: Harry N. Abrams, 1988.

Space Age Pop Music. "String Groups." 2019. http://www.spaceagepop.com/strings.htm.

Spellman, Marianne. "What We Can Learn from These Vintage School Instructional Albums." Popthomology, August 22, 2012. https://www.popthomology.com/2012/08/what-we-can-learn -from-these-vintage.html.

Spigel, Lynn. *Make Room for TV: Television and the Family Ideal in Postwar America*. Chicago: University of Chicago Press, 1992.

"Spreads Civilization." *Talking Machine World* 2, no. 7 (July 15, 1906): 5.

Stanley Bowmar Co. Advertisement. "Records for the Classroom." *Journal of Health, Physical Education, and Recreation* 38, no. 6 (June 1967): 68.

Starker, Steven. *Oracle at the Supermarket: The American Preoccupation with Self-Help Books*. New Brunswick, NJ: Transaction, 1989.

Sterne, Jonathan. *The Audible Past: Cultural Origins of Sound Reproduction*. Durham, NC: Duke University Press, 2003.

Stoever, Jennifer Lynn. *The Sonic Color Line: Race and the Cultural Politics of Listening*. New York: New York University Press, 2016.

Sturgeon, Julie, and Janice Meer. "The President's Council on Physical Fitness and Sports Revisits Its Roots and Charts Its Future." In *President's Council on Fitness and Sports: The First Fifty Years, 1956–2006*, 40–63. St. Petersburg, FL: Faircount, 2006.

Suisman, David. *Selling Sounds: The Commercial Revolution in American Music*. Cambridge, MA: Harvard University Press, 2009.

Swank, Craig. "Music Storytelling for the Young! The Imaginative World of Arthur Shimkin & Golden Records." Popboprocktiludrop, August 26, 2021. https://kimsloans.wordpress.com/tag /arthur-shimkin-and-golden-records.

Swank, Craig. "Tom Glazer: ("On Top Of Spaghetti")." Popboprocktiludrop, n.d. https:// kimsloans.wordpress.com/spotlight-tom-glazer.

Symes, Colin. *Setting the Record Straight: A Material History of Classical Music Recording*. Middletown, CT: Wesleyan University Press, 2004.

Symes, Colin. "A Sound Education: The Gramophone and the Classroom in the United Kingdom and the United States, 1920–1940." *British Journal of Music Education* 21, no. 2 (July 2004): 163–178.

Szarkowski, John. *Looking at Photographs: 100 Pictures from the Collection of the Museum of Modern Art*. New York: Abrams, 1973.

Tachi, Mikiko. "Commercialism, Counterculture, and the Folk Music Revival: A Study of *Sing Out!* Magazine, 1950–1967." *Japanese Journal of American Studies*, 15 (2004): 187–211.

Taylor, Alex. "Amway: Up from the Basement." *Detroit Free Press*, November 19, 1978, 1B.

Taylor, Timothy D., Mark Katz, and Tony Grajeda, ed. *Music, Sound, and Technology in America: A Documentary History of Early Phonograph, Cinema, and Radio*. Durham, NC: Duke University Press, 2012.

Thompson, Bradbury. *The Art of Graphic Design*. New Haven, CT: Yale University Press, 1988.

Tranquada, Jim and John King. *The Ukulele Book: A History*. Honolulu: University of Hawai'i Press, 2012.

Turner, Fred. *The Democratic Surround: Multimedia and American Liberalism from World War II to the Psychedelic Sixties*. Chicago: University of Chicago Press, 2013.

Union Trading Co. Advertisement. "Hear How Records." *Black Belt*, February 1963, 68.

Varga, George. "Obituary: Jack 'Mr. Bongo' Costanzo, Dead at 98, Collaborated with Judy Garland, Nat 'King' Cole, Marlon Brando." *San Diego Union*, August 19, 2018. https://www .sandiegouniontribune.com/entertainment/music/sd-me-music-jack-costanzo-obit-20180819 -story.html.

Victor Talking Machine. Advertisement. *Saturday Evening Post*, December 7, 1901, 22.

Vinciguerra, Thomas. "The Gamester Who Went All In." Columbia College Today (Winter 2020– 21). https://www.college.columbia.edu/cct/issue/winter-2020%E2%80%9321/article/gamester-who -went-all.

Wasson, Haidee. *Everyday Movies: Portability and the Transformation of American Culture*. Berkeley: University of California Press, 2019.

Weaver, Jennifer. "Ralph Bartholomew Jr's Postwar America." *Photo District News* 18, no. 4 (April 1998): 198.

Weinberg, Sydney Stahl. "Joyce Brothers." In Shalvi/Hyman Encyclopedia of Jewish Women, December 31, 1999. https://jwa.org/encyclopedia/article/brothers-joyce.

Weiss, Richard. *The American Myth of Success: From Horatio Alger to Norman Vincent Peale.* Urbana: University of Illinois Press, 1969.

Whyte, William H., Jr. *The Organization Man.* Garden City, NY: Doubleday, 1957.

Willis, Paul. *Learning to Labor: How Working Class Kids Get Working Class Jobs.* New York: Columbia University Press, 1977.

Wilson, John S. "Cannonball Adderley, Jazzman, Dead." *New York Times,* August 9, 1975, 15.

"Wilson Learning Announces the Passing of Larry Wilson: Founder, Speaker, and Author." Wilson Learning Worldwide, February 11, 2013. https://global.wilsonlearning.com/resources /20130411passingoflarrywilson.

Wolters, Larry. "Channel 9 Figures to get Flying Start." *Chicago Tribune,* September 14, 1964, 46.

Woods, George A. "Easing the Pain of Education." *New York Times,* March 15, 1964, X17.

Wride, Tim B. *Retail Fictions: The Commercial Photography of Ralph Bartholomew Jr.* Los Angeles: Los Angeles County Museum of Art, 1998.

Wright, Mary, and Russel Wright. *Guide to Easier Living.* Salt Lake City, UT: Gibbs Smith, [1950] 2003.

Wulf, Andrew James. *U.S. International Exhibitions during the Cold War: Winning Hearts and Minds through Cultural Diplomacy.* Lanham, MD: Rowman & Littlefield, 2015.

Wyden, Peter. *The Overweight Society.* New York: Pocket Books, 1965.

Yardley, William. "John McClure Dies at 84; Produced Classic Records." *New York Times,* June 25, 2014, A15.

Young, Steve, and Sport Murphy. *Everything's Coming Up Profits: The Golden Age of Industrial Musicals.* New York: Blast, 2013.

ILLUSTRATION CREDITS

We thank the copyright holders for granting permission to reproduce the figures. Every effort has been made to track down copyrighted images in this book. Any errors or omissions will be rectified in subsequent editions provided notification is sent to the publisher.

Courtesy of Sony Music Entertainment: Figures 1.2, 1.6, 3.6, 4.11, 4.12, 5.1, 5.5, 5.6, 6.4, 6.8, 6.12, 7.5, 7.6, 8.8, 9.6, 11.1, 11.2, 11.6, 11.7, 11.8

"RCA Victor" and the "Dog & Phonograph" courtesy of Talisman Brands, Inc., used by permission: Figures 3.6, 5.6, 6.4, 7.6, 11.2, 11.8

Courtesy of Rhino Entertainment Company: A Warner Music Group Company: Figures 3.1, 4.4, 4.5, 4.6, 4.7, 4.8, 9.3, 11.9

Courtesy of Universal Music Group: Figures 1.14, 6.14, 9.12,

Reprinted by permission of Hal Leonard LLC, Copyright © Music Minus One: Figures 0.6, 5.3, 5.4, 9.4

Courtesy GNP Crescendo Records Co., Inc.: Figure 6.1

Courtesy ABKCO Music & Records: Figure 0.1 © ABKCO Music & Records, Inc.

Courtesy Smithsonian Folkways Recordings: Figure 9.2

Courtesy of Kimbo Educational: Figure 9.10

Courtesy Jamey Aebersold Jazz; Figure 9.8 used by permission of Jamey Aebersold

Courtesy Penguin Random House: Figures 6.5, 10.2, 10.3, 10.4, 10.5

Courtesy Documentary Productions: Figures 1.12, 1.13

Reproduced by permission of *Sports Afield*, sportsafield.com.: Figure 8.14

Courtesy of Xerox Corporation: Figure 1.6

Courtesy of Boeing Digital Solutions: Figure 8.8. For reference only—not for navigational use © Boeing Digital Solutions, Inc. 2023

Courtesy of Boy Scouts of America: Figure 1.2

Courtesy Befit Enterprises, Inc.: Figure 4.3. Photograph was supplied by Befit Enterprises, Inc. JackLaLanne.com

Courtesy of McCormick & Company, Incorporated: Figure 5.8

Courtesy of The Toro Company: Figure 2.6

Courtesy of the J. Paul Getty Museum and the G. Ray Hawkins Gallery, © 2023 G. Ray Hawkins Gallery, Beverly Hills, CA: Figure 0.2

Digital Image © 2023 Museum Associates / LACMA. Licensed by Art Resource, NY: Figure 0.3

Courtesy of the George Eastman Museum. Reproduced with permission from Thomas V. Keppler: Figure 0.4

Photo by Nickolas Muray; © Nickolas Muray Photo Archives. Licensed by the Nickolas Muray Photo Archives: Figure 0.5

INDEX OF RECORDS

INDEX